APR 13 '73

PS2631
S8

88216

TERTELING LIBRARY
THE COLLEGE OF IDAHO
CALDWELL, IDAHO

P9-DUY-620

EDGAR POE THE POET

FLOYD STOVALL

Edgar Poe the Poet

ESSAYS NEW AND OLD

ON THE MAN AND HIS WORK

UNIVERSITY PRESS OF VIRGINIA

CHARLOTTESVILLE

THE UNIVERSITY PRESS OF VIRGINIA
Copyright © 1969 by the Rector and Visitors
of the University of Virginia

First published 1969

The portrait of Poe
by Samuel S. Osgood is reproduced
by courtesy of The New-York Historical Society.

Standard Book Number: 8139–0265–7
Library of Congress Catalog Card Number: 75–82532
Printed in the United States of America

88216

Preface

IN A manner of speaking, this book was begun forty years ago, for most of my ideas about Poe date from that time, but it was not completed until the day before yesterday. My ideas have matured, no doubt, but not changed significantly. After I had published several essays on Poe during the late twenties and early thirties, I was diverted to other tasks that seemed important, and that diversion lasted for three decades. When finally I could direct my attention again to Poe, I undertook to prepare an edition of his poems. Only after this work was done, two or three years ago, was I free to resume my long-interrupted critical study.

My plan was to start from the beginning and make an entirely new and comprehensive analysis and criticism of all of Poe's work. Since the essays I had previously published in periodicals were chiefly concerned with the poems and poetic theory, I did not at first intend to incorporate them in the book. As I explored the subject, however, I realized that my interest was still, as it had always been, chiefly in the poems and in the poetic theory which is inseparable from them. Since I found no reason to alter the opinions expressed in the early essays, and since to go over the same ground again would be supererogatory, I decided to include some of them and to build the rest of the book around them. This plan, I knew, would do some violence to the principle of unity; but now that the book is done I am relieved to discover less violence than I had anticipated. I have long believed, contrary to the opinions of my younger contemporaries, not only that Poe was a poet by temperament and inclination but that, directly or indirectly, he made his greatest contribution to literature in his poems and his theory of poetic art.

I had some doubts about the propriety of including the essay on "The Musiad" in a book about Poe and his work, since I am not sure that Poe wrote this humorous and satiric verse fragment. I decided to include it for three reasons principally: even if it is not all Poe's work,

TERTELING LIBRARY
THE COLLEGE OF IDAHO
CALDWELL, IDAHO

he probably had a hand in its composition; he is very nearly, if not quite, the center of interest in it; and my discussion of it throws a good deal of light on his life and activities in Baltimore between May 1829 and January 1830. I was reluctant at first to undertake an investigation of the authorship of "The Musiad," and for stimulating my interest in the problem I wish to thank David Randall, Curator of the Lilly Library at Indiana University.

I have been throughout my adult life a student of Poe's work and, from time to time, have read and reread all that he is known to have written. I think I have read also all of the more important books and essays, whether biographical or critical, published by Poe scholars. Very likely I have been influenced by the opinions of other students, and yet my own have not been in the mainstream of these opinions. I have disagreed about as often, it seems, as I have agreed with those writers who have shaped the contemporary image of Edgar Poe. So far as I am aware, the ideas expressed in these essays were formed from reading Poe's own work and antedate most of the critical works still current. Two essays contain considerable biographical information. Only a small part of this is new, but I have hoped to present data drawn from scattered sources in such a way as to give them new significance in relation to Poe's writing. Arthur Hobson Quinn's biography is the most authoritative, and I have depended largely on it, although I have also consulted his own and other sources where they have been available.

The first essay in this volume is reprinted by permission from the *Virginia Quarterly Review,* spring issue, 1967; the fourth, fifth, and sixth were first published in the University of Texas *Studies in English,* in the annual issues of 1929, 1930, and 1931, and are authorized for reprinting by the University of Texas Press. The seventh essay is reprinted from the issue of *College English* for March 1963 and is here reprinted by permission of the National Council of Teachers of English. The remaining four essays, which constitute much the greater portion of the book, were written during the past twelve months. I have made no verbal changes in any of the essays previously published except as follows: In "Poe's Debt to Coleridge" I have corrected two documentary references and slightly extended a quotation from one of Poe's reviews; and I have omitted the word "Poe's" from the title of the fourth essay and the word "Allan" from the title of the seventh. I have transferred citations of Coleridge's *Biographia Literaria* to a more scholarly text than the one originally cited, and I have altered the bibliographical style of some notes to conform with that of the rest of the book.

It would be impossible for me to remember all the people who have helped me during the long span of time since beginning these studies. For the early essays I owe most to the library of the University of Texas. For the later ones, I found the library of the University of Virginia indispensable. To the librarians of the Alderman Library of the University of Virginia, and particularly to those of the C. Waller Barrett Collection, I owe my deepest debt of gratitude. I have also had generous assistance from the librarians of Brown University, who have provided me with a Xerox copy of "The Musiad," from the Enoch Pratt Free Library of Baltimore, and from the Maryland Historical Society.

F. S.

Charlottesville, Virginia
January 29, 1968

Contents

EDGAR POE THE POET

I. Edgar Poe and the University
of Virginia

ApN INSTITUTION," said Emerson, "is the lengthened shadow of one man." This statement is particularly true of the University of Virginia, where the shadow was cast by Thomas Jefferson. He conceived the idea of it, selected the ground on which it was built, designed its buildings, employed the builders, taught workmen how to install its metal roofing, and supervised the work of construction. He hired its first professors, the majority of them young men from the English universities, planned its curriculum, made the first schedule of classes, and, as its first Rector, drew up the regulations by which it was to be governed. There were eight schools, with a professor for each school who lived in one of the pavilions on the Lawn and held his classes there. Three "hotels," so called, in the East Range and three in the West Range were occupied by the families of officials called "hotelkeepers," whose function it was to "diet," that is, to board, the students. There were 108 dormitories on the Lawn and in the Ranges.

A student might elect to attend classes in any school for which he was qualified, and paid accordingly: fifty dollars per session for attendance on one professor, sixty for attendance on two, and seventy-five for attendance on three. He paid fifteen dollars for his room if he occupied it alone, or half of that if he had a roommate. For board the hotelkeeper was allowed to charge no more than one hundred dollars. In addition to tuition and board, each student had to pay a fee of fifteen dollars for the use of public buildings and a library deposit of ten dollars. Other expenses, including fuel, clothing, and books, ran the cost of a year's attendance to $300 or more.

The first Board of Visitors was a distinguished group, including, besides the Rector, two other former Presidents, Madison and Monroe. The first session was scheduled to begin February 1, 1825, but opened late because some of the professors did not arrive from England until the middle of March. Several months before the opening date the Board had approved what Mr. Jefferson thought would be appropriate

rules governing the conduct of students. Punishments for violation of
the rules were labeled "minor" and "major." A minor punishment, such
as professorial reproof in class or dismissal from class for the day, was
imposed for inattendance at class, inattention or misbehavior in the
classroom, keeping or firing a gun on the premises, possessing or
using spirituous or vinous liquors, chewing or smoking tobacco, and
making "festive entertainment" within the precincts of the University
without the express consent of the Faculty. Major punishments were
of several orders. The more serious offenses of dissoluteness, dissipation, and playing games of chance were punishable, after the first
occurrence, with admonition and reproof, together with a warning to
parents or guardians; if the misconduct was not corrected, the student
might be refused further continuance at the University. Riotous, disor-
derly, or indecent conduct was to be punished by "interdiction of
residence within the precincts," or, in some cases, by outright expulsion. Fighting with deadly weapons, or the giving or acceptance of a
challenge to fight with such weapons, was to be punished by immediate expulsion of the offender from the University.

In spite of these regulations, there were riots, misconduct in the
town of Charlottesville, and assaults on professors and hotelkeepers
during the first year. Conditions became so bad that on October 2,
1825, the Faculty passed and sent to the Board of Visitors a resolution
stating that unless "an efficient Police" in the University was immediately established all the professors would resign. Conditions did improve, but drinking, gambling, fighting, and occasionally rioting continued through the following year and later. A total of 123 students
matriculated the first year and 177 the second, after which enrollment
declined for several years. The decline was probably a consequence of
the continuing disorders.

The second session began on schedule, but Edgar Poe arrived two
weeks late. He matriculated on February 14, 1826, and paid his fees
for attendance on two professors, Long of the School of Ancient
Languages, and Blaettermann of the School of Modern Languages.
Greek and Latin were the principal languages taught by Professor
Long, while French, German, Italian, and Spanish were taught by
Professor Blaettermann. All classes in the ancient languages met from
7:30 to 9:30 A.M. on Mondays, Wednesdays, and Fridays, and all
classes in modern languages met at the same hours on Tuesdays,
Thursdays, and Saturdays. How the professor divided his two hours of
class time among the several languages he taught I do not know, nor

have I been able to determine certainly what languages other than Latin and French were studied by Poe. The Faculty Minutes record the fact that he took the final examinations in Latin and French and was among those who excelled in each of them. Whether he took the examinations in other languages cannot be determined because only the names of those who excelled in the examinations are inscribed in the minutes. It is probable that he attended lectures in Greek with Professor Long and lectures in both Spanish and Italian with Professor Blaettermann, and it is possible that he heard some lectures in German. He demonstrated later in his published writing that he had at least an elementary knowledge of Greek, Spanish, and Italian.

The most authentic account of Poe's life in the University was written by William Wertenbaker, a student in 1826, but also then and for long afterward University Librarian, and published in the combined issue of the *Virginia University Magazine* for November and December 1868. He states that Poe attended lectures in Greek, as well as Latin, and in Spanish and Italian, as well as in French. He himself was enrolled in the School of Modern Languages, and he remembered that Poe "was tolerably regular in his attendance." Wertenbaker also recalled that Poe was commended by Professor Blaettermann in class for his verse translation of a passage from the Italian poet Tasso.

Students were expected to attend three professors unless they had permission from parents or guardians to attend two or only one. Gessner Harrison, a second-year student in 1826, was matriculated in three schools, and took the examinations in six different subjects— Greek, Latin, French, Italian, German, and Medicine—in each of which he excelled. Poe was matriculated in only two schools, presumably by permission of his foster father, and yet he states in a letter to Mr. Allan from West Point, January 3, 1831, that he had been limited to two schools because he was not provided with sufficient funds to pay tuition in three. It is evident from other letters that Poe went to the University expecting to stay two years. If he had returned, or if he had added a third school in his first year, he probably would have chosen mathematics. In the letter cited above he reminds his foster father that when he wrote from the University in 1826 for money to buy necessary books, he received no money and that the packet of books sent him contained only *Gil Blas* and the *Cambridge Mathematics* in two volumes, books, he adds, "for which I had no earthly use since I had no means of attending the mathematical lectures." At West Point he did have use for them, and he wrote Allan on November 6,

1830, asking for the *Cambridge Mathematics* and a box of mathematical instruments. In an undated letter to Allan written just before he left Richmond in March 1827, he asks for enough money to pay his passage to a northern city and support him for a month, "by which time," he promises, "I shall be enabled to place myself in some situation where I may not only obtain a livelihood, but lay by a sum which one day or another will support me at the University."

When Poe entered the University the library was housed in a room of Pavilion VII, now occupied by the Colonnade Club, but the books were moved into the Rotunda the following September. In order to withdraw books from the library a student had to present written authorization from a professor, and he could have in his possession only three books at a time. The Librarian was on hand only one hour of one day in each week to issue books to students and to receive them when they were returned. If a student wished to read in the library he had to present his request for the privilege a day in advance. On September 21, 1826, Poe wrote his foster father that the library had a "fine collection," but it would have been more accurate to call it a fine selection, for there were then not many books. Jefferson's plans called for a larger collection, but because of an unexpected shortage of funds, many of the books requested could not be acquired by 1826. The books were approved by Mr. Jefferson and doubtless reflected his personal taste as well as his judgment of what was most useful for class study. Most of the books were written in a foreign language, and the fields best represented were ancient languages, law, and medicine.

The records of the library for 1826, which still survive, show that on June 13 Poe withdrew Vols. 1, 3, and 4 of Charles Rollin's *Histoire Ancienne*, which relate to early Egyptian, Carthaginian, Persian, and Grecian civilizations, including accounts of the mythology, arts, and customs of the various peoples; and that on August 8 he withdrew Vols. 33 and 34 of the same author's *Histoire Romaine*, which deal with Caesar's Gallic Wars and the last years of the Roman Republic. The numbering of the volumes of the Roman history proves that they were a part of Rollin's *Oeuvres Complètes*, published in Paris in 1807, available in the library at that time. On August 15 he took the first two volumes of William Robertson's *History of America*, which do not go beyond the period of Spanish exploration and settlement, and on August 29 the first two volumes of John Marshall's *Life of Washington*, which carry his story only to the early period of the American Revolution. On September 12 he withdrew two volumes of Voltaire's works, recorded as 9 and 10. In the edition of Voltaire's works in the University library in 1828, and presumably also in 1826 (the Paris edition of 1817), Vols. 9 and 10 contain *La Pucelle D'Orléans, La Guerre Civile de Genève,* and various poetic epistles and other minor poems. On November 4 he withdrew Nicholas Gouin Dufief's *Nature Displayed in Her Mode of Teaching Language to Man,* in two volumes, one of which contains a French grammar and the other selections, with English aids, designed to assist the English speaking student in learning French. The book was first published in 1804 and was so popular that it ran through many editions. Gouin Dufief, a friend of Jefferson, was a refugee bookseller and teacher living in Philadelphia.

What use Poe made of the history of America and the life of Washington is not apparent, but it is obvious that he drew out Voltaire and Dufief in connection with his study of French. Very likely he wanted to see Rollin's histories to facilitate his study of Latin and Greek or to fulfill some task assigned by Professor Long. In a letter written near the end of May 1826, Poe asks Mr. Allan to send him "a copy of the Historiae of Tacitus," describing it as a small volume. Since he asks for "a copy" the book was presumably not in the Allan library but would have to be purchased. I have been unable to identify this edition, but since Tacitus was required study in his class in Latin, he may have referred to a work with the title *Five Books of the History of C. Cornelius Tacitus,* edited with Latin text and English notes by E. B. Williston. Although this book was not copyrighted until June, Poe may have seen an announcement of its forthcoming publication, with a description of its format. In a student interview published in the *Virginia University Magazine* for October 1879, William Wertenbaker is quoted as saying: "During the year 1826, there used to come into the Library a handsome young student, perhaps eighteen years old, in search of French books, primarily histories." It was Poe, doubtless pursuing his class work, for the history of France was required study along with the language and literature.

Poe's professors contributed nothing of importance to our knowledge of Poe's life at the University other than their reports of the final examinations recorded in the Faculty Minutes. Professor Blaettermann died long before Poe became well known as a literary figure and left no reminiscences of him or the University. Professor Long was a professor at the University of London after he left Virginia, and was alive in 1875, when Poe's English biographer, John H. Ingram, was collecting information wherever he could find it. In reply to his inquiry, Professor Long wrote to him on April 15, 1875: "The beginning of the University of Virginia was very bad. There were some excellent young men, and some of the worst that ever I knew. I remember well the names of both, and I think that I remember the name of Poe, but the remembrance is very feeble; and if he was in my class, he could not be among the worst, and perhaps not among the best or I should remember him." He mentions Gessner Harrison and Henry Tutwiler as his best students, but both of them had been in his classes in 1825 as well as in 1826.

Among Poe's fellow-students who later wrote about him, the most important were Thomas Goode Tucker, who was from Brunswick County, Virginia, though he later moved to North Carolina; Miles George, from Richmond, later a prominent physician in that city; and William H. Burwell, a native Virginian who in 1867 became editor of *De Bow's Magazine*, in New Orleans. Tucker was the first to write, and his reminiscences were contained in two letters written to Douglas Sherley, a student of the University, who incorporated their substance in two numbers of a series he called "Old Oddity Papers," published in the *Virginia University Magazine* in March and April 1880. Tucker recalls that he and Poe spent much time in the library reading the histories of Lingard and Hume—most likely their histories of England during the Roman occupation—and were familiar with English poetry from Chaucer to Scott; that Poe was excellent in Latin and French but read Greek indifferently; and that, though he rarely prepared his lessons in advance, his brain was so active and his memory so good that he needed only a few minutes of study before class in order to make the best recitation. Nevertheless, he says that while Gessner Harrison and Henry Tutwiler studied hard and observed all regulations, he and Poe and their "rollicking set of jovial companions" were "much given to nonattendance at lectures and entertaining a good-humored disregard of all restraints and regulations imposed by the Faculty." He tells a good story about a considerable number of students who in May 1826 fled to the Ragged Mountains and remained there for days to escape a summons by the sheriff to the Albemarle grand jury, which was investigating reports of students gambling in the University and in Charlottesville. The main features of this story are confirmed by the minutes of the Faculty and other University records, but Tucker's statement that Poe was the ringleader of the band is unconfirmed and probably fictitious. He describes Poe as short in stature, compact, bow-legged, quick in his movements, and athletic, and adds that "he had about him the air and action of a native-born Frenchman." He remembers Poe as "very mercurial in his disposition and exceedingly fond of peach and honey." He would drain his glass without obvious pleasure, and then be thrown into a state of excitement that found vent in a "continuous flow of wild, fascinating talk." He states that Poe roomed on the Lawn with Miles George until the two had a fight, after which he moved to No. 13 West Range, where he had no roommate.

The testimony of Miles George is perhaps more accurate. In a letter, elicited by Ingram's inquiries, from Dr. George to the sculptor E. V. Valentine, dated May 18, 1880, he admits that Poe first lived on the Lawn, that he and Poe had a fight but were soon friends again, and that after the fight Poe moved to the West Range. He denies, however, that they were ever roommates, he having lived on East Lawn and Poe on West Lawn. He says that he was often in Poe's room both on the Lawn and in West Range. He differs with Tucker on two other points. He does not remember that Poe's excitement was the consequence of his drinking, but rather that being by nature of an excitable temperament, he drank to calm himself. He also remembers Poe as short, compactly set, and bow-legged, as Tucker described him, but as "of rather a delicate and slender mould," weighing about 130 to 140 pounds. If his legs were bowed it was so slightly as to escape notice and did not affect the symmetry of his figure or the "ease and grace of his carriage." Dr. George's letter, from the Ingram Collection, was published by Professor James Southall Wilson in the *Alumni Bulletin* for April 1923.

There is a legend of uncertain origin that Poe's room in West Range was No. 17. This legend is still occasionally revived, though Tucker's statement that it was No. 13 is now generally accepted as correct. It is supported by the recollection of Jesse Maury, who was still living in 1899 when his testimony was recorded by Professor Charles W. Kent and later published in his volume compiled to commemorate the unveiling of the Zolnay bust of Poe. Maury was not a student, but his father had the contract to deliver wood to Conway's hotel at the corner where the offices of the *Virginia Quarterly Review* are now located, and he remembered that his father's workmen regularly unloaded the wagons at the woodpile, which was just back of the West Range block containing dormitories 5, 7, 9, 11, 13, and 15. This block was known in Poe's time as "Rowdy Row." No. 17 was in the block across the alley to the south.

William Burwell's recollections of Poe were first published in the New Orleans *Times-Democrat,* May 18, 1884, under the title "Edgar A. Poe and His College Contemporaries," and was reprinted in the *Alumni Bulletin* for April 1923. A clipping of the newspaper item is in the Ingram Collection, and bears Ingram's notation in pencil that Burwell reports nothing except what he got from the *Virginia University Magazine* articles based on Tucker's reminiscences, which he terms "imaginative." Burwell describes Poe as about five feet and two or three inches in height, "somewhat bandylegged, but in no sense muscular or apt at any physical exercises." This statement underestimates Poe's known height by five or six inches. That Poe was athletic is demonstrated by the fully authenticated episode of his swimming down the James River in 1825 against a strong tide for a distance of six miles.

Many of the discreditable legends about Poe, including the charge that he led a dissolute life while at the University, had their beginning in the errors and falsehoods of Rufus W. Griswold, his literary executor. In his obituary article, signed "Ludwig," in the New York *Tribune,* October 9, 1849, two days after Poe's death, Griswold asserts that Poe entered the University in 1825 and there "led a very dissipated life, the manners of the College at that time being extremely dissolute." In his "Memoir," published with the third volume of his edition of Poe's works in 1850, Griswold further distorts the facts with the following statement:

In 1822, he returned to the United States, and after passing a few months at an academy in Richmond, he entered the University at Charlottesville, where he led a very dissipated life; the manners which then prevailed there were extremely dissolute, and he was known as the wildest and most reckless student of his class; but his unusual opportunities, and the remarkable ease with which he mastered the most difficult studies, kept him all the while in the first rank for scholarship, and he would have graduated with the highest honors, had not his gambling, intemperance, and other vices, induced his expulsion from the University.

Griswold's dates are all wrong, and so is most of the rest of his account of Poe at the University. Students were not graduated, in our sense of the word, in 1826; they were only certified as having completed certain courses. There is no evidence that Poe had any vices other than gambling and drinking; and these, I am convinced, have been exaggerated. By his own confession, he gambled, and like most other students at that time he occasionally drank and doubtless at times became more or less intoxicated, but he managed to remain for the full session of ten months without being expelled, suspended, or reprimanded, and his name was never mentioned in the minutes of the Faculty until after the final examinations, and then only to record his superior work in his classes.

Tucker's reference to Poe's nonattendance at lectures and his disregard of Faculty regulations is therefore not borne out by the records. It may be also that Tucker's account of the flight of Poe with others to the Ragged Mountains is not accurate in every respect. In Poe's letter to John Allan, written near the end of May 1826 while he was a student, he has this to say:

Soon after you left here the Grand Jury met and put the students in a terrible fright—so much so that the lectures were unattended—and those whose names were upon the Sheriff's list—travelled off into the woods & mountains—taking their beds & provisions along with them—there were about 50 on the list—so you may suppose the College was very well thinn'd —this was the first day of the fright—the second day "A proclamation" was issued by the faculty forbidding "any student under pain of a major punishment to leave his dormitory between the hours of 8 & 10 A.M.—(at which time the Sheriffs would be about) or in any way to resist the lawful authority of the Sheriffs"—This order however was very little attended to —as the fear of the Faculty could not counterbalance that of the Grand Jury—most of the "indicted" ran off a second time into the woods—and upon an examination the next morning by the Faculty—Some were reprimanded—some suspended—and one expelled—James Albert Clarke from Manchester (I went to school with him at Burke's) was suspended for two months. Armstead Carter from this neighborhood, for the remainder of the session—And Thomas Barclay for ever—

This account agrees in general with the record of the Faculty Minutes, which show that the date of the "proclamation" was May 9, and that among the students required to remain in their dormitories were James A. Clarke, Charles Peyton, Thomas G. Tucker, J. A. Carter (presumably the one Poe calls Armstead), Thomas Barclay, and William Burwell. There were only twenty-five names on the list—not fifty, as Poe may have supposed—and his own name was not there. Poe was correct about the expulsion of Barclay and the suspension of Carter and Clarke. This action took place on May 11. The other statements in Poe's letter about student troubles are corroborated also by the minutes of the Faculty meetings on May 24 and 25. If Poe went with the students who fled to the Ragged Mountains it was evidently not as ringleader and apparently not from fear of the sheriff; it might have been for fear he would be called as a witness, or it might have been only for the fun of it or because he was better acquainted with the area than other students. The discrepancy between Poe's estimate of fifty and the Faculty's list of twenty-five might be accounted for on the same ground.

More or less in agreement with Tucker's statement that Poe belonged to a "rollicking set of jovial companions," James A. Clarke is reported to have said in an interview published in a Richmond newspaper November 29, 1885, a clipping of which is in the Ingram Collection: "He was a pretty wild young man and took much interest in athletic sports." Clarke was pretty wild himself, as his suspension bears witness. His remark about Poe's interest in athletic sports may refer not so much to his activities at the University as to an earlier time in Richmond. He remembered Poe's famous swim in the James River, though he did not witness it. Another Richmond man, David Bridges, who was interviewed at the same time, and who had also gone to school with Poe at Burke's, was a witness to the swim and says he swam with Poe part of the way, but gave out. There was little opportunity for the display of athletic prowess by students at the University in 1826 unless in fist fights. Poe's alleged wildness is almost certainly an exaggeration. The fact that despite his shortage of funds Poe had no roommate suggests a love of privacy and perhaps a temperamental lack of congeniality inconsistent with the legend of his wildness. Tucker himself says that he was not gregarious and chose to have only a few companions. Miles George, in his letter to Valentine previously quoted, was nearer the truth in saying: "He was very excitable and restless, at times wayward, melancholic and morose, but again—in his better moods frolicsome, full of fun and a most attractive and agreeable companion."

In a letter to Allan dated February 4, 1829, while Poe was still in the army, he said he offered no excuse except youth and inexperience for what he termed the "infamous conduct" of himself and others at the University; but he added: "It was however at the commencement of that year that I got deeply entangled in difficulty which all my after good conduct in the close of the session (to which all there can testify) could not clear away." This difficulty may have been pecuniary, leading first to honest debts and then to gambling in a desperate effort to raise money. The phrase "close of the session" seems to refer to the last three months, for in the letter of January 3, 1831, he protested to Allan: "Had you let me return, my reformation had been sure—as my conduct the last 3 months gave every reason to believe—and you would never have heard more of my extravagance." This is borne out by his excellent performance in the examinations and by his letter to Allan September 31, 1826, from the University, in which he says that though only a first-year student, he will have to stand his examinations along with the second-year students. He thinks this hardly fair. Then he adds: "I have been studying a great deal in order to be prepared, and dare say I shall come off as well as the rest of them, that is—if I don't get frightened." It should be remembered in this connection that the students that Professor Long remembered as his best, Gessner Harrison and Henry Tutwiler, were two of these second-year students with whom Poe was competing.

Except in the reports of the examinations, Poe's name was mentioned only once in the Faculty Minutes, and this was after the session had officially closed. The Faculty met on December 20, 1826, to investigate the Proctor's charges that hotelkeepers had been drinking and gambling with students in their dormitories. The Proctor submitted the names of nine students who were "supposed to possess knowledge of the facts." Poe was one of the nine, all of whom were questioned by the Faculty at that meeting. Six of the nine, including Poe, stated that they had not heard until now of hotelkeepers drinking and gambling with students, and were dismissed without comment. The other three stated that they had heard of such conduct but had not seen it. None of these students had ever been called before the Faculty for misconduct. The next day the Faculty examined the hotelkeepers, and it was brought out that several of them had gambled with students. These were chiefly the hotelkeepers in the East Range, including Major Spotswood. Edwin Conway was the only one of the West Range hotelkeepers who was suspected, and it was not proved that he gambled, though he admitted that he had once played cards with students in one of the dormitories. Since in 1826 students were permitted to choose the hotel where they boarded, it is impossible to say whether Poe boarded at Conway's hotel, which was nearest to Room 13, or at some other.

We know very little about the debts Poe contracted while a student. A letter from Major Spotswood to John Allan, published in Quinn's biography, dated May 1, 1827, states that although Poe did not board with him he owed him a debt for the use of his servant. In the Ellis-Allan Papers in the Library of Congress there is an itemized bill for clothing amounting to $68.46. The bill is dated December 4, presumably of 1826, and was rendered by Samuel Leitch, Jr., who was the authorized agent in Charlottesville of the Richmond firm of Ellis and Allan. This bill, as Quinn shows, was not paid as late as June 28, 1828. There is in the University of Virginia Library a promissory note, a gift of Mrs. James Southall Wilson, signed "E. A. Poe," and made out to Dan'l S. Mosby & Co., for the amount of $41.36. There is nothing in the note to indicate what the debt was contracted for. Daniel S. Mosby & Co. may be the same establishment that is referred to several times in the minutes of the Faculty as "Mosby's," or "Mowsby's shop," and seems to have been a confectionery in or near Charlottesville where drinks both vinous and spirituous were sold, and where students were wont to congregate. In one case the drinking was said to have been done in a back room at Mosby's. If drinks were the principal commodity dispensed at Mosby's, which seems probable, Poe may have incurred the debt by a too-lavish entertainment of his friends there.

Students gambled off the precincts of the University as well as in their dormitories. Mention is made in the Faculty Minutes of gambling over Jones's book store, which may have been between the University and Charlottesville. Whether there was gambling also at Mosby's I have been unable to determine. It is not known to whom Poe owed gambling debts, nor can we be sure of the amount of the debts, though they were once estimated by James Galt, a beneficiary of John Allan's will, as high as $2500. Wertenbaker, a disinterested party, thought he remembered, in 1869, that Poe had told him in 1826 that his total debts amounted to $2000, and that he intended to pay them, including the gambling debts, which he considered debts of honor. In his letter to Allan January 3, 1831, Poe may refer to these gambling debts when he says: "You would not let me return because bills were presented to you for payment which I never wished nor desired you to pay." If they were ever paid, I have found no record of when or how.

Poe is known to have been a member of the Jefferson Society, for his name appears in the minutes of one of its meetings in the capacity of secretary. Both Burwell and Tucker speak of his writing. Burwell recalls that Poe "delighted and entertained" his friends by reading his own poems, and Tucker says that friends often filled Poe's room and "scarcely breathed as they eagerly listened to some story" he had written. For a while he was nicknamed "Gaffy" after the hero of one of his stories, which he destroyed. Burwell and others remembered Poe's skill at drawing, which he demonstrated on the walls of his room to such effect that his friends were in doubt whether in future life he would be painter or poet. It is possible that he wrote his 400-line poem "Tamerlane" while at the University, and perhaps also some of the short poems of his first small volume, which was printed in Boston in the spring or early summer of 1827. Apparently no prose fiction written at the University has survived. The only use he ever made of his University experience in later writing was in two stories: "William Wilson" (1839), where the scenes of drinking and gambling by students of Eton and Oxford may have been projections of comparable scenes he remembered at the University of Virginia, and "A Tale of the Ragged Mountains" (1844), in which he speaks of residing near Charlottesville in the fall of 1827—the date an error for 1826. It is a mistake to read into these episodes, as some have done, any factual details of Poe's biography. In the earliest (1837) version of "Mystification," a humorous tale, there is a paragraph, later omitted, in which the narrator mentions a number of incredible things he has seen, among them the following: "I have seen an ox-cart, with oxen, on the summit of the Rotunda." This is interesting in view of the fact that in 1887 and again in 1965 students really did place a cow on top of the Rotunda. "Tamerlane," the story of a Mongol conqueror of the fourteenth century who sacrificed love for ambition, may reflect something of Poe's disappointment that his Richmond sweetheart, Sarah Elmira Royster, became engaged to another man while he was at the University, and later married him, but the resemblance is slight.

Poe's second volume of poetry was published in 1829 and his third in 1831, but they passed into temporary oblivion almost without notice. From August 1836 to January 1837, he was editor of the *Southern Literary Messenger,* in Richmond, and at least one issue of the magazine during this period was reviewed in the *Virginia Advocate,* a Charlottesville paper, but I have found no printed evidence that he was, as a literary figure, known to the students or faculty of the University before his death. There was not even a notice of his death in the *Jefferson Monument Magazine,* a student monthly published from October 1849 to June 1851, unless it was in the issue of November 1849, which is missing from the file in the University library. In the issue of this magazine for February 1850 appears the first student composition definitely inspired by Poe. This is a poem entitled "A Travestie." Underneath the title is the following sentence in quotation marks: "The Jester having encountered a piece of POEtry, endeavoureth to give a grotesque shadow of the same." It is a rather good parody of "The Raven," the first of many to be published in later issues of this magazine and its successors. The only other mention of Poe in this magazine is an insert at the bottom of a page of the April issue following, which reads: "Poe called a beautiful woman 'a perpetual hymn to the Deity.'"

There was no student magazine from June 1851 to December 1856, when the first issue of the *University Literary Magazine* appeared. In February 1858 the name was changed to *Virginia University Magazine,* and under this name it continued until April 1861. During these years a great many articles on Poe, several parodies, and some poems influenced by him appeared. By 1856 most of Poe's writing was available in the Griswold edition of four volumes, and the poems and selections from the prose tales were more readily accessible in single volumes. Interest in him and his works was evidently considerable among the students at this period. In the magazine for February 1857 there is an article called "The Literary Man," which describes the "would-be literary man" of the University as a pale, nongregarious, pipe-smoking fellow who wears a collar like Byron and thinks the only true poet the world ever saw was not Shakespeare or Tennyson but "a young man, not long deceased, and formerly at the University of Virginia, named Edgar Allan Poe." Students of this type, the writer continues, are often seen coming from the library with dusty books, but "it is a perpetual source of regret to them that the library does not keep pace with the times, that the aforementioned Poe & Co. are not to be found there. Those who are lucky enough to belong to the 'Jeff' take immense pleasure in looking over old records to see the minutes signed 'Edgar A. Poe, Secretary, Jefferson Society.'" In their rooms the table is covered with books, and there "Poe's works always find a place, and Macaulay's Essays." Other articles in the magazine compare Poe with Byron, quote from Griswold's "Memoir" and accept as true his charge that Poe was dissolute, though brilliant. An article in December 1858 calls him "the most gifted poet and the most unfortunate man in America," contrasting his "exalted genius" with his "dark moral obliquity." This is the kind of criticism students might also have read in John M. Daniel's article on Poe in the *Southern Literary Messenger* for March 1850, in George Gilfillan's uninformed and slanderous article in the *London Critic* that was reprinted in several periodicals in this country in 1854, and in the author's book, *A Third Gallery of Portraits,* in 1855. There were more accurate and more friendly articles on Poe by Lowell, George Graham, and others who knew him, but they had far less impact on the public mind than the writings of Griswold and his followers. Nevertheless, from about this time, students began to show more interest in Poe's poems, tales, and criticism than ever before. Two articles published in 1860 discuss with intelligence some of Poe's critical theories, and in April of that year a writer has interesting things to say of "The Raven" and *Eureka* as examples of the pathetic and the abstruse, which he identifies as the two dominant characteristics of Poe's work.

After its suspension in 1861 because of the Civil War, the *Virginia University Magazine* was not resumed until December 1867. By this time, if not before, the writings of its now distinguished alumnus were available in the library, for William Wertenbaker says in 1868, in an article already referred to, that "Mr. Poe's works are more in demand and more read than those of any other author, American or foreign, now in the Library." Yet there were fewer articles on Poe in the magazine during the ten years following 1867 than there had been during the four years 1857 to 1860. In an article on University alumni in October 1870, the writer names Poe as the "proudest and foremost upon our roll of honor." Another writer in January 1872 condemns Griswold's treating "William Wilson" as if it were a remorseful confession by Poe of his own misdeeds, and criticizes Southerners for reading with apparent approval books about Poe that besmirch his name while his own writings "moulder on the booksellers' shelves." Looked at in the most favorable light, however, it must be admitted that Poe was until 1880 known chiefly as a somewhat Byronic personality and as the author of "The Raven." If other poems were sometimes mentioned in the magazines they were likely to be "Ulalume," "Annabel Lee," or "The Bells." There was not a great deal of interest in any of his stories except the two connected with his experiences at the University—"William Wilson" and "A Tale of the Ragged Mountains." Several critical works were mentioned, including "The Philosophy of Composition"—probably because it relates to "The Raven"—and an item in *The Literati* called "Fancy and Imagination." Rather surprisingly, considering the time and place, there is a very competent article on *Eureka.*

An article called "Poe and the University of Virginia" was published in the issue for April 1903 in which the author estimates that the magazine had printed between 1885 and 1900 as many as ninety contributions which bear upon Poe's life and writings or show traces of Poe's influence on their style. There are more imitations than in any earlier period, but in most of the poems and stories named in this article the traces of Poe's style, it seems to me, are very tenuous. Serious student interest in Poe was greater between 1885 and 1900 than between 1867 and 1885, but less than during the four or five years immediately preceding the Civil War.

A number of factors combined to increase interest after 1885. The first was the publication that year of Woodberry's biography of Poe. Another, which conduced also to increased interest in literature generally, was the establishment of the first School of English in 1883. Before then the University offered little encouragement toward the study of modern literature. Even more important was the endowment of the Linden Kent Memorial School of English Literature in 1893, with Professor Charles W. Kent at its head. Under Professor Kent's leadership, the University of Virginia became one of the very first institutions of higher education to offer courses in American literature.

By this time Poe had become famous, and interest in him at the University merged with the general interest. Therefore it need not be pursued further here. I should like, however, in closing, to mention a few special honors which the University and its faculty and students have conferred on Poe.

In 1897 the Poe Memorial Association was organized, largely through the efforts of Professor Kent and his colleague Professor James A. Harrison. They raised a considerable sum of money and engaged the well-known sculptor Julian Zolnay to prepare a bronze bust of Poe. The bust was completed in 1899 and placed, together with a collection of books by and about Poe given chiefly by Professor Harrison, in the Poe Alcove of the Library in the Rotunda. On October 7, fifty years after Poe's death, the bust was unveiled with appropriate ceremonies which were later memorialized in a special volume edited by Professor Kent. In 1902 Harrison, who taught Anglo-Saxon and was head of the School of Teutonic Languages but was interested also in American literature, edited and published in seventeen volumes the *Complete Works of Edgar Allan Poe*, a landmark in Poe scholarship. In 1904 the Raven Society was organized, honoring Poe, and was authorized to furnish No. 13 West Range in the style of dormitories in Poe's time and to use it as a meeting place. In 1909 the University celebrated the centennial of Poe's birth with elaborate ceremonies, where tributes in prose and verse were read and afterward published in a memorial volume. The same year the Board of Visitors authorized the establishment of the Edgar Allan Poe School of English, co-ordinate with the Linden Kent School and later to be combined with it to form the Department of English. Beyond question, the year 1909 marked the peak of Poe's fame at the University of Virginia, and perhaps also in the entire country. The name of Poe still has a kind of magic, and the false image created by Griswold still survives in the popular mind, but his literary reputation is now and must remain in the custody of the informed critic and scholar.

II. Poet in Search of a Career

I

WHEN Poe left Charlottesville, probably on December 21, 1826, he could not have foreseen the uncertain future that lay before him. He owed not only gambling debts but also debts for purchases made and money borrowed. In his letter to Allan from West Point, January 3, 1831, he said he owed "money borrowed of Jews in Charlottesville at extravagant interest" to pay for books, a hired servant, wood, washing, "and a thousand other necessaries."[1] He did not desire his foster father to pay his gambling debts, although he considered them debts of honor, but he did expect him to discharge his more legitimate obligations, including the cost of some fine clothes purchased from Samuel Leitch just before he left Charlottesville. The full extent of these obligations was not known by Allan until later, and Edgar was welcomed home by his family and friends in the cheerful spirit of the Christmas season. There is good reason to believe that he still hoped to be allowed to return to the University in a few weeks to begin a second session there.

But this hope was soon blasted; just how soon it is not possible to say. Thomas H. Ellis, the son of John Allan's partner, published a long letter in the Richmond *Standard* May 7, 1881, on the occasion of the death of Allan's second wife. He charged Poe, on secondhand evidence, with bad conduct and among other things, said:

> Mr. Allan went up to Charlottesville, inquired into his ways, paid every debt he thought ought to be paid, and refusing to pay some gambling debts (which Mr. James Galt told me, in his lifetime, amounted to about $2,500) brought Edgar away in the month of December following, and for a time kept him in Ellis & Allan's countingroom (where they were engaged in winding up their old business) —thus attempting to give him some knowledge of book-keeping, accounts, and commercial correspondence.[2]

[1] *The Letters of Edgar Allan Poe*, ed. John Ward Ostrom (2 vols., with consecutive pagination; Cambridge, Mass., 1948), pp. 39–42 (hereafter cited as *Letters*). This letter was misdated by Poe, "1830" for "1831."

[2] From a newspaper clipping in the Ingram Collection, Alderman Library, University of Virginia.

There are several statements in this passage which, as Poe's most reliable biographer has suggested, must be questioned.[3] The amount of the gambling debts may be exaggerated; Allan did not pay all the debts that an honest merchant should have considered worthy of payment; and there is at least some ground for doubting that Edgar was put to work in the counting room of Ellis and Allan. One other part of the statement, which Quinn does not mention, should also be examined: that is that Allan paid the debts before December and that he "brought Edgar away" in that month. Allan did make two visits to Charlottesville while Edgar was a student there, and both of these are mentioned by Edgar in his only two surviving letters to Allan written from the University. In neither is there the slightest hint of discontent on the part of either Poe or his foster father. The letters are chatty and rather affectionate in tone. The first visit occurred shortly before May 9, the date of a "disturbance" among the students mentioned by Poe in his first letter, written in May, probably in the latter part of the month. The second visit, mentioned in Poe's letter dated September 21, 1826, occurred between May 24 and August 1. In this letter Poe says a student named Wickliffe was "in suspension" at the time of Allan's visit. The Faculty Minutes reveal that Charles Wickliffe was suspended by the Faculty on May 24, the period of suspension to end on August 1.[4] I find no evidence that Allan visited Edgar after August 1, or that he came after him at the end of the session.

It is not known just when Allan learned the full truth of Edgar's indebtedness, but there can be little doubt that this knowledge was the chief source of their bitter quarrels during the three months following Edgar's return to Richmond. Evidence has been presented by several biographers of a period of serious friction between them two years before Edgar entered the University. Quinn conjectures, on the basis of a letter written by Allan to Poe's brother Henry, that Poe had learned as early as 1824 of Allan's marital infidelities and had reproached him for them.[5] Whatever the cause may have been, it appears that by 1825, when Allan inherited a fortune from his uncle William Galt, the earlier feelings of confidence and affection between them had to some extent been restored. It would have been natural for Poe to expect to inherit part of this fortune after Allan's death, and natural also for him to indulge his taste for books, good clothes, and

[3] Arthur Hobson Quinn, *Edgar Allan Poe, A Critical Biography* (New York, 1941), p. 109.

[4] For further details, see the preceding essay, "Edgar Poe and the University of Virginia."

[5] Pp. 89–90.

little extravagances not inappropriate in the son of a wealthy merchant. It would have been no less natural for Allan's habitual parsimony to lead him to withhold ready cash which he knew Edgar would spend freely. In sending him to the University with insufficient funds or, in any case, funds barely sufficient to pay his initial expenses, leaving him no pocket money, he might have expected that Edgar would use his credit for reasonable additional expenses during the session and that the potential creditors in Charlottesville would exercise restraint in extending credit. He could hardly have made two visits to Charlottesville without learning that Edgar was spending more money than he himself had provided, although it is certain that he did not learn of the gambling debts, which Poe's fellow-students would have wished to keep secret.

One may be sure that Ellis's statement that Allan refused to pay "some" of these gambling debts falls short of the fact, for since he did not pay Samuel Leitch for Edgar's purchase of clothing it is not likely that he would have paid any gambling debts whatever. The amount of these debts cannot be precisely estimated. William Wertenbaker, Poe's fellow-student in 1826, remembered years later that Poe told him he owed about $2,000, an estimate which probably included all debts, whether from gambling, purchases, or borrowing. Moreover, Poe may have been bragging to Wertenbaker. Knowing his tendency to exaggerate his youthful exploits, even his vices, we may perhaps scale down the figure of $2,000 somewhat and be nearer the truth. In matters of serious import Poe's statements can usually be accepted as true. Many of his statements in his letter to Allan January 3, 1831, have been checked with known facts and proved to be accurate. It may be assumed, therefore, that he was telling the truth when he says that before he "became desperate and gambled" he applied to James Galt, a prosperous young relative of John Allan and like him a beneficiary under the will of William Galt, who declined to lend him money. In the same letter Poe admits that he "became dissolute" although he "never loved dissipation." But it is clear from the context that to become dissolute, as he used the term, was to gamble, and that his sole dissipation was his gambling. Poe used the same terms when he gave Griswold material for a biography, but Griswold—and most of the world following him—have interpreted them in a way Poe never intended.

When Edgar returned from the University his gambling was apparently not known to his friends in Richmond; the students who had

gambled would have preferred to keep the fact from public knowledge and therefore would hardly have solicited payment from Allan.
Leitch and others whose claims were more legitimate, however, were
not slow to act, and Allan's refusal to pay these debts made things
difficult for Edgar, as is evident from a phrase in the letter cited above
relating to the early months of 1827: "Every day threatened with a
warrant, &c." Poe was probably referring to these threats when he said
in an earlier letter, dated February 4, 1829, written from Fortress
Monroe: "You will remember how much I had to suffer upon my
return from the University."[6] This was not to be the last time Poe
would be threatened with arrest and imprisonment for debts his foster
father refused to pay.

Though Poe's University debts were the initial and principal cause
of his breach with Allan, there were doubtless other reasons. Thomas
Ellis may have been right in saying that Allan put Poe to work in the
counting room of Ellis and Allan to give him business training, but it
is not likely that Poe worked willingly or long at this job. Poe's letters
to Allan from 1827 to 1831 throw some light on the question. After a
violent quarrel with Allan on Sunday, March 18, 1827, which continued the next morning, Poe left the house without money or personal
belongings. Later that day, in a letter dated simply "Monday," he asks
for a little money with which to buy food and lodging and requests
that his trunk, containing his clothes and books, be sent to the Court
House Tavern. In this letter he gives explicit reasons for his going:

Since I have been able to think on any subject, my thoughts have
aspired, and they have been taught by *you* to aspire, to eminence in public
life—This cannot be attained without a good Education, such a one I
cannot obtain at a Primary school—

A collegiate Education therefore was what I most ardently desired, and I
had been led to expect that it would at some future time be granted—but
in a moment of caprice you have blasted my hope—because forsooth I
disagreed with you in an opinion, which opinion I was forced to express—

Again, I have heard you say (when you little thought I was listening and
therefore must have said it in earnest) that you had no affection for
me—You have moreover ordered me to quit your house, and are continually upbraiding me with eating the bread of idleness, when you yourself
were the only person to remedy the evil by placing me to some business—

You take delight in exposing me before those whom you think likely to
advance my interest in this world—

[6] *Letters,* pp. 13–14.

You suffer me to be subjected to the whims & caprice, not only of your white family, but the complete authority of the blacks—these grievances I could not submit to; and I am gone—[7]

The ambiguous phrases in the above quotation are those relating to "eminence in public life," to an opinion which Poe says he was forced to express, and to his idleness because his foster father would not place him in "some business." Eminence in public life in Virginia in Poe's time could certainly not be attained through clerking, bookkeeping, or any operation connected with a mercantile establishment. Just what Poe had in mind by "public life" is not clear, but since it was to require a collegiate education we may assume it was the law, medicine, literature, or something else on a social level with these pursuits. The opinion he was forced to express surely related to the problem of his profession and may have been his determination to achieve eminence as against Allan's desire to have him go into business. This raises the question, of course, of what Poe meant by placing him in "some business." There is no escape from ambiguity here, but taken in context the words could not mean the kind of business that Ellis says Poe had already been placed in without success. It follows also that in charging Allan with "exposing" him before those who might advance his interest Poe had in mind not business executives but men of eminence such as John Marshall and William Wirt, both of whom had long been resident in Richmond, though often absent on official duty in Washington. Also both were acquaintances, if not friends, of John Allan. There were numerous others, perhaps less eminent, who might have advanced Poe's fortunes in public life. Poe closes his letter by asking for enough money to defray the expense of travel to "some of the Northern cities" and to live on until he can place himself "in some situation," as he expresses it, "where I may not only obtain a livelihood, but lay by a sum which one day or another will support me at the University."

Allan answered this letter the day it was received, probably Tuesday. He devoted his letter chiefly to an explanation of what he meant by "the charge of eating the Bread of idleness," saying that it "was to urge you to perseverance & industry in receiving the classics, in perfecting yourself in the mathematics, mastering the French &c. &c. how far I succeeded in this you can best tell."[8] Quinn says, "This can

---

[7] *Ibid.*, pp. 7–8.

[8] *Edgar Allan Poe Letters Till Now Unpublished in the Valentine Museum,* with Commentary by Mary Newton Stanard (Philadelphia, 1925), pp. 67–68 (hereafter cited as *Valentine Letters*).

hardly refer to the period after Poe's return to Richmond," but he gives no reason for his opinion.[9] My own opinion, on the contrary, is that it could refer to no other period. Conjecturally, I should say that Allan put Poe to work in the Ellis and Allan counting room, as Ellis says, but that Poe complained and quit the work, and that Allan then proposed that he continue the study of the classics and resume the study of mathematics, which he had discontinued when he entered the University. Since these studies could have been of little or no use to him in the business world, Allan must have proposed them as an alternative to the forbidden second year at the University. If so, he was not directly opposed to Poe's preparing for a public career but only to his using plans for such a career as an argument for returning to the University. Poe's "idleness" probably consisted of nothing worse than his spending his time writing and revising poems.

Poe's second letter to Allan was written on Tuesday before he received the reply to his first. In it he again asked for his trunk, and this time he requested the gift or loan of the specific sum of twelve dollars for passage to Boston. Evidently his plans on Tuesday were more definite than they were the day before, for he added, "I sail on Saturday."[10] His going to Boston suggests that he was intent on pursuing a literary career. Allan's stress on the classics and mathematics—the latter particularly—would indicate that his choice for Poe was a professional career such as medicine or the law. A businessman in the early nineteenth century would normally have no patience with a son, even an adopted one, who aspired to a career in creative writing, and least of all poetry.[11]

It is fairly certain that Poe sailed, as planned, on Saturday, March 24. Whether he proceeded directly to Boston or stopped off at Baltimore or Philadelphia is not known. Neither can we be sure whether he paid his passage money or worked his way, but it seems probable that he got the money for the journey either from Allan himself or through Mrs. Allan. Thomas Ollive Mabbott speculates on the possibility that Poe visited Baltimore between March 24 and May 1, 1827. He cites as possible evidence nine lines of verse, which he thinks are in Poe's handwriting but which are unsigned, in the album of Octavia Walton, who has added the date, "May the 1st, 1827." Another poem, signed

---

[9] P. 115.   [10] *Letters*, pp. 8–9.
[11] Hervey Allen suggests the possibility of such a disagreement between Allan and Poe. See *Israfel: The Life and Times of Edgar Allan Poe* (New York, 1927), I, 191 ff.

"E. A. P.," addressed to Margaret Basset and in her album now in the Lilly Library at Indiana University, he thinks was written by Poe in 1829 rather than in 1827 as has sometimes been claimed.[12] These are interesting possibilities, but the facts remain uncertain. Poe may have arrived in Boston as early as April 7, but all that we know certainly is that he was in Boston on May 26, when he enlisted in the army under the name of Edgar A. Perry, and that he had been in the city long enough to make the acquaintance of another young man, a printer by the name of Calvin F. S. Thomas, and to prepare his manuscripts for printing. The little book was probably printed in July, since it was noticed as a new book in the August number of the *United States Review and Literary Gazette*. It is represented on the title page as being "By a Bostonian," which was literally true in the sense that Poe was born there. It is not known how many copies were printed, but it had practically no sale, and copies are now extremely rare.

It is tempting to speculate on when these poems were written,[13] but little can be known beyond what is fairly obvious. The title page was certainly designed after Poe arrived in Boston, and the quotation on the title page may refer to his own situation at the time:

> Young heads are giddy, and young hearts are warm,
> And make mistakes for manhood to reform.—Cowper.[14]

As a rule, however, Poe's epigraphs relate not to himself but to the poems they introduce. Here, for example, the giddy heads and warm hearts, as well as the mistakes, are those of Tamerlane and the speakers in most of the short poems of the 1827 volume. The Preface contains three short paragraphs. The first begins with the following sentence: "The greater part of the Poems which compose this little volume, were written in the year 1821-2, when the author had not completed his fourteenth year." In the second paragraph he says that in "Tamerlane" he has "endeavoured to expose the folly of even *risking* the best feelings of the heart at the shrine of Ambition." The

---

[12] See the Introduction to his Facsimile Text Society Edition of *Tamerlane and Other Poems* (New York, 1941), pp. xii–xvii.

[13] The list of printed works where such speculation has been made is too long to be detailed here. For some enlightened comment on the subject, see Mabbott's introduction, *ibid*.

[14] The lines are 444–445 of *Tirocinium; or, A Review of Schools*, inscribed by the author to the Rev. William Cawthorne Unwin, the tutor to his own two sons. The poem praises the education of boys by private tutoring instead of by schools. Poe could have read it, with *The Task,* in a small volume of 1825.

third paragraph informs the reader that though the poet is not indifferent to the success of his poems, "failure will not at all influence him
in a resolution already adopted." These are the significant statements
of the Preface.

Poe's misstatement as to the date of composition was the first of
several involving these and other poems. Writing to John Neal in the
autumn of 1829, he said he was "not yet twenty," though he was
within a few months of twenty-one. He also said, "I am about to
publish a volume of 'Poems'—the greater part written before I was
fifteen." In the biographical sketch he provided Griswold for insertion
in the first (1842) edition of *The Poets and Poetry of America,* he gave
1811 as the year of his birth, and he made no mention of the three
early editions of his poems. In the Philadelphia *Saturday Museum* for
March 4, 1843, seventeen of Poe's poems were printed (including
selections from "Al Aaraaf"), with notes and a biographical sketch by
H. B. Hirst based on memoranda provided by Poe.[15] The following
passage appears just before the lines "To Helen": "He wrote verses as
soon as he could write at all. His first poetical publication, however,
was 'Al Aaraaf, Tamerlane, and Minor Poems. By a Virginian.' Of this,
the first edition was published (in pamphlet form) in Boston, before
he had completed his fifteenth year. Some of his best pieces, among
others the subjoined lines to Helen, were composed two years previously." Following the poem it is specifically stated that this poem
was composed "by a boy of fourteen," and that a "second edition" was
published in 1829, and a third "during the author's cadetship at West
Point." In a letter to Lowell, October 19, 1843, Poe says he is sending
him a copy of the *Museum* with his "life and portrait," adding: "The
former is true in general—the latter particularly false. It does not
contain the faintest idea of my person."[16] Perhaps the account of his
life in this paper is "true in general," but the statements in the passage
I have quoted are all specifically untrue. One can understand that in
1843, with his growing dislike of New England, he should wish to
change "By a Bostonian" on the title page of the 1827 pamphlet to "By
a Virginian," but the other misstatements of fact are not so easily
explained. Poe must have marked out some passages of the life sketch

---

[15] As explained in Poe's letter to F. W. Thomas, February 25, 1843, *Letters,* pp.
223–225. This material, with minor differences, was first published in the *Museum*
on February 25.

[16] Lowell did not use this, but another portrait painted by A. C. Smith of
Philadelphia, which has since become well known. It is the frontispiece to Killis
Campbell's edition of the poems.

before sending it to Lowell for his article in *Graham's Magazine* for
February 1845. There we are told simply that Poe "had published (in
1827) a small volume of poems, which soon ran through three editions." This is still untrue, but nearer the truth than the *Museum*
sketch. Lowell's essay retains, however, the statement that "To Helen"
was written at the age of fourteen.

We know from the testimony of his fellow-students that Poe was
writing poems and stories while at the University of Virginia, and it is
probable that he had written some verse, like many another youth, by
the time he was fourteen. It is beyond belief, however, that "To
Helen" existed in anything like finished form before 1830, since it was
not included in either the 1827 or the 1829 volume. Because the theme
of "Tamerlane" is the conflict between love and ambition, it seems
likely that it was begun while Poe was at the University but not
completed until after he returned to Richmond and learned that Sarah
Elmira Royster, with whom he is said to have been in love, had
engaged herself to another man. Some of the short poems—"Dreams"
and "Evening Star," for two examples—might have been composed as
early as 1825, though surely not in 1821 or 1822. John Allan objected
to Edgar's ambition to become a poet, but he could hardly have taken
this seriously before the boy reached sixteen or seventeen.

Besides "Tamerlane" the 1827 volume contained nine short poems,
three of which were not reprinted by Poe in later editions. These were
"Dreams," "Evening Star," and a poem without title, later called by its
first line, "The Happiest Day—the Happiest Hour." Another, "Invita-
tion," was given the title "To ____ ____" in 1829 and afterward "A
Dream within a Dream." The poems which were reprinted were revised extensively. The short poems were grouped in a section following "Tamerlane" called "Fugitive Pieces." After this section there were
several pages of notes to "Tamerlane." They contribute little to the
understanding of the poem except to explain the source of the hero's
name in the historical conqueror Tamerlane, also known as Timur
Bek. They were dropped from all later editions.

Very little is known of Poe's daily life in the Army. He was assigned
to Battery H. 1st U.S. Artillery, then stationed at Fort Independence,
Boston. He was transferred with his unit to Fort Moultrie, near
Charleston, South Carolina, where it arrived November 18, 1827. A
little more than a year later it was transferred to Fortress Monroe,
Virginia, and arrived there December 25, 1828. Poe was promoted to
the rank of sergeant major on January 1, 1829, but before that he had

decided he wanted to be discharged. His first known letter to Allan after he left Richmond is dated December 1, 1828, from Fort Moultrie. It refers to a letter from Poe's immediate superior officer, Lieutenant J. Howard, either to John Allan or to Poe himself, which had been sent by a Mr. John O. Lay to Richmond and given to Allan for his perusal. We learn from Poe's letter to Allan that Lieutenant Howard had promised him his discharge "solely upon a re-conciliation with yourself." To this proposal Allan replied directly to Mr. Lay saying that Poe "had better remain as he is until the termination of his enlistment"; this reply was conveyed through Lieutenant Howard to Poe. Poe's letter of December 1, 1828, seems to have been written at the insistence of Lieutenant Howard. Quinn says, "Evidently there had been previous correspondence" between Poe and Allan, but a careful reading of Poe's letters does not appear to support this statement.[17] Receiving no reply to the letter of December 1, Poe wrote again on December 22 and on February 4, 1829. In the third letter he requests Allan to assist him, through his personal acquaintance with William Wirt or General Winfield Scott, to secure admission to the West Point Military Academy. It is evident from the other letters that he had thought of this before, or that it had been suggested to him by Lieutenant Howard, but that he had dismissed it for the time being as either impracticable or not to his taste. He proposed it now as a last resort to escape the final three years of his term of enlistment. The move proved successful, but only, one suspects, because the death of Mrs. Frances Allan on February 28, 1829, had softened Allan's heart to the extent of sending for Poe and asking that he be granted a week's leave. Poe was discharged, effective April 15, 1829, after he had secured a substitute to complete the period of his enlistment. Afterward he told Allan that he had to pay a bounty of $75.00—much more than was customary—because he felt he could not wait until someone offered himself for less.

All of Poe's officers wrote letters, dated April 20, praising his conduct and services while in the Army. Poe took these to Washington with him early in May, where he presented his credentials to Major John Eaton, Secretary of War.[18] John Allan also wrote, on May 6, but the tone of his letter was so cold and condescending that it would

[17] Pp. 129–135; also pp. 742–743, where records of the War Department are cited in a letter from the Adjutant General.

[18] Quinn, pp. 134–137.

certainly have chilled the bearer to the bone if he had seen it.[19]
Having presented his credentials, Poe went on to Baltimore, perhaps
on May 7 or 8, where he renewed his relationships with his relatives
there and awaited the notice of his appointment.

II

This notice was slow in coming, but in the meantime he made the
most of his leisure to prepare a second edition of his poems. On May
20 he wrote to Allan saying he had found his grandmother, the aged
widow of General David Poe, and other relations, had called on
William Wirt (who had moved to Baltimore the preceding month)
several times, and had been introduced to many gentlemen of "high
standing" in the city.[20] One of the visits to Wirt was on the morning of
May 11, when he left with him a poem, presumably "Al Aaraaf," for
criticism. Professing his inability to judge modern poetry, Wirt returned the poem the same evening and suggested to Poe that he
consult Robert Walsh, the editor of the *American Quarterly Review,*
in Philadelphia.[21] Poe promptly took his manuscript to Philadelphia,
probably May 12 or 13, and after a talk with Walsh delivered it to the
publishing house then known as Carey, Lea and Carey, together with
an undated letter to Isaac Lea, in which he described his principal
poem.[22] The main portion of this description is quoted here in full:

Its title is "Al Aaraaf"—from the Al Aaraaf of the Arabians, a medium
between Heaven & Hell where men suffer no punishment, but yet do not
attain that tranquil & even happiness which they suppose to be the
characteristic of heavenly enjoyment.

> Un no rompido
> Un dia puro, allegre, libre
> Quiera—
> Libre de amor, de zelo
> De odio, de esperanza, de rezelo—

I have placed this "Al Aaraaf" in the celebrated star discovered by
Tycho Brache which appeared & dissapeared so suddenly—It is represented as a messenger star of the Deity, &, at the time of its discovery by

[19] *Valentine Letters,* pp. 110–111. For Poe's letters, see *Letters,* pp. 9–15.
[20] *Letters,* pp. 16–17.
[21] *Valentine Letters,* pp. 131–132. The original manuscript is credited to the
Boston Public Library.
[22] *Letters,* pp. 18–19.

Tycho, as on an embassy to our world. One of the peculiarities of Al Aaraaf is that, even after death, those who make choice of the star as their residence do not enjoy immortality—but, after a second life of high excitement, sink into forgetfulness & death—This idea is taken from Job— "I would not live always—let me alone"—I have imagined that some would not be pleased (excuse the bull) with an immortality even of bliss. The poem commences with a sonnet (illegitimate) a la mode de Byron in his prisoner of Chillon. But this is a digression—I have imagined some well known characters of the age of the star's appearance, as transferred to Al Aaraaf—viz Michael Angelo—and others—of these Michael Angelo as yet, alone appears. I send you parts 1rst 2d & 3d. I have reasons for wishing not to publish the 4th at present—for its character depends in a measure upon the success or failure of the others.

This description of "Al Aaraaf" must be discussed in some detail. Part of it, together with additional material, was used in the edition of 1829 as a note to line 173 of Part II. The first sentence of the note is almost identical with the first sentence quoted above. The lines of verse are verbally identical except that in the letter Poe omits the word "sueno" at the end of the first line. The rest of the note, however, is somewhat different, and is quoted here for comparison:

Sorrow is not excluded from "Al Aaraaf," but it is that sorrow which the living love to cherish for the dead, and which, in some minds, resembles the delirium of opium. The passionate excitement of Love and the buoyancy of spirit attendant upon intoxication are its less holy pleasures—the price of which, to those souls who make choice of "Al Aaraaf" as their residence after life, is final death and annihilation.

The idea of sorrow and the idea that passionate love is unholy in Al Aaraaf do not appear in the letter, and the reference to Job in the letter is omitted in the note.

The lines in Spanish, which Poe quotes in both the letter and the note as five connected lines, are lines 26–27 and 39–40 from "Vida Retirada," by the sixteenth-century monk Luis Ponce de León. In the scholarly edition of Ponce de León's *Obras Poéticas*, by P. José Llobera (Madrid, 1932), the lines appear as follows:

> Un no rompido sueño
> un día puro, alegre, libre quiero;
>
> . . . . .
> libre de amor, de celo,
> de odio, de esperanzas, de recelo.

This may be translated: "I desire an uninterrupted sleep, a day that is clear, happy, free; . . . free of love, of envy, of hopes, of fear." The sentiment fits very well the theme of "Al Aaraaf." The sense of some of the lines Poe omitted in his quotation does not fit. It may be assumed, therefore, that some of his variations from his original were deliberate, though others were the consequence either of ignorance of the language or careless copying—more likely the latter. Poe's use of "z" for "c" in two words may be accounted for by his using an early text.[23]

There are other errors in Poe's letters—for example, "dissapeared" and "Brache" for "Brahe"—which was probably written in haste. The sonnet referred to is the one printed without title at the beginning of the 1829 volume, afterward called "Sonnet—To Science." It is called "illegitimate" presumably because the rhyme sequence does not conform either to the Spenserian or Shakespearean forms but has elements of both.[24]

Aside from its title, Poe's poem has little in common with the conception of al aráf as it is described by George Sale in his "Preliminary Discourse" to the Koran.[25] In his letter to Carey, Lea and Carey, Poe says he took the idea which then seemed to him central in the poem—that certain people, not caring for an immortality of bliss, choose Al Aaraaf, where after a second life of high excitement they sink into forgetfulness and death—from the Book of Job. Poe quotes a portion of the sixteenth verse of Chapter 7, but to set it in its context I quote here all of verses 13 through 16:

> 13 When I say, My bed shall comfort me, my couch shall ease
>   my complaint;
> 14 Then thou scarest me with dreams, and terrifiest me
>   through visions:

[23] It is not possible to identify the edition Poe used. The *Poesías*, edited by Ramón Fernández, was published in Madrid in 1790 as Vol. X of a collection called *Parnaso Español* that was widely distributed. It is not listed in the 1828 catalogue of the University of Virginia library, but could probably have been found in the libraries of Baltimore. He might, of course, have found the passage in an anthology or textbook.

[24] Quinn is quite mistaken in saying (p. 162, note 34) that Poe here "reveals his habit of making references without care." He supposes that Poe's phrase "a la mode de Byron in the prisoner of Chillon" refers to the form of Byron's sonnet, whereas it obviously refers merely to the fact that, like Byron, he places a sonnet before a long poem as a kind of Preface.

[25] See "An Interpretation of 'Al Aaraaf,'" in the present volume. The Koran (London reprint, 1821), with George Sale's "Preliminary Discourse," is listed in the 1828 catalogue of the library of the University of Virginia. Probably it was available when Poe was a student.

15 So that my soul chooseth strangling, and death rather
   than my life.
16 I loathe it; I would not live alway: let me alone; for
   my days are vanity.[26]

There is nothing in Poe's letter to suggest that the forgetfulness and
second death in Al Aaraaf are punishment for guilt, nor is there
anything in the verses quoted to suggest that Job wished to die for any
other reason than that he was weary of life. I leave to theologians the
question whether Job believed in immortality or not. In the letter Poe
makes a clear distinction between an immortality of heavenly bliss on
the one hand and a second life of excitement followed by forgetfulness and annihilation on the other.[27] In choosing a second life of
excitement one chooses eventual annihilation in preference to an
immortality of bliss. In the published poem, however (II, 176–177,
263–264), Angelo and Ianthe "fell" because they had forfeited Heav-
en's "grace" by indulging in the excitement of passionate love and
consequently not hearing God's message conveyed through Nesace
and Ligeia. They were "guilty" spirits, and their annihilation was a
punishment, not an escape from the weariness of life on earth. Al
Aaraaf was a place to which one might hope to escape from earth, as
the poet had exclaimed only a few lines earlier:

> And there—oh! may my weary spirit dwell—
> Apart from Heaven's Eternity—and yet how far from Hell!

Whether the full name "Michael Angelo" appeared in the manuscript
sent to Carey, Lea and Carey or only "Angelo" as it is in the poem
there is no way of knowing. There are several reasons for dissociating
the Angelo of the poem from the historical Michelangelo: Angelo is
called "young" whereas Michelangelo lived to be nearly ninety; the
one was Greek, the other Italian; and, to make identification more
difficult, Poe represents the earth as flying from its course and bursting
into flame at the time of Angelo's death—a catastrophe which, fortunately, had not happened at the time the poem was written. Originally
Poe may have thought of Michelangelo for the poem and then
changed the character to "Angelo" to avoid these inconsistencies.

It is tempting to try to distinguish in the published poem the three

[26] Quoted from the annotated edition of the Bible by Thomas Scott, in 6 vols.
The 1827 edition is listed in the catalogue of the University of Virginia, 1828.

[27] The second death mentioned in the letter must mean the same as "annihilation" in Poe's note to l. 173 of pt. II of the poem, quoted above.

parts which he says he sent to Carey, Lea and Carey. The task would be easier if Poe had indicated the number of lines in his manuscript. We know only that he thought it too short to make a book, and so he proposed to include with it some short poems. It would be my guess —and I can do little better than guess—that the first fifteen lines of Part I were not in the manuscript, but that the rest of it, as printed, constituted essentially the first part in the manuscript version. That would be approximately 145 lines. Lines 1 through 173 of Part II of the finished poem may have existed, except for slight changes, as the second part of the manuscript. As Killis Campbell says in his note to line 174, "This line clearly introduces a new stage in the story."[28] The third part of the manuscript must have begun there. It must have consisted primarily of the story of Angelo and Ianthe, which continues to the end of the poem, with the possible exception of lines 174–177 and 261–264, which concern their guilt and punishment, and lines 234–236, the destruction of the earthly world. So defined, the third part would have contained approximately 80 lines. I suspect this part underwent more drastic revision and cutting than the other parts before the poem was published. There are inconsistencies in the poem that may be the consequence of Poe's changing his original design to sustain a new thematic pattern. The idea of making the poem a vehicle for suggesting his aesthetic theory had probably not occurred to Poe before May 1829.[29]

In the letter he speaks of not wishing to publish the fourth part yet, as if it had been written, but it is very doubtful that it then existed except in the merest fragments. In any case, nothing of the kind indicated was ever published. I believe he was ambitious to make his poem into something like an epic, a *Paradise Lost* in reverse, representing the escape from a wearisome world into an Eden of tranquillity and eventual oblivion. His footnotes prove that he had been reading Milton rather carefully, not only *Paradise Lost* but the minor poems and even the Latin poems.

It seems probable that after writing the letter described above Poe made a second trip to Philadelphia. In his letter to the firm, July 28, 1829, he mentions "a short interview, at your store," at which Mr. Lea suggested that he might attempt something for the *Atlantic Souvenir*, an annual published by them.[30] Since Poe wrote to Allan from Balti-

---

[28] *The Poems of Edgar Allan Poe* (Boston, 1917), p. 190.

[29] See "An Interpretation of 'Al Aaraaf,'" sect. III.

[30] *Letters*, p. 27. No contribution by Poe to the *Atlantic Souvenir* has been discovered.

more on May 20 and did not mention these publishers it must be presumed that the interview occurred after that date. Yet it could not have occurred later than May 27, for on May 29 Poe wrote to Allan again from Baltimore and asked him to subsidize the publication of his poems to the extent of $100, saying that he "had no reason to think" Carey, Lea and Carey would not decline publication unless guaranteed against loss. It is clear from this letter that Poe had been informed of the terms on which Carey, Lea and Carey would publish his poems. Poe concludes, "I shall wait anxiously for your answer."[31] The answer was not long in coming. Allan's reply has been lost, but the manuscript of Poe's letter of May 29 in the Valentine Museum bears the following endorsement in Allan's handwriting: "replied to Monday 8th June 1829 strongly censuring his conduct—& refusing any aid."[32] Still hopeful, Poe appealed again to his foster father on June 8 in a letter now lost, and again on June 25. In this last letter he said he had not withdrawn his manuscript from the publishers, pending Allan's decision. This decision apparently was transmitted in Allan's letter to Poe dated July 19 (now lost but referred to in Poe's note of July 26), for Poe wrote to Carey, Lea and Carey on July 28 requesting the return of his manuscripts, explaining that he declined to publish at his own expense because he had "made a better disposition" of his poems. This may have been wishful thinking, for it is not likely that he had any dependable means of publication by the end of July. It is possible, however, that he had already consulted Hatch and Dunning, and that they or others, William Gwynn, for example, might have given him some encouragement.

We hear nothing more of the manuscripts until October 30, when Poe wrote to Allan, who apparently had asked to see them: "I would have sent you the M. S. of my Poems long ago for your approval, but since I have collected them they have been continually in the hands of some person or another, & I have not had them in my own possession since Carey & Lea took them—I will send them to you at the first opportunity."[33] This statement is probably true in the sense that Poe had not had all the manuscripts in his own hands at one time since he had taken "Al Aaraaf" to Philadelphia about the middle of May. On

---

[31] *Letters*, pp. 16–17, 19–20.   [32] *Valentine Letters*, p. 121.

[33] *Letters*, pp. 21–22; 24–26. The mention of "Carey & Lea" indicates that when the firm of Carey, Lea and Carey was reorganized in September as two separate firms—Carey and Lea and Carey and Hart—it was the former that retained Poe's manuscript, no doubt because Poe had dealt chiefly with Isaac Lea. For details of the reorganization see p. 97 note 71.

May 18, 1829, the Baltimore *Gazette and Daily Advertiser* published
39 lines (194–201, 214–220, 237–260) drawn from Part II of "Al
Aaraaf," with the following prefatory paragraph:

Al Aaraaf, among the Arabians, a medium between Heaven and Hell, is
supposed to be located in the celebrated star discovered by Tycho Brahe,
which burst forth in one night upon the eyes of the world, and disappeared
as suddenly.—Michael Angelo is represented as transferred to this star,
and speaking to the "lady of his unearthly love" of the regions he had left."[34]

It cannot be determined from the documents available whether the
lines were removed from the manuscript before it was sent to Carey,
Lea and Carey or copied from it for submission to the paper. Gwynn
may have had in his possession the entire manuscript of "Al Aaraaf" at
one time, probably after it was returned to Poe by Carey, Lea and
Carey in August, and before it was delivered to Matchett and Woods,
printers for Hatch and Dunning, two or three months later.[35]

Since Poe did not send his short poems to Philadelphia with the
manuscript of "Al Aaraaf," there was nothing to prevent his submit-
ting them separately to magazine editors. How many he sent out there
is no way of knowing, but we do know that he sent "Fairyland" (with
the title of "Heaven") to John Neal and later (with its usual title) to
N. P. Willis. Neal commented kindly on the poem and printed two
extracts totaling thirteen lines in the September number of the *Yankee*. In a rather contemptuous boast of how he habitually burned
manuscripts submitted to him, Willis, in "The Editor's Table" of the
American Monthly Magazine for November 1829, spoke of reading
four lines of Poe's poem just before it went up in flames, and quoted
the lines. If Poe saw this comment he apparently did not take
offense.[36]

It is almost certain that when Poe wrote to Allan on October 30 his
manuscripts—all of them—were already in the hands of Hatch and
Dunning of Baltimore, for he told Allan in a letter on November 18
that the poems "will be printed by Hatch & Dunning of this city upon
terms advantageous to me they printing it & giving me 250 copies of
the book:—I will send it on by Mr. Dunning who is going immediately

[34] *The Gazette and Daily Advertiser* was published by William Gwynn, by
whom Poe's cousin, Neilson Poe, was then employed. These lines were discovered
and reprinted by Kenneth Rede in "Poe Notes from an Investigator's Notebook,"
American Literature, V (March 1933), 49–54.

[35] For more information on Poe's publishers and printers, see "Poe and 'The
Musiad,' " pp. 85–87 and 97 note 71, in the present volume.

[36] See also pp. 80–81.

to Richmond."[37] *Al Aaraaf, Tamerlane, and Minor Poems* was published in December or late November 1829, but exactly when would be hard to determine. Poe must have expected it to be printed soon after his letter of November 18 if his "immediately" may be taken seriously. He wrote to John Neal at an uncertain date, probably in October, thanking him for appreciating his poem "Fairyland," and for expressing confidence in his powers as a poet, "the very first words of encouragement," he says, "I ever remember to have heard." He says he is sending Neal an extract from "Al Aaraaf" describing the palace of Nesace, "the presiding Deity."[38] He sent, in fact, not only those lines (II, 11–39) but also three extracts from "Tamerlane" and one from "A Dream within a Dream," in all 120 lines. Neal printed them all in the December *Yankee,* together with some encouraging words about the young poet.[39]

Poe wrote to Neal on December 29 expressing his thanks and saying, "I wait anxiously for your notice of the book."[40] The notice Poe expected was not the one Neal printed with the extracts in the December *Yankee,* which he must have seen, for he says in the same letter, "You will see that I have made the alteration you suggest—'ventur'd out' in place of *peer-ed.*" Since the 1829 edition has this change, Poe must have sent Neal a copy of the book along with his letter, or earlier, and awaited a review of that. No other notice appeared in the *Yankee,* but an anonymous review was published in an unidentified Baltimore newspaper. Randolph W. Church, Virginia State Librarian, reprinted this review in the summer issue of the *Virginia Cavalcade* in 1955.[41] The chief critical passage in the review, which is altogether favorable, follows:

The object, at present, is to offer our tribute of admiration and regard to the Author of "Al Aaraaf, Tamerlane, and Minor Poems," which have

[37] *Letters,* p. 34. The printing was done by Matchett and Woods, a firm not organized till near the end of October. See pp. 85–86.

[38] *Letters,* pp. 32–33.

[39] New Series, No. 3 (Dec. 1829), 295–298. The periodical had been for several months published in Boston under the title the *Yankee and Boston Literary Gazette.*

[40] *Letters,* p. 35.

[41] V, 4–7. Mr. Church informs me that a clipping of this review was once in the possession of the late J. H. Rindfleisch and that he made a photographic copy of it during the 1930's. The clipping, he thinks, may have been lost at some later date. It is not among the other items of the Rindfleisch Collection now in the Virginia State Library. The extracts from this review in the present essay are printed with Mr. Church's permission, which is gratefully acknowledged.

recently been issued from the press in this city. We view the production as
highly creditable to the Country. Throughout, there runs a rich vein of
deep and powerful thought, clothed in language of almost inimitable
beauty and harmony. His fancy is rich and of an elevated cast; his
imagination powerfully creative. There is no laboured attempt at effect; no
immoderate use of epithets; no over-burdening the idea with words, no
cant, no nonsense.

The reviewer then quotes lines 1–17 from Part I and lines 112–127
from Part II of "Al Aaraaf" and also the first 28 lines of "Fairyland," of
which he says: "Its conception is truly grand, and its versification
highly ingenious." He concludes by expressing the hope "that the
author will receive that pecuniary remuneration which he so richly
merits, and which we are confident a public, when once it has examined the foundation of his claims, will cheerfully and amply confer."

Church comments: "Was the review or the reviewer known to Poe?
It is almost inconceivable that both were not." I quite agree. I can
think of only three or four people who might have written such a
review. One, of course, is Poe himself; yet I am inclined to dismiss that
possibility as inconsistent with Poe's habits and also because the style
is not noticeably like his. Another is Poe's brother, although there is no
reason for supposing he did it except that he was Poe's brother and
therefore would wish to praise the poems. A more likely candidate is
Poe's close friend at that time, Lambert A. Wilmer, a newspaperman
well acquainted with the editors and literary men of Baltimore and
probably living there at the end of 1829. If he did it, Poe himself
might have been a collaborator, or at any rate may have offered
suggestions.[42] William Gwynn might have published the review in his
newspaper, the *Gazette,* and indeed might have written it himself,
although I doubt that. Still another, and perhaps the most likely,
candidate is John Neal. The chief obstacle to crediting him with the
review is that he was in Boston at the time. Yet he might have written
it as an act of good will and, not wishing to take the responsibility for
enthusiastic praise of the poems, sent it to Poe for insertion anonymously in a Baltimore newspaper. If Neal was the author of the
review, Poe would, of course, have informed his family of the fact.
Neilson Poe said in a letter to his cousin Josephine Clemm on January
26, 1830: "Edgar Poe has published a volume of Poems one of which is
dedicated to John Neal the great autocrat of critics—Neal has accord-

---

[42] For a more detailed discussion of Wilmer's relationship with Poe and their
possible collaboration on another poem, see "Poe and 'The Musiad.'"

ingly published Edgar as a Poet of great genius etc.—*Our* name will be a great one *yet.*"[43] This tends to support Neal's authorship.

There were two other notices of the book. A short comment among the "Literary Notices" was made by Mrs. Sarah Josepha Hale in the *Ladies' Magazine* for January 1830. Parts of the poetry, she thinks are boyish and feeble, but other parts "of considerable length" remind her of Shelley. She concludes that the poet must be very young but "is evidently a fine genius." A longer review was published by John H. Hewitt early in 1830 in an issue of the *Baltimore Minerva and Emerald,* which is not now extant. In the eyes of the modern reader Hewitt damages himself more than Poe when he confesses his inability to make sense out of "Al Aaraaf" and compares the rhythmic movement of the poem to "travelling over a pile of brick-bats." But "Tamerlane" and the short poems find more favor in his eyes, and he quotes two short poems and a few lines from Ligeia's song in "Al Aaraaf."[44]

This edition of Poe's poems is better bound and better printed than his 1827 volume. In addition to the general title page, there is a separate title page for each of the two long poems and one for the group of short poems which reads "Miscellaneous Poems." There is no general preface, but each section has some brief introductory material. After the title "Al Aaraaf" in the first section there are four mottoes or epigraphs, each printed on a separate page, which seem to suggest the character of the poem. The first one reads as follows:

> Entiendes, Fabio, lo que voi deciendo?
> Toma, si, lo entendio:—Mientes, Fabio.

This may be translated: "Do you understand, Fabio, what I am saying?" "Yes, of course, I understand it." "You lie, Fabio." No source is given. The spelling "voi" for "voy" suggests an early work, but I have not been able to identify it. The second is from *Comus*, line 122: "What has night to do with sleep?" Poe substitutes "has" for Milton's "hath." The third is represented as a "Dedication," and is said to be from Cleveland, but I have not found it among his poems: "Who

---

[43] Quoted by Quinn, p. 165, from a manuscript copy in the handwriting of Amelia F. Poe in the Enoch Pratt Library, Baltimore. The underlined "Our" and "yet" were sly hints by a lover who afterward married the lady he was writing to.

[44] Hewitt printed portions of this review in *Shadows on the Wall* (Baltimore, 1877), pp. 41–43, and it has since been printed from manuscripts at Emory University in "Recollections of Poe, by John Hill Hewitt," ed. Richard Barksdale Harwell, *Emory Publications, Sources and Reprints,* Ser. V (1949), pp. 22–24.

drinks the deepest?—here's to him."[45] The fourth is in quotation marks
but no source is indicated: "A star was discovered by Tycho Brahe
which burst forth, in a moment, with a splendor surpassing that of
Jupiter—then gradually faded away and became invisible to the
naked eye." The source has no significance; it might have been an
encyclopaedia or any of various works on astronomy available to Poe.
All have significance, however, in the interpretation of "Al Aaraaf."
The Spanish quotation, if it is a quotation, is a sly challenge to the
prospective reader's ability to understand the poem, a challenge many
readers have professed themselves unable to meet successfully. The
quotation from *Comus* vaguely suggests the theme of the poem, but
the one credited to Cleveland is a bit puzzling because it is frivolous.[46]
The fourth quotation is essential to the understanding of "Al Aaraaf"
and appears, with slight revisions, in all later texts. The first and third
were omitted in all later texts and the second was omitted after
1831.

On the page immediately preceding the title "Tamerlane" in the
second section the word "Advertisement" is centered in large type.
Under it is the statement: "This Poem was printed for publication in
Boston, in the year 1827, but suppressed through circumstances of a
private nature." On the page opposite this advertisement appears the
dedication: "To John Neal This Poem Is Respectfully Dedicated." The
poem as printed here is reduced from its originaal 406 lines to 243 lines,
and the notes are omitted altogether. These and other revisions made
a vastly better poem of "Tamerlane." On the page following the
section title "Miscellaneous Poems" are two epigraphs:

> My nothingness—my wants—
> My sins—and my contrition—
> SOUTHEY E PERSIS.
>
> And some flowers—*but no* bays.
> MILTON.[47]

[45] I looked in *The Poems of John Cleveland*, ed. John M. Berdan (New Haven,
1903, 1911). It may be in an early edition I have not seen.

[46] Al Aaraaf is not a land of enchantment like the dark forest in which Comus
ruled, but neither is it a sunlit world such as ours. Poe admired *Comus* and in the
"Letter to Mr. _____ _____" in the 1831 volume rated it superior to *Paradise Lost*.
In *Politian*, a little later, he has Lalage quote, with minor variations, two lines
from *Comus*: "It in another climate, so he said, / Bore a bright golden flower, but
not i' this soil!" The frivolous quotation from Cleveland might prove to be significant if we knew its context.

[47] I suppose "e Persis" is Poe's way of saying "from the Persian," but why he
chose to put it that way I do not know. The lines are the last two of a short poem

These epigraphs, as altered, were perhaps an attempt to disarm criticism. The first poem of this section is called "Preface." It is the same poem later titled "Romance." Besides "Romance" four new poems appeared in this volume, the most important being "Fairyland," already mentioned. For the two long poems and several of the short ones, this edition is important, because Poe made it, not the 1831 edition, the basis of his text in the edition of 1845.

We do not know how many copies were printed, whether all printed copies were bound, or what exactly were the terms of publication. The language of Poe's letter to Allan on November 18, 1829, suggests that Hatch and Dunning paid the costs of printing and binding and gave Poe 250 copies in lieu of royalties. In view of the unwillingness of Carey, Lea and Carey to risk anything to publish them, this seems unlikely to be the whole truth. I suspect that Poe paid for the printing himself, or promised to pay, and by this means became the owner of 250 copies. Hatch and Dunning might then have agreed to sell the books and to reimburse Poe out of the proceeds if they proved sufficient. If Allan supplied funds or a guarantee for the printing, which is doubtful, it must have been because he was impressed by the favorable notice of John Neal, then an important man in American literary circles. Poe would have furnished him with Neal's printed notices of the poems and also with that of Mrs. Hale. If Allan did not back the book, it is somewhat more than possible that William Gwynn did.[48]

Turning now from the poems to their author, it is well at this time to review the question of Allan's contribution to Poe's support from May to December 1829. The evidence must be gleaned from Poe's

---

with the title "Imitation from the Persian," first published in the *Bijou* (a London Annual) for 1828. Poe substitutes dashes for Southey's internal commas and an exclamation point after the second line. The quotation from Milton is from "An Epitaph on the Marchioness of Winchester," but Poe has altered the line to suit his own purpose. In context the line reads as follows:

> "Here be tears of perfect moan
> Wept for thee in Helicon,
> And some flowers, and some bays,
> For thy hearse to strew the ways."

The first two of these lines, with the initial "Here" changed to "There," are quoted as part of Poe's note to l. 181 of pt. II of "Al Aaraaf": "Unguided Love hath fallen —'mid tears of perfect moan."

[48] For a fuller discussion of this matter, see "Poe and 'The Musiad,'" pp. 84–87.

letters to Allan and from Allan's endorsement on the manuscript letters as recorded in the *Valentine Letters*. On Poe's letter of May 20, Allan indicates that he gave Edgar $50 when he left Richmond early in May, that he remitted him $100 on May 18, and that he paid his draft (mentioned in Poe's letter) for $50.[49] In Poe's letter of July 26 he acknowledges receiving a letter with money on July 22, probably $50, and another $50 in Allan's letter of August 19. On November 18 Poe acknowledges Allan's check for $80.00. These sums total $380. The record of Poe's expenditures is less definite. On August 10 he wrote Allan, "I can obtain decent board lodging & washing with other expenses of mending &c for 5 & perhaps even for 4½ $ per week." Whether he had lived so cheaply during the preceding three months is doubtful. He informed Allan on June 25 that his cousin Edward Mosher had robbed him while he was asleep in the same room with him at Beltzhoover's Hotel. The robber took $46, but Poe says he recovered $10 the next night, so the net loss was $36. He also paid a note for $50 which he had signed at the time he had hired a substitute for his place in the army the preceding April.[50] Presumably his travel expense from Richmond to Washington and on to Baltimore would not have been paid from the $50 Allan gave him when he left home. The only other expense for traveling would have been the one trip, or perhaps two, from Baltimore to Philadelphia. When he made the trip from Baltimore to Washington described in his letter of July 26, he walked both ways, "having paid away $40 for my bill & being unwilling to spend the balance when I might avoid it." But this $40 must have been his bill for room and board, perhaps at Beltzhoover's Hotel. Just when Poe returned to Richmond after December 29, 1829, we have no record, but since he and Allan seem to have been on friendly terms at this time and no other letters from Poe are on record until May 3, 1830, it seems very likely that he was allowed to return at the end of December. If so, he would have been away for nearly eight months, or about 32 weeks. Calculated at five dollars a week, his room and board would have amounted to $160. Adding to that expense the $36 which he presumably never recovered from Edward Mosher and

[49] *Valentine Letters*, p. 126. For Poe's letters, see *Letters*, pp. 16–34.

[50] In a letter to Sergeant Samuel Graves, the substitute mentioned, on May 3, 1830, Poe speaks of debts both to Graves and to a Sergeant Griffith which were still unpaid, but these must have been personal loans not connected with the payment of his substitute.

the $50 he paid in discharging the debt for his army substitute, we have a total of $256. This would leave a balance, for all other expenses, of $124 out of the $380 received from Allan.[51] It does not seem possible that he could have saved enough from this amount to pay for the printing of his book or any considerable part of it.

III

Poe's trip to Washington in July must have been made at the urgent request of his foster father, who suspected him of not making a serious effort to gain admission to West Point. In Washington Poe was told that he had not been appointed for June because there were more applicants than places to be filled, but he was encouraged to hope that he might be admitted for September and assured of admission for June 1830. Notice of his appointment came to him at Richmond on March 30, 1830, and Allan gave his permission the next day. Poe signed articles agreeing to serve the United States for five years unless sooner discharged, as stated in John Allan's letter to the Secretary of War, dated May 31, 1830.[52]

Poe probably returned to Richmond at the end of December 1829 or the beginning of January 1830. Quinn cites the Ellis and Allan records, which show that Allan ordered some clothes for Poe on January 8, which he would hardly have done unless Edgar was then at home.[53] The exact date on which Poe left Richmond is uncertain. On May 3, 1830, he wrote to Sergeant Graves and foolishly spoke of John Allan as being "not very often sober." Several months later Graves sent the letter to Allan. In self-justification Poe wrote Allan, on January 3, 1831, that he had written the letter to Graves "within a half hour after you had embittered every feeling of my heart against you by your abuse of my *family*, and myself, under your own roof—and at a time when you knew my heart was almost breaking."[54] How Allan abused his family there is no way of knowing, but he may have questioned the moral character of his parents because they were actors, or he may

---

[51] He had to pay board during this period in Baltimore, for he writes on July 15, "I am incurring unnecessary expense as Grandmother is not in a situation to give me any accommodation."

[52] This letter is printed in Hervey Allen's *Israfel*, I, 265.   [53] P. 166, note.

[54] *Letters*, pp. 36, 41–42.

have reiterated his suspicion, first expressed in his letter to Henry in 1824, that Poe's sister Rosalie was illegitimate.[55] But apparently it was not the abuse that caused Poe's heartbreak. What was it then? Is it possible that Poe was then still hopeful of a reconciliation with his foster father and that he was reluctant to leave home again and go to West Point under the conditions laid down by Allan? Poe had no stomach for the army, even as an officer, and Allan surely knew it, but he saw in the Academy an excuse to withdraw the slender support that he had given Poe while he awaited admission. Poe had left Richmond before May 21, for on that date Allan addressed a letter to him at Baltimore and enclosed a note for twenty dollars.[56] He probably did not leave, however, until near the middle of the month, since Allan ordered on May 13 "for E. Poe 4 blankets," presumably for Edgar to take with him to the Academy.[57]

How did Poe occupy his time during the four months he was in Richmond in the winter and spring of 1830? He may have spent some time reviewing for the entrance examinations at West Point, but he could not have anticipated much difficulty with them since they were chiefly in mathematics and French, in both of which he was already proficient. He had his own room at the Allan house and, no doubt, a good many books, his own and Allan's. But he must have missed the libraries of Baltimore, especially the Baltimore Library Company, which, according to records surviving in the Maryland Historical Society, possessed eight or nine thousand well-selected volumes. Many, perhaps most, of these were lost in 1835 in the burning of the Athenaeum building where they were housed. From the list of acquisitions we can see that it contained books only of the highest quality in all fields, including literature. It was as good as the library of the University of Virginia when Poe was there, and perhaps better for his purposes. In Baltimore he could have read all the masterpieces of classical literature, the best of modern literature in English, French, and other languages, and learned works in all fields. This was a subscription library, and the list of subscribers included no member of Poe's family until 1838, when Neilson Poe became a subscriber. However, any reader, whether a subscriber or not, was free to use the

[55] This letter is quoted by Quinn, p. 89, from a copy found in the Ellis and Allan Papers in the Library of Congress. There is of course no evidence now, if there ever was, that Rosalie was illegitimate.

[56] Mentioned in Poe's letter to Allan from West Point, June 28, 1830, *Letters,* pp. 37–38.

[57] Quinn, p. 166, note 1.

books in the reading rooms, and since Poe was not regularly employed, it is fairly certain that he spent many hours there between May and December 1829, as well as in later years.

There was a small library in Richmond, also a subscription library, owned by the Richmond Mercantile Library Association, but it could not have offered much enrichment. An existing catalogue dated November 15, 1839, lists fewer than 400 volumes. So far as they went, the books were excellent, including histories of the ancient worlds—such as Greek, Roman, Egyptian, Persian—Aristotle's *Rhetoric* (Thomas Taylor's translation), *The Ruins* and *Travels in Syria and Egypt* by Volney, and a *History of England* by Hume and Smollett. One of the books he must have read, here or elsewhere, was *France*, by Lady (Sydney) Morgan, whom he was to mention later in the Introduction to the "Tales of the Folio Club." The Richmond library received sixteen current periodicals, including the London *Quarterly Review*, the *Edinburgh Review*, and *Blackwood's Edinburgh Magazine*, all of which he had probably been reading in the rooms of the Library Company of Baltimore. It is quite possible that John Allan was a regular subscriber to one or more of these journals. Whatever the extent of his reading, however, Poe must have had time for writing, too, and the reading would normally have stimulated his creative intelligence. It is more than likely that some of the new poems published in his next volume were composed during these months in Richmond.

Since Edgar still had a few friends in Richmond, including Thomas Bolling, who had been at the University with him, and Robert M. Sully, nephew of the painter Thomas Sully, he doubtless spent some time with them. On January 19, the Richmond *Whig* reported that *Al Aaraaf, Tamerlane, and Minor Poems* had been "just received"—probably from the hand of the poet himself. The paper repeated some of Neal's praise and announced that the book was for sale at Sanxey's bookstore.[58] It is a fair guess that as many of these books were given away by the author as were sold by Sanxey.

On leaving Richmond, Poe went first to Baltimore, but he seems not to have remained there very long since Allan's letter of May 21 had to be forwarded to him at West Point. When he replied from West Point on June 28, he had completed his entrance examinations, which were certainly not difficult. He had received Allan's letter, with $20, three

[58] Mary E. Phillips, *Edgar Allan Poe—the Man* (Philadelphia, 1926), I, 358–359.

days before, presumably on June 25, but he said it had been "lying
some time" in the West Point post office. Poe undoubtedly called for
this letter as soon as he arrived in West Point, but how long it had
been there must be a guess. If "some time" is estimated at two weeks
we get about June 10 as the possible time of its arrival. It should have
reached Baltimore before the end of May. Presumably Henry sent it
on so that it would reach West Point at about the time he expected
Edgar to arrive there. It would appear that Allan did not foresee Poe's
early departure from Baltimore, and that Henry expected him to
arrive at West Point sooner than he did.[59]

Where was Poe between the time he left Baltimore and the time he
arrived at West Point? Hervey Allen says he "probably went by way
of Philadelphia to New York, and thence to West Point," and thinks he
may have arranged for the publication of his sonnet "To Science" in
the Philadelphia *Casket* for October.[60] Probably he did go to Philadelphia, though he need not have gone there to arrange for the reprinting
of the sonnet, for his friend Wilmer was in Philadelphia at that time.
He was an employee of Samuel Atkinson, who published both the
Saturday Evening Post and the *Casket*, and could have arranged with
Poe by letter for the printing of the poem. Perhaps Poe already had in
manuscript all the poems he was to include in his third volume and
stopped in Philadelphia to see Carey and Lea, or other publishers,
about bringing it out. Not succeeding in Philadelphia, he would
naturally have tried to persuade a publisher in New York. One of the
New York publishers he might have called on at the time was Elam
Bliss, who later did publish the book. It was to contain about 300 lines
of new poetry. Poe may have composed or revised some of these after
he arrived at West Point, but he had but little space or time there in
which to court the Muse. He lived with two roommates in camp or in
a barracks room perhaps ten by fourteen feet and was obliged to fulfill
the requirements of drill and classes at least until the end of
December.[61]

Poe was sent at once to Camp Eaton on the Hudson, where from

---

[59] For Poe's letter of June 28, see *Letters*, p. 37.   [60] *Israfel*, I, 267.

[61] In the report of Richard M. Johnson for the Committee on Military Affairs to
the House of Representatives, May 17, 1834 (reprinted as an appendix in Benson
J. Lossing's *Cadet Life at West Point*, Boston, 1862, pp. 327–367), we find (p.
345): "Under the existing regulations, the cadets are encamped in the months of
July and August, during which period the instruction is exclusively military. The
remaining ten months are passed at the institution, where not less than nine, nor
more than ten, hours are daily devoted to study."

July 1 to August 30 he lived with three other cadets in a tent and spent most of his day on the drill grounds. Regulations were strict, and many of his fellow cadets were arrested for infractions, but Poe's name does not appear on the records for any offense.[62] During the remaining four months of the year he might have found some time for writing, for the regulations then provided that "during the first six months, the studies are confined to the French language and the mathematics,"[63] and Poe was proficient in these. In the examinations given at the end of this period, on January 3, 1831, which one fourth of the class normally failed, Poe did well, "standing three in French and seventeen in mathematics in a class of eighty-five successful examinees."[64] Even with his proficiency Poe must have done some studying. If we can believe the reminiscences of his fellow cadets, Poe's only writing while at the Academy was the composition of lampoons on officers and faculty for the amusement of his friends.[65] One of these lampoons was published by Henry B. Hirst, apparently with Poe's consent, in the Philadelphia *Saturday Museum* on February 25 and again on March 4, 1843.[66]

Poe could have found some time for writing after these examinations, for on the very day they were given, January 3, he wrote to Allan that he would from that day neglect his studies and duties, and if Allan did not give his permission for him to resign he would leave without it after ten days.[67] Poe did not leave the Academy after ten days, but he did begin to absent himself from parades and roll calls on January 8 and from classes on January 17. He was tried by the Court Martial on February 8, adjudged guilty, and ordered dismissed from the Academy, effective March 6, 1831.[68] Why did Poe deliberately provoke his dismissal? In the letter of January 3 he wrote Allan: "When I parted from you—at the steam-boat, I knew that I should never see you again." Nevertheless, in an earlier letter, of June 28, 1830, he had addressed his foster father in the old affectionate way as

[62] See Carlisle Allan, "Cadet Edgar Allan Poe, U.S.A.," *American Mercury*, XXIX (Aug. 1933), 446–455. Allan had access to the Academy records.

[63] See Lossing (Appendix), p. 347.   [64] Allan, p. 453.

[65] See Thomas W. Gibson's account of Poe at West Point in *Harper's Magazine* for November, 1867, the article by Carlisle Allan cited above, and various biographies.

[66] This is included among the poems attributed to Poe in Floyd Stovall's *Poems of Edgar Allan Poe* (Charlottesville, Va., 1965), hereafter cited as *Poems*. See the text on p. 141 and the notes on pp. 296–297.

[67] *Letters*, pp. 39–42.

[68] See the records of the War Department printed by Quinn, pp. 742–744.

"Dear Pa," and reported: "I find that I will possess many advantages & shall endeavor to improve them. Of 130 Cadets appointed every year only 30 or 35 ever graduate—the rest being dismissed for bad conduct or deficiency. The Regulations are rigid in the extreme."[69] Even as late as November 6, 1830, he wrote to Allan (addressing him this time as "Dear Sir," but signing himself "Yours affectionately"): "I have a very excellent standing in my class—in the first section in every thing and have great hopes of doing well. I have spent my time very pleasantly hitherto—but the study requisite is incessant, and the discipline exceedingly rigid." He sends his respects to "Mrs. A," the second Mrs. Allan, whom John Allan had married on October 5, 1830, and regrets that they did not visit West Point while they were in New York.[70] Between this date and the date of Poe's letter of January 3, John Allan had received from Sergeant Graves the letter Poe had written the preceding May 3, and had become so angry that he wrote Poe forbidding any further communication between them.[71] Assuming that he could at least reply, Poe reviewed their relationship at some length, defending himself as best he could for what he did at the University of Virginia,[72] and added: "You sent me to W. Point like a beggar. The same difficulties are threatening me as before at Charlottesville—and I must resign." It would appear that Allan provided no allowance for Poe to supplement his meager pay as a cadet. Most parents or guardians must have provided such an allowance, for we learn that one regulation of the Academy "limits the allowance of money by parents and guardians," and places the specified sum in the custody of the superintendent. We learn also that in 1834, and presumably also in 1830, "The monthly pay of the cadets . . . is $28.20; from this deductions are made, in conformity with the regulations, for boarding, clothing, books, etc.; the balance which the cadet may receive in each, seldom exceeds $4.50 per month."[73] The stated purpose of restricting

[69] This statement is confirmed by reliable sources. In an address by Francis H. Smith, Superintendent of the Virginia Military Academy, delivered at West Point on June 12, 1879, on "West Point Fifty Years Ago," he said that Colonel Thayer, the Superintendent at West Point from 1817 till 1833, was criticized in Congress because "his discipline was counted too stern." Speaking of his own class, he said also: "We commenced fifty years ago with a class of 130; we graduated 43." This address was published as a pamphlet (New York, 1879).

[70] *Letters*, pp. 38–39.

[71] Allan's letter is not extant, but it is referred to by Poe, who must have replied to it promptly.

[72] For this story, see "Edgar Poe and the University of Virginia."

[73] This and the preceding quotation are taken from pp. 348 and 359 of the

the allowance was to improve the conditions of study and promote equality in dress and the manner of living among the students, but certainly it was not intended to create hardship. Poe may have been inclined toward extravagance, but there is no reason to doubt his statement in his letter of November 6 that, as he had no deposit, his "more necessary expenses" had run him into debt.

IV

Poe left the Academy on February 19 and wrote to Allan from New York two days later, saying that in traveling from West Point without a cloak he had caught a violent cold and was otherwise ill: "I feel that I am on sick bed from *which* I never shall get up." He appealed to Allan's sense of justice for help, but there is no evidence that he received it.[74] Poe may have imagined he was sicker than he really was, but the shaky handwriting of the manuscript, as reproduced in the *Valentine Letters,* indicates that he was either ill or in a state of nervous excitement. At any rate he recovered and wrote on March 10 to Colonel Thayer asking for a recommendation in behalf of his wildly conceived idea of going to Paris in the hope of an appointment to the Polish army. In his letter to Allan of February 21 he said he had written to his brother Henry but could expect no help from him. If this letter or Henry's reply, if he made one, had survived we might have a more reliable account of Poe's condition after leaving West Point.

Needless to say, he did not go to Paris or join the Polish army. Woodberry says that on March 7, the day after his formal dismissal, Poe was "penniless, since only twenty-four cents remained to his credit." It may be presumed that Poe's salary was continued until this time so that it would be sufficient to meet his debts on the records of the superintendent. This does not preclude the possibility that Poe had some money when he left on February 19. Woodberry quotes from a letter written to him on July 1, 1884, by General Allan B. Magruder, who had been a cadet in Poe's time, which indicates that most of the cadets subscribed seventy-five cents each for a copy of a

---

report of Richard M. Johnson, in Lossing (Appendix). In H. Irving Hancock's *Life at West Point* (New York, 1902), p. 17, we read: "From 1802 to 1845, the pay of the cadets had been sixteen dollars per month, with two rations per day added." See also Quinn, p. 173.

[74] *Letters,* pp. 43–44.

new edition of Poe's poems, perhaps under the delusion that the book would be a collection of satires and lampoons. Since, if General Magruder's account is true, the superintendent allowed the subscription price to be deducted from the cadets' pay, the entire sum may have gone directly from the superintendent to the publisher without passing through Poe's hands. This would be the more likely if, as Magruder thought, the publisher, Elam Bliss, came to West Point and bargained with Poe over the cost of publication. If Bliss did go to West Point for this purpose, it is most likely that he went before January 8, when Poe began to neglect his duties.[75] It may well be that Poe's manuscript was already in the hands of the printer, Henry Mason, 64 Nassau Street, when he arrived in New York City.

Poe gave his third volume the simple title *Poems* and designated it the "Second Edition," ignoring the 1827 volume and obviously counting the 1829 volume the first edition. It may be recalled that in the 1829 volume he inserted an "Advertisement" before the title page of "Tamerlane" stating that though that poem was "printed for publication" in 1827 it was suppressed for reasons of a private nature. In his own view the poem had been published for the first time in 1829. Under the name of the author on the title page of the 1831 edition is the following: "Tout le monde a raison.—Rochefoucault."[76] This epigraph—"Everybody is right"—applies to the book as a whole, but I am not sure what Poe meant by it unless it was addressed cynically to prospective reviewers. The dedication page follows the title page and reads as follows: "To the U. S. Corps of Cadets this volume is respectfully dedicated." Poe could hardly have done less in recognition of the advance subscriptions which made the publication of the

---

[75] See George E. Woodberry, *The Life of Edgar Allan Poe* (Boston, 1909), I, 77–79. Because he was dismissed, Poe received no allowance for travel. Had he been allowed to resign with Allan's consent, he says in his letter of February 21, he would have received $30.35 for mileage.

[76] I have been unable to find this quotation in La Rochefoucauld's *Pensées, Maximes, et Réflexions Morales*, ed. Aimé-Martin in 1864 (a revision of the 1822 edition by Louis Aimé-Martin). It is possible that Poe saw it in some still earlier edition, for there were many, with numerous variants. My colleague Professor Joseph M. Carrière suggests that it might have been taken from a sentence—"Quand tout le monde a tort, tout le monde a raison"—from Act I, scene 3 of the play *La Gouvernante* (1747) by Nivelle de La Chaussée. Poe might have taken only the part of the quotation that suited his purposes, though I doubt that he did in this case. But if it is from Nivelle de La Chaussée, why did he attribute it to La Rochefoucauld? The use of "t" for "d" in the spelling of La Rochefoucauld's name is not an error. The name was sometimes spelled that way in Poe's time and before, and is so spelled in Rees's *New Encyclopaedia* (1810).

poems possible. The table of contents follows and, after that, a page with the word "Letter" in large type in the center. This is a title page for the prose introduction in the form of a "Letter to Mr. ___ ___" (later called "Letter to B___"), presumably his publisher Elam Bliss. Between the page with the word "Letter" and the first page of the prose introduction is the following epigraph, which seems to apply specifically to the contents of the "Letter":

> Tell wit how much it wrangles
> In fickle points of niceness—
> Tell wisdom it entangles
> Itself in overwiseness.
>   *Sir Walter Raleigh.*[77]

We see in "The Letter to Mr. ___ ___" how, in Poe's opinion, Wordsworth, particularly in his Preface to the *Lyrical Ballads,* "wrangles" in "points of niceness," and how Coleridge's wisdom becomes entangled in "overwiseness." Coleridge, he says in the "Letter," "goes wrong by reason of his very profundity." The imagination, he thinks, is more dependable than wit or wisdom.

The volume contains ten poems, six of them new. The first, here called "Introduction," is a much extended version of the poem entitled "Preface" and placed first in the section of the 1829 volume called "Miscellaneous Poems." In 1845 Poe changed the title to "Romance." The original poem had 21 lines, the 1831 version 66. The 45 new lines were not reprinted, and in all later versions Poe returned to the 1829 text with but minor revisions. "Fairy Land," also reprinted from the 1829 edition, is similarly expanded: from 46 to 64 lines.[78] In this case

[77] Except that Poe changes "she" to "it" in the third line and "herself" to "itself" in the fourth, the quotation is verbally identical with lines 43–46 of Raleigh's poem "The Farewell" as printed in *The Works of Sir Walter Raleigh* (8 vols.; Oxford, 1829), VIII, 725–726. A note introducing "The Farewell" states that the poem "has been given as written by Sir Walter Raleigh, the *night before his execution,* but it had already appeared in Davison's 'Rhapsody' in 1608; and is also to be found in a MS collection of Poems in the British Museum, which has the date of 1596." In Davison's text the poem is called "The Lie." The most significant variation in the Davison text is that the second line quoted by Poe has "tickle" instead of "fickle." The Davison text is printed as a note in the collected *Works,* and Poe may have seen it.

[78] The title "Fairyland" appears as one word in the 1829 volume; in the 1831 volume it is also one word in the table of contents and on the title page, but appears as two words at the head of the text of the poem. In the 1845 edition Poe introduced the hyphen, and the poem is usually referred to as "Fairy-Land." The title as two words, hyphenated or not, seems more suitable to the content and tone of the poem.

some of the original lines were dropped and others drastically revised. However, as in the case of "Romance," in later printings Poe preferred to restore, with minor revisions, the text of 1829. The untitled sonnet, later "Sonnet—To Science," is printed as part of "Al Aaraaf" and is not separately listed in the table of contents. If it is counted, the 1831 volume contains eleven poems. The principal change in the text of "Al Aaraaf" is that the first fifteen lines of the 1829 version are dropped or much revised. Otherwise the poem shows only minor changes, though these are numerous. In 1845, the next complete printing of the poem after 1831, he returned to the text of 1829. The text of "Tamerlane" was considerably revised and expanded in several places. Two poems, "The Lake— To _____" and "To __ __," later "A Dream within a Dream," were incorporated, with some revision, into the body of "Tamerlane." Again, he returned to the 1829 text of "Tamerlane" in later editions.

As stated earlier,[79] two of the original four epigraphs before "Al Aaraaf" were omitted in 1831; namely, the Spanish verses, which suggest that the reader will not understand the poem, and the line dedication from Cleveland, "Who drinks the deepest?—here's to him," which might be taken as a frivolous note. Both were omitted, I suspect, because they were out of keeping with the serious tone of the poem. Also omitted were the "Advertisement" and the dedicatory page to John Neal before "Tamerlane," and—since the 1831 edition had no section of "Miscellaneous Poems"—the title page and the two epigraphs for that section of the 1829 volume.

The six new poems were "To Helen," "Israfel," "The Doomed City," "Irene," "A Paean," and "The Valley Nis." Since "Fairy Land" is inserted between the third and fourth of these, I can see no significance in the order in which they are introduced in the volume. It may be that "Introduction" and "Fairy Land" are changed from their original versions because the poet considered them new poems. If he did, he might have intended a thematic and structural link between "Fairy Land," in which the moon "Has sent a ray down with a tune," and "Irene," in which the moon "hums" within Irene's ear. As later revised, both poems retain the moon as a factor, but without personification; the moon is an influence, but it does not speak or "hum" a tune.

---

[79] On p. 38 above.

Killis Campbell says in the bibliographical note to his edition (New York, 1936) of the 1831 volume for the Facsimile Text Society that "it was in this little book that Poe first made it convincingly clear to the world that a new poet had been born in America." This is perhaps an overstatement of the superiority of the 1831 edition over that of 1829. It is possible that Campbell was thinking more of the six new poems as they became after later revisions than of their 1831 text. It is true that "To Helen" and "Israfel" appear here in something like their final form, but "The Doomed City" (later "The City in the Sea"), "Irene" (later "The Sleeper") and "The Valley Nis" (later "The Valley of Unrest") were extensively revised and vastly improved in later texts, and "A Paean" (later "Lenore") was almost completely rewritten.

Perhaps the most obvious development in the 1831 edition is the greater emphasis, especially in the prose "Letter," on poetic theory. This theory had been symbolically expressed in "Al Aaraaf," as I have said in my essay on that poem, but it is made more explicit here in the "Letter" and even in the poems, particularly in "To Helen" and "Israfel." It seems that Poe's critical sense developed rapidly between the time he was discharged from the army and the time he left West Point. Although we cannot always trust the memory of his fellow cadets who wrote many years later, I cite here, for what they may be worth, the accounts of two of them as to Poe's literary activity at the Academy. Timothy Pickering Jones remembered that Poe dictated verses to him lampooning the officers and had him post copies about the barracks. Thomas W. Gibson recalled that Poe interested himself in literary criticism, "or more properly speaking caviling," whether Shakespeare, Byron, Addison "or the latest poetaster—all came in alike for his critical censure. I never heard him speak in praise of any English writer, living or dead."[80] The arrogant tone of the "Letter to Mr. ___ ___" lends support to Gibson's statement; but despite his caviling, Poe manages there not only to express a very high opinion of Wordsworth and Coleridge, but to formulate a few of the critical ideas which later he developed into a distinctive aesthetic theory. Gibson, of course, might have confused some of his West Point memories with what he knew or heard of Poe's rough handling of some authors in his reviews of the late thirties and forties.

The exact date on which the 1831 *Poems* was published cannot be determined. It might have been at any time between the middle of

[80] Quoted by Carlisle Allan, pp. 451–452.

March and the end of April. Since he wrote to Colonel Thayer on March 10 that he had "no longer any tie" to bind him to his native country, Poe must have expected his book to appear soon after. Certainly he would not have thought of leaving the country without seeing it. He returned to Baltimore before May 6, when he wrote to William Gwynn about employment. Apparently the book had not been noticed in the periodicals at that time. It was briefly reviewed in the New York *Mirror* on May 7, and it was noticed in the Philadelphia *Casket* for May, which probably came out near the middle of the month.[81] The review in the *Mirror*, probably written by its editor, George P. Morris, is generally favorable. It begins: "The poetry of this little volume has a plausible air of imagination, inconsistent with the general indefiniteness of the ideas. Every thing in the language betokens poetic inspiration, but it rather resembles the leaves of the sybil when scattered by the wind." He quotes the last lines of "The Doomed City" as "less incomprehensible than most in the book, although the meaning is by no means perfectly clear." He also quotes three other lines from the same poem (lines omitted from later editions) to compare them unfavorably with Coleridge's "Ancient Mariner." His longest quotation consists of eighteen lines from "Fairy Land," which he says are also obscure. Apparently the only fault found by the reviewer with Poe's verse was its obscurity, a fault often alleged since. The notice in Atkinson's *Casket* reads as follows: "We extract the following poetry from a small 18mo. volume of poems by Edgar A. Poe, a part of which was published in a former edition. The author is, we believe, a member of the U. S. Corps of Cadets, as the volume is dedicated to that body." After this note, three complete poems are quoted without comment: "To Helen," "Irene," and the sonnet preceding "Al Aaraaf," the last having previously appeared in the 1829 edition. The publisher might have sent a copy to the *Mirror* for review, but since there were no reviews published in the *Casket*, it seems more probable that Poe sent his friend Lambert Wilmer a copy of the book and that Wilmer

---

[81] The *Casket* did not print book reviews. Campbell, in the bibliographical note to his facsimile edition, says this issue was published about May 15. In my own investigation of the probable date, I have found only one bit of evidence; that is a brief account in the issue of February 1831 of a solar eclipse that occurred on February 12 of the same year. For that month, at least, the publication date was not before the middle. Mabbott has told me that it was also noticed about the same time in the *Saturday Evening Post*, but I have not seen the issue in which the notice appeared.

selected the poems to be reprinted, possibly with Poe's approval. At that time Wilmer was writing for both the *Saturday Evening Post* and the *Casket*. So far as I know, no other contemporary notices of the 1831 edition have been discovered.

It is not likely that Poe received much in the way of royalties from Elam Bliss, but since he probably got enough in subscriptions to pay for the publication, the little he did receive would have been his. He wrote to William Gwynn on May 6 that he no longer looked to John Allan for support and that he was ready to settle down in Baltimore at a regular job.[82] There is no surviving evidence that Gwynn helped him find employment, but it is likely that he did put him in the way of occasional part-time work. Quinn suggests that Poe did "unidentified hack work for newspapers." Writing was the kind of work he was best fitted to do, but he might also have been willing, for the time being, to do clerical work for Gwynn's *Gazette* or other papers. At any rate, he wrote Allan on October 16, saying that though wretchedly poor he is out of debt and for once has no favor to ask. He was, I believe, sincere in speaking of his foster father's "forbearance" and "generosity," while admitting "the most flagrant ingratitude" on his part, and in recalling with nostalgia the mutual affection they once felt. It may be, of course, that Poe anticipated his future need of help and was preparing the ground for it. His brother Henry had died on August 1 preceding, and Edgar, in a sense, filled his place in the household of Mrs. Clemm and the aged Mrs. David Poe, who still drew a small pension.

Whatever sense of security Poe may have felt, he lost it within a month for on November 18 he wrote again to Allan requesting $80 to pay a debt for which he says he had been arrested eleven days previously.[83] The debt, he says, was "incurred as much on Hy's account as on my own about two years ago." Two years before would have been about the time of the publication of the 1829 volume of his poems. Perhaps the debt was associated with the printing of the poems, though it is hard to see how Henry could have been involved

---

[82] Probably he returned to Baltimore about May 1, for he told Gwynn: "I would have waited upon you personally but am confined to my room with a severe sprain in my knee." The context of the letter suggests that he had been back several days.
[83] *Letters*, p. 47. In this letter Poe speaks of Allan's "late kindness," which might possibly mean that Allan had made some reciprocal gesture after Poe's overture of October 16, but it is more likely that he refers to some pecuniary help given indirectly by Allan in response to his letter of February 21 from New York.

in that transaction. Poe was apparently not put in jail,[84] but it is not certain that his debt was paid with Allan's money. Receiving no response to his first appeal, Poe wrote again on December 15 and on December 29. Meantime Mrs. Clemm also wrote begging Allan to assist Edgar. Although Allan did not write to Poe or send any money directly, he endorsed Poe's letter of December 15 as follows: "Wrote on the 7th Decr. 1831 to John Walsh to procure his liberation & to give him $20 besides to keep him out of further difficulties & value on me for such amt. as might be required—neglected sending it on till the 12th Janr. 1832. Then put in the office myself."[85] Did Poe's creditors receive their money from Allan through John Walsh, or did he find other means to pay them? In his next, and last, letter to Allan, dated April 12, 1833, he begins by saying: "It has now been more than two years since you have assisted me, and more than three since you have spoken to me."[86] It had, of course, been only fifteen months since Allan said he had mailed the letter authorizing help for Poe. It is not likely that Poe would have deliberately misrepresented the elapsed time, since Allan knew as well as he how long it had been. This raises the question again whether Poe may refer to some unrecorded assistance which Allan had provided in response to his letter of February 21, 1831. That would have been "more than two years" before. If Allan had sent money then, the fact might have accounted, in part, for the bitterness of his endorsement on the letter, which he made more than two years afterward: "Apl 12, 1833. It is now upwards of 2 years since I received the above precious relict of the Blackest Heart & deepest alike destitute of honour & principle every day of his life has only served to confirm his debased nature—Suffice it to say my only regret is in Pity for his failings—his Talents are of an order that can never prove a comfort to their possessor."[87] This comment on Poe was inscribed by Allan just a few weeks after he had finished his will with its codicils. He must have been rereading Poe's letters with some qualms of conscience and made the comment in an attempt at self-jus- tification. He died within a year, leaving Poe nothing. It is not surprising that he did not answer Poe's letter of April 12, which he would have received a few days after making the harsh annotation on Poe's old letter.

[84] Quinn, after investigation, reports no record of Poe's having been in jail (p. 190).

[85] *Valentine Letters,* p. 300. Mrs. Clemm's letter is printed on p. 295.

[86] *Letters,* pp. 49–50.   [87] *Valentine Letters,* p. 268.

V

In his letter of April 12, Poe assured Allan that, though he was in need, he had not been idle. In fact he must have been pretty busy since returning to Baltimore. Between May and December 1831, he wrote at least five tales for submission in the Philadelphia *Saturday Courier* contest, which was first announced on May 28. The competition closed December 1, and the winner was announced on December 31. Eighty tales were submitted. Poe's five tales were published in the *Courier* in the course of the year 1832: "Metzengerstein" on January 14; "The Duke de L'Omelette," later "The Duc de L'Omelette," on March 3; "A Tale of Jerusalem" on June 9; "A Decided Loss," later "Loss of Breath," on November 10; and "The Bargain Lost," later "Bon-Bon," on December 1. The prize-winning story, "Love's Martyr," by Delia Bacon, was published on January 7, and since "Metzenger-stein" came out the following week, we may assume that it was runner-up in the competition.[88]

"Metzengerstein," perhaps the best of the five tales, well exemplifies the style he later called "arabesque," though it has elements also of the "grotesque." The other four tales are in the grotesque style, though they have elements of the arabesque. James Southall Wilson argued that these tales and others written between 1831 and 1835 "were meant as deliberate burlesques and satires."[89] Doubtless this is accurate enough in an article aimed at the readers of a popular magazine, but the generalization needs qualification. I think Poe's primary aim was humor, not satire. He found episodes and situations to his purpose in contemporary fiction—in Disraeli and Horace Smith, for two exam-

[88] These tales were first discovered in the *Courier* by Killis Campbell and announced in an article in the *Dial*, February 17, 1916. They were reprinted with an introduction by John Grier Varner in *Edgar Allan Poe and the Philadelphia Saturday Courier* (Charlottesville, Va., 1933). With them he also included a later tale, published in the *Courier* on October 14, 1843, with the title "Raising the Wind; or, Diddling Considered as One of the Exact Sciences." When this was reprinted in the *Broadway Journal* on September 13, 1845, the first part of the title was omitted. It has been suggested that it might have been submitted for the contest in 1831 and had lain in the *Courier's* editorial offices through the intervening years. This is not likely, since the tale bears stylistic features of a later time. It is possible, however, that it was written in 1831 or 1832, kept by Poe or returned to him by the *Courier*, and afterward revised.

[89] "The Devil Was in It," *American Mercury*, XXIV (Oct. 1931), 215–220.

ples—but I doubt that he was seriously trying to ridicule the works he imitated. They were burlesques, yes, but not satires, strictly speaking, and certainly not ill-humored ones. "The Duke de L'Omelette" is probably a good-humored satire on N. P. Willis, as I have noted elsewhere.[90] It contains one obvious jibe at Coleridge: the cresset in the Devil's apartment hung by a chain with "its upper end lost, like Col__e, *parmi les nues*." Poe may also, in that story, as Ruth Leigh Hudson has said, have "mimicked the tone of flippancy" of Disraeli's novel *The Young Duke* (1830) and "ridiculed the extravagance of his characterization by exaggerating it to the ludicrous,"[91] but he was not writing satire because the pleasure to be derived from reading Poe's story is not in the least dependent on a knowledge of Disraeli's.

Wilson calls "A Tale of Jerusalem" a burlesque "of a whole novel," which he identifies as Horace Smith's *Zillah; a Tale of the Holy City* (1829). The tale is a burlesque, but not of the whole novel; Poe has merely borrowed a single episode, a very minor one, and a few striking phrases for local color.[92]

"A Decided Loss" is an extravaganza that is sufficiently grotesque, but so far as I can tell there is no specifically directed satire in it. It has generally been supposed that the mention of "Hewitt's 'Seraphic, and highly-scented double extract of Heaven, or Oil of Archangels' " is a jibe at J. H. Hewitt, the reviewer of Poe's 1829 volume, but that is improbable since the context makes it clear that the man who had lost his breath, which he says was "remarkably sweet," thought he had recovered it when he smelled Hewitt's perfume, a bottle of which he had accidentally spilled. I suspect Hewitt's "Oil of Archangels" was advertised in the newspapers of 1831–32. When Poe reprinted this tale in the *Broadway Journal* on January 3, 1846, he substituted "Grand-jean's Oil of Archangels," and I should expect to find it advertised and popular in 1846. The hero's discovery that he could make the guttural tones used by the actors in *Metamora* and *Miantinimoh* is not satire

---

[90] See "Poe and 'The Musiad,' " p. 99; see also the essay by K. L. Daughrity referred to there.

[91] "Poe and Disraeli," *American Literature*, VIII (Jan. 1937), 402–416; see p. 408 especially. See also David H. Hirsch, "Another Source for Poe's 'The Duc De L'Omelette,' " *American Literature*, XXXVIII (Jan. 1967), 532–536.

[92] This episode is the substitution of a pig for a sacrificial lamb by the Romans while besieging Jerusalem. J. G. Varner has shown that the pig episode is basically the same as one found in the *Talmud*, though Poe probably did not find it there. See "Poe's *Tale of Jerusalem* and the *Talmud*," *American Book Collector*, VI (Feb. 1935), 56–57.

but humor designed to make the most of contemporary theatrical hits.[93]

"The Bargain Lost" is a humorous variant of the Faust story. Insofar as it is a satire, it is directed at philosophers in general and Platonic philosophers in particular. Voltaire, who is mentioned by his real name, François Marie Arouet, is very much to the Devil's taste; he calls him "a clever fellow." There is no sign of bitterness or ill will in any of these tales, which were written in good humor and high spirits. In a certain sense, they constitute a sort of comic interlude in Poe's work between the poetic creativity of his youth and the more professional writing of his maturity.

For the biographer the year 1832 is the most serious lacuna in the record of Poe's life. What was he doing while these tales were being printed in the *Courier*? There has been much speculation, but little is known. There have been rumors and legends: that Poe made a trip to Europe, that he had two or three love affairs in Baltimore, and that he visited Richmond and abused his foster father and the second Mrs. Allan.[94] I am convinced that he did not go to Europe, I doubt seriously that he went to Richmond, and I am inclined to dismiss as gossip most or all the stories of his love affairs. There is good reason to believe that Poe lived with his Aunt Maria Clemm from May 1831 until he returned to Richmond in the summer of 1835; her residence was in Wilks Street until late 1832 or early 1833, and after that in Amity Street.[95] In his "Recollections of Edgar A. Poe," Lambert Wilmer said that when he knew Poe in Baltimore, "His time appeared to be constantly occupied by his literary labors; he had already published a volume of poems, and written several of those minor romances which afterwards appeared in the collection called 'Tales of the Grotesque and Arabesque.' He lived in a very retired way with his aunt, Mrs. Clemm."[96] The volume of poems referred to was the 1829 edition and

[93] *Metamora* was written by J. A. Stone especially for Edwin Forrest, whose booming voice was suited to produce the gutturals of the Indian hero. It was first presented in New York on December 15, 1829, and was repeated frequently there and in other principal cities for several years. *Miantinimoh* was a dramatization of Cooper's *The Wept of Wish-ton-Wish* and was presented in Philadelphia (where the *Courier* was published) in May 1831 and later.

[94] The most convenient source for these legends is Hervey Allen's *Israfel*, I, 329–343.

[95] See Quinn, pp. 188 and 205; and May Garrettson Evans, "Poe in Amity Street," *Maryland Historical Magazine*, XXXVI (1941), 363–368. Poe seems to have lived in a boarding house or hotel while he was in Baltimore in 1829.

[96] First printed in the Baltimore *Daily Commercial*, May 23, 1866. It was

the "minor romances" were undoubtedly the five tales published in the *Courier*. Wilmer came back to Baltimore, after an absence of perhaps two years, in January 1832 to edit the *Saturday Visiter*. He remained as editor about eight months, until approximately October 1832. Later in the article Wilmer says: "My intercourse with Poe was almost continuous for weeks together. Almost every day we took long walks in the rural districts near Baltimore, and had long conversations on a great variety of subjects." Since, as I have pointed out elsewhere,[97] Wilmer was editing country papers in or near Elkton, Maryland, from the time he left Baltimore in 1832 until he returned late in 1834, the long walks with Poe occurred almost certainly during the year 1832. These facts about Wilmer can easily be established independently of his recollections by reference to authentic records of the newspapers he edited.

As Quinn suggests, some of Poe's earliest work may be hidden in the columns of Baltimore papers.[98] It may be that yet undiscovered tales and poems were published also in the literary weeklies, some of which have not survived. On August 4, 1832, Lambert Wilmer wrote editorially in the *Saturday Visiter* that he had read "some manuscript tales" written by Poe, and praised them "for originality, richness of imagery and purity of the style." He added that with Poe's permission he might publish one or two of them in the *Visiter*.[99]

What specific tales and poems Poe wrote during the year 1832 it is now impossible to say. Poems that might have been written that year include two acrostics, one titled "Elizabeth" and the other untitled, which he inscribed in the album of his cousin Elizabeth Herring; the poem "Serenade," published in the *Saturday Visiter* under his own name on April 20, 1833; the two poems "To ___" and "Fanny," both

---

reprinted by T. O. Mabbott in the little volume containing a facsimile of Wilmer's poem *Merlin* (New York, 1941), pp. 29–34.

[97] "Poe and 'The Musiad,'" p. 96.

[98] P. 209. In Poe's letter to White, May 30, 1835, he mentions a review of the *Southern Literary Messenger* written by him for the Baltimore *Republican* and suggests that he would like to be authorized to write also for the *American*, which he says has a better class of readers. Four such reviews have been found and reprinted, three in the *Republican* and one in the *American*. See the articles by T. O. Mabbott and David K. Jackson in *Modern Language Notes*, XXV (1920), 374, and L (1935), 251–256.

[99] Quoted by Quinn, pp. 194–195, from the file of the *Visiter* in the Maryland Historical Society. Apparently Wilmer did not publish any of the stories, perhaps because his troubles with the proprietors of the *Visiter* began about the time of this editorial and soon led to his resignation.

signed "Tamerlane" and published in the *Visiter* on May 11 and 18; and "Latin Hymn" and "Song of Triumph," as they appear in the manuscript tale "Epimanes" that he submitted on May 4, 1833, to the *New England Magazine*.[100] In his letter to the editors, sent with the manuscript of "Epimanes," he wrote: "It is one of a number of similar pieces which I have contemplated publishing under the title of 'Eleven Tales of the Arabesque.' They are supposed to be read at table by the eleven members of a literary club, and are followed by the remarks of the company upon each. These remarks are intended as a burlesque upon criticism. In the whole, originality more than any thing else has been attempted. I have said this much with a view of offering you the entire M. S."[101] Unfortunately, the remarks by the members have not survived. If they had we might be able to settle the question of whether the burlesques are satirical or merely humorous.

In addition to "Epimanes," these eleven "Tales of the Arabesque" must have included also the five which had previously been published in the *Courier*. The six new tales, including "Epimanes," may have been the ones that Wilmer had read in manuscript the preceding summer. They also might have been the same six tales Poe submitted in the summer of 1833 for a prize offered by the *Saturday Visiter*, then edited by John H. Hewitt.[102] The six tales were submitted under the group title "Tales of the Folio Club," and Latrobe later remembered them as a "small quarto bound book."[103] The only tales of which he remembered the titles were "MS. Found in a Bottle" and "A Descent into the Maelstrom." Since the latter was not published until May 1841, the correctness of Latrobe's memory has been questioned. A

[100] For these poems and the facts of their publication, see *Poems*, pp. 130–134, 142–143, 290–294, 297–298. "Epimanes" was, after 1840, called "Four Beasts in One."

[101] *Letters*, p. 53.

[102] The story of this episode in Poe's life is too well known to need repetition here. See Quinn, pp. 201–204, and John E. Semmes, *John H. B. Latrobe and His Times, 1803–1891* (Baltimore, 1917), pp. 558–564.

[103] Quinn quotes the letter written by the contest judges to the publishers published in the *Visiter* for October 12, in which they speak of Poe's offerings as "Tales of the Folio Club." The same issue announces that a volume entitled *Tales of the Folio Club* will be published by subscription. However, Kennedy's note on Poe's letter of November [19?], 1833, the original of which is in the Peabody Institute, states in reference to Poe's mention of his manuscript then in the hands of Carey and Lea: "This refers to the volume of tales sent to Carey & Lea—'Tales of the Arabesque &c.'—being the series submitted for the prize, for which one was chosen, and the others at my suggestion sent to Carey & Lea. J. P. K." James A. Harrison, *The Life of Edgar Allan Poe* (New York, 1902), p. 2, prints this note but erroneously prints "two series" and "two others."

manuscript in the Griswold Collection in the Boston Public Library contains Poe's introduction to the Folio Club, a brief description and characterization of its eleven members, and all but the first two paragraphs of a story then called "Siope—A Fable," and later "Silence—A Fable." The manuscript seems to be a fragment consisting of four pages numbered 10 and 11 and 61 and 62. The major portion of "Siope" is on the last two pages and Poe's introduction on the first two. Presumably there were originally fifty pages of manuscript in between; if so, they might have contained the ten remaining tales. Assuming that the eleven original "Tales of the Folio Club" are the same as the eleven "Tales of the Arabesque," we can identify all but one. There were the five previously published in the *Saturday Courier* and, in addition, "Epimanes," "MS. Found in a Bottle," and "Siope—A Fable." Two others are fairly sure: "Lionizing," first published in the *Southern Literary Messenger*, May 1835, and "The Visionary," later called "The Assignation," which first appeared in *Godey's Lady's Book*, January 1834. If we do not accept "The Descent into the Maelstrom" as the eleventh—and I do not think we should—we can choose from among the following, all included in the 1840 edition of *Tales of the Grotesque and Arabesque* and all first published in 1835 in the *Messenger:* "Berenice" in March, "Morella" in April, "Hans Phaal" in June, and "King Pest" and "Shadow. A Parable" both in September. By counting all these as "Tales of the Folio Club" in their expanded form, but omitting "A Descent into the Maelstrom," we have the sixteen which Harrison designated and printed first in his edition of Poe's works. If we add "A Descent" or some other tale, we have the number of seventeen which Poe told Harrison Hall in a letter on September 2, 1836, he had written.[104] The five or six stories beyond the original eleven might have been written after October 1833, but there is no way of fixing the dates of composition. Some attempts have been made to identify the narrator of each story with a specific member of the Folio Club as they are described in Poe's Introduction, but those who have published their views do not agree. The problem is not pursued here because it is beyond the scope of the present essay.[105]

[104] *Letters*, pp. 103–104. Poe told Hall that all seventeen were published in the *Messenger*. Actually he had published only fourteen tales there at that time.

[105] See T. O. Mabbott, "On Poe's Tales of the Folio Club," *Sewanee Review*, XXXVI (April 1928), 171–176; and J. S. Wilson, "The Devil Was in It," *American Mercury*, XXIV (Oct. 1931), 215–220.

Poe was introduced to the members of the committee that awarded the *Visiter* prizes, and Kennedy especially took such an interest in him and his work that their meeting may fairly be said to have been the turning point in Poe's life. The following entry appears in Kennedy's journal for November 11, 1833: "In July last I was appointed together with John Latrobe & Dr. Miller, a committee, by the editors of the Saturday Morning Visiter to decide upon a prize tale and poem. Early in October we met for this purpose and having about a hundred tales and poems. The prize for the tale was given to Edgar A. Poe, having selected 'A Ms. found in a bottle' from a volume of tales furnished by him. This volume exhibits a great deal of talent, and we advised him to publish it. He has accordingly left it in my possession, to show it to Carey in Phila."[106] At some time between the date of this entry and April 1834, Kennedy delivered Poe's manuscript to Carey and Lea, either in person or by mail. He was encouraged to expect its publication for he wrote to T. W. White on April 13, 1835, about Poe: "He has a volume of very bizarre tales in the hands of Carey & Lea, in Philadelphia, who for a year past have been promising to publish them."[107] Poe had written Kennedy about November 19, 1834, asking him if he could induce Carey and Lea "to aid me with a small sum in consideration of my M.S. now in their hands." He wrote again on December 19, asking if Kennedy had received his letter.[108] Kennedy replied on December 22:

I requested Carey immediately upon the receipt of your first letter to do something for you as speedily as he might find an opportunity, and to make some advance on your book. His answer let me know that he would go on to publish, but the expectation of any profit from the undertaking he considered doubtful—not from want of merit in the production, but because small books of detached tales, however well written, seldom yield a sum sufficient to enable the bookseller to purchase a copyright. He recommended, however, that I should allow him to sell some of the tales to the publishers of annuals. My reply was that I thought you would not object to this if the right to publish the same tale was reserved for the volume. He has accordingly sold one of the tales to Miss Leslie for the "Souvenir," at a dollar a page, I think with the reservation mentioned—and has remitted me a draft for fifteen dollars which I will hand over to you as soon as you

---

[106] This manuscript journal of J. P. Kennedy is now in the Peabody Institute, Baltimore, and is quoted by permission.
[107] Woodberry, I, 109–110.   [108] *Letters*, pp. 54–55.

call upon me, which I hope you will do as soon as you can make it convenient. If the other tales can be sold in the same way, you will get more for the work than by an exclusive publication.[109]

Poe undoubtedly collected his $15, but no tales were published in the *Souvenir* then or later. Evidently he became discouraged, for he wrote Kennedy on March 15, 1835, enclosing an advertisement for a teacher in the public schools and asking him for help in getting the appointment: "In my present circumstances such a situation would be most desirable."[110] Nevertheless he continued to write. Kennedy wrote T. W. White, in the letter of April 13, cited above, "Poe did right in referring to me." He said that Poe was then "at work upon a tragedy, but I have turned him to drudging upon whatever may make money, and I have no doubt you and he will find your account in each other." It is clear from this letter that White had liked the stories he was publishing and had written to Kennedy with some idea of offering Poe editorial work.[111]

This brings us to the conclusion of Poe's search for a career. His work for the *Southern Literary Messenger* continued and increased, and in June White invited him to come to Richmond to assist in editing the magazine. Poe made the move sometime between July 20 and August 20, 1835. He had come to realize that he could not earn a living by writing poetry, however good it might be, and that even fiction of the kind he was willing to acknowledge would be a slim resource. The position of editor offered him the security of a regular salary with some time for creative work. It was the best arrangement he could hope for under the circumstances. From that time on, Poe's career was that of an editor and reviewer, to which fiction writing was only supplemental. As for his poetry, he wrote only five or six new poems during the succeeding ten years, although he never lost interest in it, and he continued to revise and republish his earlier work. It was only after his career as an editor was over, at the end of 1845, that he

[109] Woodberry, I, 105–106.

[110] *Letters*, p. 56. At various times afterward Poe attempted to secure a salaried position as teacher or government worker, but without success.

[111] "Berenice" had been published in the March issue and "Morella" in April. The tragedy Poe was at work on was *Politian*. The unfinished manuscript is in the Pierpont Morgan Library. He surely began this dramatic poem long before April 1835. "The Coliseum" is made a part of the play in the manuscript, and since it was the *Visiter* prize poem it must have been composed before October 1, 1833. It belongs near the end of the play, which was planned, if not written, in sequence. It may be surmised, therefore, that some of the scenes had been written as early as 1833 or even 1832.

had the freedom to devote himself again to poetry. He proved to be an excellent editor, but he was too stern a critic to be popular, and he never achieved the editorial independence required for the full development of his critical abilities. He is now most esteemed as a writer of short stories, but by temperament and inclination he was first and always a poet. He turned to fiction and adopted the career of a magazine editor from sheer necessity, not from choice.

III.   Poe and ''The Musiad''

THE prose satire of Edgar Allan Poe is well known though not always admired, and there is an occasional satiric note in his acknowledged poems, particularly in some of the early ones. A few poems that are primarily satiric have been attributed to him. He is said to have written lampoons for the amusement of his fellow cadets against some of the officers and instructors at West Point while he was a student there in 1830 and 1831, and some competent scholars believe that he wrote, perhaps before 1827, a satiric poem, "O, Tempora! O, Mores!," first published in 1868.[1] Still another satiric poem, or poetic fragment, has been attributed to him. This is a pamphlet of eight pages, the title page of which reads: "The MUSIAD or NINEAD, a Poem. By DIABOLUS. *Edited by* ME. Baltimore: 1830." Following the "Editor's Preface" in prose there are 101 lines of pentameter verse arranged in rhyming couplets except that in one instance three lines are made to rhyme. Numerals in parentheses before nineteen of the lines were apparently meant to refer to notes that either are lost or were never printed. On the title page of this unique copy, under the date, appears in pencil the letter "M," which is the initial of the person who catalogued the pamphlet for the Brown University Library. Under the last line of verse appears the following, also in pencil: "Collated—imperfect—?—13S°°." Under that again there is the letter "M," signifying that the cataloguer made the collation on September 13, 1900.[2] (See facsimile facing page 66.)

Only one copy of this pamphlet is known to exist, and that is in the Library of Brown University. It came into the possession of C. Fiske Harris, a notable collector of early American poetry, in 1874 or earlier,

---

[1] See *The Poems of Edgar Allan Poe*, ed. Floyd Stovall (Charlottesville, Va., 1965), pp. 137–141 for the text of the poems, and pp. 294–297 for editorial comment.

[2] For this explanation of the pencil notes, and for other help, I am indebted to Miss Barbara Hobson, Assistant Special Collections Librarian at Brown University.

for it is listed in his *Index to American Poetry and Plays in the Collection of C. Fiske Harris* (Providence, 1874), item 972: "? Diabolus. The Musiad or Ninead. Balt. 1830. 8°." Harris died in 1881, and his collection was acquired by his cousin Senator Henry Bowen Anthony, also a collector, who died in 1884, leaving the collection to Brown University. One would naturally expect this pamphlet to have passed with the rest of the collection through Senator Anthony to Brown University, but it is not listed in John C. Stockbridge's *Anthony Memorial Catalogue of the Harris Collection of American Poetry*, published in 1886. If it did not reach Brown University until 1900, the date it was collated and catalogued, where had it been since Harris published his *Index* in 1874? Perhaps it was lost or misplaced temporarily in the collection.

If more than the one copy ever existed, a second was seen in Baltimore, in the Library of the Maryland Historical Society, in 1876. On June 6 of that year William Hand Browne wrote to Poe's English biographer John H. Ingram: "I have been shown to-day in the liby. of Maryland Histl. Socy. an 8pp. pamphlet containing a satirical poem called 'The Musiad or Ninead. By Diabolus. Published by Me. Baltimore, 1830.'" The librarians of the Maryland Historical Society have looked for this pamphlet there several times during the last half dozen years but have found no trace of it. This suggests the possibility that there was never but the one copy and that the one Browne saw in Baltimore was the same as that owned by Harris, who, in that case, must be supposed to have left it temporarily at the Historical Society Library in the hope that its author might be identified. Probably it remained there until it was restored to the Brown University Library.[3] If there was only one copy, the chances are greater that the poem was printed in a unique copy from an incomplete manuscript. Another possibility is that the manuscript was complete with notes and that the printing of a preliminary copy was interrupted for some reason and never completed, the manuscript being later lost or destroyed. This would explain the numerals referring to notes that were never printed.

[3] William Hand Browne was born in Baltimore, December 31, 1828. In 1876 he was, or had recently been, editor of the *Southern Magazine*, and in 1879 he became the Librarian at Johns Hopkins University. But in the 1850's he was in the commission business in Baltimore. C. F. Harris had also been in the commission business in New York during the 1850's, so that it is not improbable that they were acquainted. Browne's letter to Ingram is in the Ingram Collection at the University of Virginia.

Harris suggested that Mrs. Whitman consult John Neal about "The Musiad," and she wrote to him on November 11, 1874. She sent him a copy of the poem, or substantial quotations from it, and expressed her conviction that Poe wrote it. She had, she said, consulted "a literary gentleman" of Providence, who told her that "if Poe did not write it *himself* it must have been written by John Neal." Neal replied that he did not write the poem and had not heard of it before, but added, "I think, with you, that the lines you send were written by Poe himself."[4] On May 19, 1876, Mrs. Whitman wrote to Ingram saying that Harris "wishes to know if you can find in the National Collection the pamphlet of which I spoke to you summer before last, called the Musiad or Ninead, by Diabolus, which was published in Baltimore in 1830 . . . I wrote to John Neal about it. The notes were torn off. Mr. H. thinks we might find something of great interest in them. I think I wrote to you about it." I have found no mention of "The Musiad," however, in Mrs. Whitman's letters to Ingram in 1874. She may have confused it with Poe's 1827 volume, *Tamerlane and Other Poems*. She did write to Ingram about that on July 21, 1874, saying that Harris had shown her a copy of the 1831 edition which he had obtained at a book sale in New York, and that he has "sought for many years for the edition said to be published in 1827, but can find, as yet, no trace of it."[5] Neither Ingram nor any other biographer of Poe mentions "The Musiad."

The poem was reprinted for the first time in 1964 in Randall's account of the formation of the Lilly Collection of Poe, already mentioned, and it is to be included with other poems attributed to Poe in Thomas Ollive Mabbott's forthcoming edition of Poe's poems. For the convenience of the reader, the title page, preface, and poem are reprinted here from the original at Brown University. Line numbers have been added for the purpose of reference ("me" in line 9 and "Gywnn" in line 90 are obviously misprints for "we" and "Gwynn").

[4] Mrs. Whitman's letter to Neal and his reply are in the Lilly Library at Indiana University. They are printed in David A. Randall, *The J. K. Lilly Collection of Edgar Allan Poe* (Bloomington, Ind., 1964), pp. 49–50.

[5] These letters are in the Ingram Collection. Harris had bought Poe's third volume, *Poems* (1831), in March 1869 at the sale of Albert Gorton Greene's collection, but no other work by Poe. See Roger E. Stoddard's pamphlet, *C. Fiske Harris, Collector of American Poetry and Plays* (Providence, 1963), pp. 5–11.

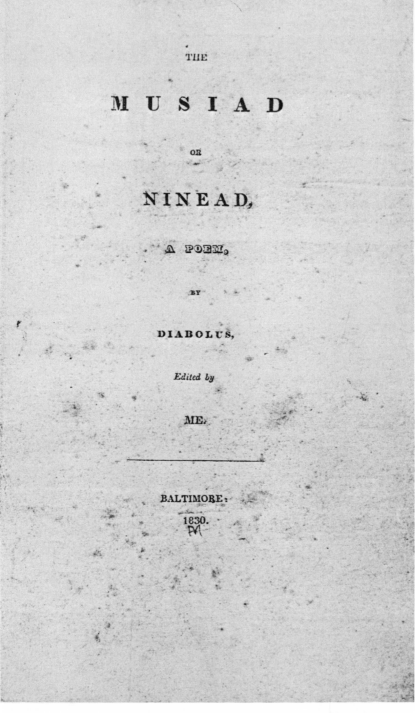

THE

MUSIAD

OR

NINEAD,

A POEM,

BY

DIABOLUS,

Edited by

ME.

BALTIMORE:

1830.

Title page of *The Musiad* (1830). Reproduced from the original in the Brown University Library

THE

MUSIAD

OR

NINEAD,

A POEM,

BY

DIABOLUS,

Edited by

ME.

———————

BALTIMORE:

1830.

EDITOR'S PREFACE.

The following poem was left (in MS.) some weeks since, at my Printing-Office, by a gentleman, whom, from his extreme taciturnity, I, at the time, suspected of some sinister design. It was closely done up in a canvass envelope, and labelled in a large Italian hand which my oldest devil confessed himself unable to decipher—partly because, as he afterwards observed, it was much too plain and self-evident. The stranger wished 500 copies to be printed immediately, saying that he would send for them on the Monday ensuing. I hinted my desire of looking into the packet, sur le champ, with a view of profiting by his personal experience in the reduction of a fortress whose outworks promised so formidable a resistance—The reply in the negative sounded very much like a growl. So contemptuous an answer, from so diminutive a man, induced me to raise my hand for the purpose of knocking him down: but, as he looked me straight in the face, I abandoned my original intention, not forgetting, however, to embrace that opportunity of scratching my head, it being a maxim with me, as with Epictetus, that mistakes cease to be such when turned to any reasonable account.

The gentleman soon after moved towards the door, and since, because of his singular assurance, I could not help fancying him a moneyed man, I stood prepared, as I have been taught, to return his bow in departing—but the stranger departed without bowing—and the effort, on my side, to regain my natural position without an obeisance destroyed my equilibrium, and prostrated me on the floor. Since then I have neither seen nor heard of this personage, and the unaccountable obstinacy with which my diaboli defend his reputation together with a strong smell of sulphur on the staircase incline me to think him no better than he should be. Still I would not have ventured to issue the books (which were printed) altho' urged so to do as a security for my own bill, and that of the surgeon who in my fall strongly suspects the co-operation of a tail, were I not perfectly convinced that the satire is harmless, in as much as the persons satirized are, for the most part, as far beyond injury as my housekeeper's eggs.

MUSIAD

Why not a Muse will deign to dwell with us—   1
Why Moore shall make a poem—and Dawes a fuss
I sing: or will, if God will grant the power
To Rufus Dawes to hold his tongue one hour.

Muse! whom before thy fellow flock had flown   5
I hid, betimes, to be my love alone,
Tell how thy sisters one eventful day
Whom chance did bring, mischance did fright'n away,
Since when unmus'd we write—for write me must—
(1) Bards will not starve, and tradesmen will not trust.   10

The cloth had been removed: o'er Chian wine
(2) With Moore and Wordsworth sat the stately nine:
It was not late enough by half an hour—
The lights were dim—the Chian wine was sour—
Wordsworth was very dull—too little to drink!   15
(3) Tom Moore look'd up to sigh—and down to think—
An awful silence reigned which dared to break
Not ev'n Tom Moore, till thus Thalia spake.
"To list to reason may the nine refuse
"No longer, Muses! ye, who love the Muse!   20
"Twice yesterday, and once again to-day
(4) "Invokes our aid a Yankee roundelay."

She paus'd—"I know," said Moore—"I think," said Clio,
"We'd better pay them a short visit, heigho!"
"Adjust their claims—look over what they write"—   25
Added Melpomene; said Tom Moore "try it:"
"Unless we fairly see we cannot judge"
Observed Calliope; said Tom Moore, "fudge!"
"I think, then, Wordsworth, Moore, with your consent
(5) We'll go" said Clio—"the devil!" said Tom:—they went.   30

A sea-like murmur round our nation spread—
Muses among us! life among the dead!
(6) And heads were scratched, as on that day which gave
Miss Frances Wright the world to deafen, and save.
And let them scratch! be mine nil admirari—   35
(7) Miss Wright is very right—the six foot fairy!
And Mrs. Royall, tho' of tenderer stuff,
For democrats is royalty enough.

What temple have we for the Muses fit?
What court for mind? what tribunal for wit?   40
There dwell (where Chesnut proves, to all who see,
(8) Of a right line the possibility—
Where gilded tomes the passer-by invite
If rich, to read—if better off—to write—
Where nonsense, gratis, from a foreign land   45
Is by new fools admir'd at second hand—
Where dust is very scarce and folly thickens)
(9) A goose, and two of Mother Carey's chickens:
There lit the nine—thence loud the rumour rings
(10) "To night we will assay what ev'n M'Henry sings."   50

Blue were the stockings—blue the candlelight
In the blue room where sat the nine that night—
Where sat the nine! and good Lord! how they sat?
(11) Did Captain Basil e'er see the like of that?
On books! how little do the Muses know   55
Of what we think most holy here below!
Only behold! Melpomene, the wench
Is sitting on Hadad, instead of bench!
See! Polyhymnia lolls upon a super—
—Fine copy of the last new lie of Cooper!   60
And Erato is in a corner, serving
Her nether parts with an old tale of Irving!

(12) While Patrick Henry, Wirt, is thinking now
      Calliope a lighter load than thou!
      He would have died to set the country free—   65
      But oh! to die so damned a death in thee!

      The nine were seated as I sang before—
      Willis was there, and bowed—what could he more?
      (He rang the bell as he came thro' the door)—
(13) Willis! whose shirt-collar—whose look—whose tone is   70
      The beau-ideal fancied for Adonis!
      "Ladies!" he said, and blush'd, "behold in me
      "(I'm scarce of age) an early devotee!
      "I sing—the Muses bid, and why be mute?
      "I dance—the Muses dance—I play the flute—   75
      "I play the fool—the devil—and, better yet,
(14) "I damned a Token, soon will a Gazette—
      "To low ambition and the pride of kings
(15) "I leave the rest and write unwritten things!"
      Next Pickering came, and grieved, fond youth! to see   80
      A sad example more, poor Nat! in thee
      Of those who, bat-like, blind with open eyes
(16) Will not write sense, and dare not sonnetize.
(17) Next Poe who smil'd at reason, laugh'd at law,
      And played a tune who should have play'd at taw,   85
      Now strain'd a license, and now crack'd a string,
      But sang as older children dare not sing.
      Said Clio "by all the wise, who can admit
      "Beardless no goat a goat—no wit a wit,
(18) "Say! did not Billy Gywnn, the great, combine   90
      "With little Lucas to put down thy line?
      "And thou! thy very heart is on thy toy!
      "Thy red-hot lyre will burn thee—drop it, boy!"
      While yet he stood a trump was heard—a shout—
(19) And Sumner, Lincoln, Fairfield shov'd him out—   95
      "Yield!" said the youth, and shov'd—"respect your betters,
      "And bow to names of two and twenty letters."
      What tho' his neckcloth sat somewhat awry,
      In a fine frenzy roll'd the poet's eye—
      His high thoughts were—if not his coat—his own,   100
      And all Apollo trembled in his tone.

Since the pamphlet was published anonymously and no objective
evidence exists that I have found that would identify the author or

authors of either the poem or its preface, his or their identity must be discovered, if at all, through circumstantial and internal evidence. On the basis of such evidence I am inclined to believe, though I cannot state positively, that Poe wrote both the poem and the preface, possibly with the collaboration of his friend Lambert A. Wilmer. The question is both important and complicated; to present the evidence fairly, pro and con, it is necessary to enter into a detailed analysis of the contents of the pamphlet.

II

Any moderately well-informed person in Baltimore in 1830 would have understood most of "The Musiad" readily enough, but readers now will feel the need of some explanatory comments. It will be remembered, of course, that in 1820 Sydney Smith raised the embarrassing question, Who reads an American book? and that for the next twenty years this question was extensively discussed in American periodicals. The poet of "The Musiad" begins with the assumption that the Muses had never visited America although its poets were regularly invoking them; hence the decision by the Nine to come to this country, interview its poets, and "adjust their claims." We learn in the second stanza that they have visited America as planned but have been frightened away by some "mischance"—that is, all except one, whom the poet of "The Musiad" has hidden and kept, and whom he now invokes. The story to be told, presumably, will explain the "chance" that brought the Muses to America and the "mischance" that frightened them away. It is not clear what this "chance" was unless it was the fact, stated in lines 21–22, that Yankee poems had invoked the Muses "twice yesterday, and once again to-day." The rest of the poem concerns the visit. Because we never arrive at the "mischance" or the departure of the Muses, it may be assumed that the poem is incomplete as printed.

In view of the stated theme of "The Musiad" one might expect it to be national in character—to survey the entire field of American poetry, and perhaps other forms of writing as well, since Clio, the Muse of History, Thalia, the Muse of Comedy, Melpomene, the Muse of Tragedy, and Calliope, the Muse of Heroic Poetry, figure prominently as urging the visit to America. As it has been preserved, however, the poem is local in character. In the New York *Mirror,* October 9, 1830, a critic, under the section "American Literature," presumably George P. Morris, the editor, made the following judgment of American poets: "When we have named Bryant and Halleck, Percival, Hillhouse, Dana and Sprague, with perhaps one or two others, we have named all whose works really do their country honour." None of these names appear in "The Musiad." The poets who are named, unless we accept Willis, were connected in one way or another with Baltimore and Philadelphia.

The action of the poem begins with the nine Muses sitting, "o'er Chian wine," after a dinner with Moore and Wordsworth. The wine was Chian, no doubt, because the island of Chios was once claimed as Homer's birthplace. Wordsworth was present because he was presumably, in the eyes of the writer, the best known living British poet after Moore. Southey was then out of fashion, and Coleridge was not yet well known as a poet, though widely recognized as a critic and philosophical writer. There is a bit of satire in the line "Wordsworth was very dull—too little to drink!"

Thomas Moore, however, is an active character and is treated with respect by the satirist, who proposes to sing "Why Moore shall make a poem—and Dawes a fuss."[6] There may be obscure allusions to Moore's earlier poems in lines 28–30, in the two exclamations "fudge!" and "the devil!" In 1818 Moore published *The Fudge Family in Paris. Edited by Thomas Brown, the Younger.*[7] This is a document in the interminable literary war between the Whigs and the Tories after Waterloo, presented as a clever mixture of satire and good humor in a series of versified letters exchanged between members of the Fudge family and their friends. There is no parallel between the contents of "The Musiad" and "The Fudge Family in Paris," but to readers of 1830 Moore's exclamation would seem peculiarly appropriate. A cheap edition of *The Works of Thomas Moore, Esq.,* had been published in

[6] Moore was in America in 1804, visiting, among other places, Philadelphia, where he was entertained by Joseph Dennie, editor of the *Port Folio,* and other admirers, who made life agreeable for ten days. See H. M. Jones, *The Harp That Once*—(New York, 1937), pp. 80–82.

[7] *The Works of Thomas Moore* (New York, 1825), V, 5–116. This was first published in London in 1818 and went through eight editions within the year. Moore had first used this pseudonym a few years earlier in the popular *Intercepted Letters, or the Twopenny Post-Bag (ibid.,* pp. 231–272). It was borrowed from the late seventeenth-century satirist Thomas Brown "of facetious memory," as Addison described him. See Benjamin Boyce, *Tom Brown of Facetious Memory* (Cambridge, Mass., 1939); also *Letters of Thomas Moore,* ed. W. S. Dowden (Oxford, 1964), I, 256–257.

six small volumes in New York in 1825. If the exclamation "fudge!" alludes to this poem, it may well be that the exclamation "the devil!" alludes to "The Fudger Fudged; or, The Devil and T***y M***e (London, 1819)," with which some unidentified partisans of the Tory cause replied to Moore.

There is another possible allusion to Moore in lines 51–52: "Blue were the stockings—blue the candlelight / In the blue room where sat the nine that night." The term "blue stocking" was often applied to literary ladies in the early nineteenth century and may for this reason have been used in reference to the Muses. But the room was also blue, and there is something extraordinary in the manner of the Muses' sitting, for they all sat on books, and one of them was using a tale of Irving in a very disrespectful manner. Volume V of the New York edition of Moore's works, which contained "The Fudge Family in Paris," contained also "M. P., or, The Blue-Stocking (pp. 127–230)," a comic opera first produced at the Lyceum Theatre, London, in 1811. It is in part a political satire and in part a satire on learned ladies and on contemporary books. Three of the main characters are Sir Charles Canvas, a member of Parliament, Lady Bab Blue, a "scientist" by pretension, modeled on Mrs. Malaprop, and Leatherhead, who operates a circulating library in connection with his bookstore and publishing business. With the sentimental love stories we have no concern here. Leatherhead is called "that venerable Chamberlain of the Muses," and two of the more important scenes take place in his library, another just outside. Lady Bab has written a poem on sal ammoniac entitled "The Loves of Ammonia" and offered it to Leatherhead for publication.[8]

The "blue room" where the Muses sat—the "temple" most fit for a "court of mind" and a "tribunal of wit"—was the bookstore of Carey, Lea and Carey, on Chesnut[9] Street, in Philadelphia. "Mother Carey's chickens" is a term sailors are said to have used for stormy petrels; in the poem it refers to the two sons of Mathew Carey, Henry C. and Edward L., who were associated with Isaac Lea in 1829 in the publishing and bookselling firm of Carey, Lea and Carey. The "goose" presumably refers to Lea, the son-in-law of Mathew Carey. Among

[8] Some of Webster's earlier dictionaries state that sal ammoniac is "said to have been prepared originally from camel dung near the shrine of Jupiter Ammon." Murray's *New English Dictionary* has the following quotation from Beckford's *Vathek* (1786): "The camels, which had been left unmolested to make sal ammoniac."

[9] Regularly spelled without the middle "t" in the 1820's and 1830's.

quotations in the *New English Dictionary* illustrating the meaning of "Mother Carey's chickens" is the following from Captain Cook's *Voyages* (1790): "Another sort, which is the largest of the petrels, and called by seamen, Mother Carey's goose, is found in abundance." A son-in-law, Lea was appropriately "Mother Carey's goose" to distinguish him from the sons. At that time Carey, Lea and Carey was probably the largest publisher in America, and perhaps also the largest importer of foreign books for republication and retail sale. The foreign books "by new fools admir'd at second hand" may refer to books republished in America, but it may, and perhaps more properly, refer to those reviewed in the *American Quarterly Review*, which then, and later, dealt severely with American poets. In a review of Samuel Kettell's *Specimens of American Poetry* in that journal for September 1829, the reviewer feels he must "deprecate and resist the attempt to exalt" even the best American poets "to the height of the great British classics." He also suggests that "our countrymen would possibly be more meritorious and distinguished *in the end*, if they took the resolution of confining themselves to the perusal of the British galaxy, discarding their indigenous stock, together with nearly all the British verse of the present century."[10]

The allusions to Frances Wright, Mrs. Royall, and "Captain Basil" are interesting in themselves and helpful in establishing the date of composition of "The Musiad." Fanny Wright became a sensation in the summer of 1828 when she first began to give public lectures. Mrs. Frances Trollope heard her second lecture, given in Cincinnati in July, and noted her "tall and majestic figure" and the "wonderful power of her rich and thrilling voice."[11] Her radical ideas on slavery, marriage, and politics received much attention in the newspapers from 1828 until her departure for England on July 1, 1830. She first lectured in Baltimore on five successive nights in late November or early December 1828. That city, she wrote her sister, "has been the stronghold of priestcraft for some years past." There was fear of public

---

[10] The *American Quarterly Review*, as a business enterprise, was allied with Carey, Lea and Carey. Robert Walsh, whom Poe had consulted about a publisher for his poems was the editor, but James McHenry was the principal reviewer and probably the author of this review. See *Letters of Edgar Allan Poe*, ed. J. W. Ostrom (Cambridge, Mass., 1948), I, 18–23. This work will hereafter be referred to as *Letters*.

[11] *Domestic Manners of the Americans*, ed. Donald Smalley (New York, 1949), pp. 70–73. John H. Hewitt remembered her as "tall, for a woman, and rather masculine" (*Shadows on the Wall*, Baltimore, 1877, p. 45).

disturbances, but none occurred. She was often called the "Priestess of Beelzebub" and the "Angel of Infidelity." By the summer of 1829 she was notorious if not famous throughout the country. Mathew Carey, though a staunch Catholic, had been the first to publish her play *Altorf*, in 1819, and the play had been performed at the Park Theatre in New York in February 1819, during her first visit to America. On July 4, 1829, she delivered an address "to a crowded audience" in "one of the largest theatres in Philadelphia."[12]

Mrs. Anne Newport Royall was less famous nationally than Fanny Wright but much better known in Baltimore and Philadelphia. She was born in 1769 in Maryland, spent her childhood in backwoods Pennsylvania, went to Virginia after her father's death, married William Royall there in 1797, and was widowed in 1813. Deprived later of her rights to her husband's property, and after years of poverty, she became a successful writer of travel books and moved to Washington. Her biographer describes her in her prime as "a sweet-natured, large-minded, witty, and wonderfully observant woman."[13] Her chief fault was the intolerance of intolerance which led her sometimes to become abusive. John H. Hewitt describes an unpleasant visit from her while he was editor of the *Minerva,* and he recalls her as "a squatty, round-faced, sharp-nosed, thin lipped little woman."[14] But Samuel C. Atkinson, editor of the Philadelphia *Saturday Evening Post,* liked Mrs. Royall and was liked by her. In the *Post* for June 13, 1829, she is quoted as saying she had called on Mr. Atkinson in his office and praised him. In the issue of October 31 she is reported as then visiting Philadelphia. The editor had had a brief interview with her and found her "affable as ever." She had just published the second volume of *Mrs. Royall's Pennsylvania,* the first having come out in June. Later that year she was arrested in Washington on the ridiculous charge of being "a common scold." After a long and equally ridiculous trial,

[12] These facts are drawn chiefly from William Randall Waterman's *Frances Wright* (New York, 1924), pp. 163–183, and A. J. G. Perkins and Theresa Wolfson's *Frances Wright, Free Enquirer* (New York, 1939), pp. 245–255. According to J. Thomas Scharf and Thompson Westcott, *History of Philadelphia* (Philadelphia, 1884), I, 624, the address on July 4 was delivered in the Walnut Street Theatre, and her last lectures were given on two successive Sunday evenings in September 1829.

[13] Sarah H. Porter, "The Life and Times of Ann Royall, 1769–1854," *Records of the Columbia Historical Society of Washington, D.C.,* X (1907), 10. This work was expanded and published as a book in 1909 (Cedar Rapids, Iowa), where Mrs. Royall's first name is correctly spelled "Anne."

[14] *Shadows on the Wall,* pp. 23–26. This would probably have been in 1829.

which was not settled until midsummer 1830, she was convicted and
fined $10 and required to keep the peace for a year. Frequent reports
of this trial were published in the Baltimore and Philadelphia newspapers. Mrs. Royall was known to be a personal friend of Secretary of
War John H. Eaton and of his wife, the former Peggy O'Neil, against
whom the wives of other members of President Jackson's cabinet
made scandalous charges; this was not calculated to improve Mrs.
Royall's social status in official Washington. Poe might be expected to
have taken a special interest in this case because, in an effort to secure
his appointment to West Point, he went to Washington about July 23,
1829, where he had a personal interview with Eaton.[15] The statement
in lines 37–38 of the poem that Mrs. Royall is "royalty enough" for
democrats alludes to her well-known social and political theories, but
also perhaps to the rumor that her father, William Newport, was an
illegitimate scion of the royal Stuarts. She is reported to have taken
notice of this rumor only once, saying: "I am of noble blood but I
consider no title so honorable as that of American citizen. I have no
desire to claim alliance with royalty."[16]

The "Captain Basil" of line 54 refers to Captain Basil Hall, a British
writer of travel books, one of which, *Skimmings; or a Winter at
Schloss Hainfeld in Lower Styria,* Poe reviewed favorably in the
Southern Literary Messenger, October 1836. The poet of "The Mu-
siad" had in mind Captain Hall's *Travels in North America in the
Years 1827 and 1828,* which was originally published in three volumes
in Edinburgh and London during the summer of 1829 and reprinted
by Carey, Lea and Carey shortly thereafter in two volumes. In the
New York *Mirror* it was announced on August 22 as "in press of
Carey, Lea & Carey." The book relates how the author arrived in New
York May 15, 1827, went to Niagara Falls and Canada, and then back
through New York, Philadelphia, Baltimore, on through the South to
New Orleans, and back up the Mississippi to New York, where he
embarked for England July 1, 1828. He liked Philadelphia, especially
complimenting its libraries and learned societies. He comments on the
efficiency of Carey, Lea and Carey in republishing new English books,
but charges that Americans do not buy the more important foreign
books but only those that have proved or are likely to prove popular.
He is usually sensible and fair in his comments on America, and these
do not justify the impression conveyed in the poem that he has
reported seeing marvels. Most likely the poet refers particularly to

---

[15] As related in Poe's letter to John Allan, July 26, 1829; *Letters,* I, 24–26.
[16] Porter, p. 6.

what Hall had to say about publishing in Philadelphia, and about Carey, Lea and Carey especially.

The other literary names in the poem may best be taken up as they occur. Rufus Dawes, the first American poet mentioned, was evidently a great talker, though not a prolific writer. Hewitt, his friend and associate in Baltimore, says of him: "In short, none of our native poets have gained so enviable a reputation upon so small a number of publications as Dawes, if I except Sprague and Richard Wilde; the *quality*, not the *quantity*, placed him among the most favored of our bards."[17] On the other hand, N. P. Willis, who had been well acquainted with Dawes in Boston in 1827–28, wrote of him in the "Editor's Table" of his *American Monthly Magazine*, August 1829, that although all acknowledge he is a genius, "the truth is that the main part of Dawes's celebrity, like Coleridge's, is based upon his conversation. . . . He is out of reach—editing a paper in Baltimore."[18] In his "Autography" in *Graham's Magazine*, November 1841, Poe says of Dawes: "He seems to have been infected with a blind admiration of Coleridge—especially of his mysticism and cant."[19] Like Bryant, Willis, and Longfellow, Dawes had published poems in the U.S. *Literary Gazette* about 1825, but his first volume did not appear until 1830. It contained one poem of moderate length and thirty-three short ones. Later he published two long poems which were collected in 1839 in a volume entitled *Geraldine, Athenia of Damascus, and Miscellaneous Poems*, which Poe reviewed in *Graham's* for October 1842.[20] His judgment was that the shorter poems "have the merit of tenderness," but that the long poems are bad; "Geraldine," he declares, is "a mere mass of irrelevancy." In the "Autography," referred to above, he called "Athenia of Damascus" pompous nonsense.

The next poet mentioned, James McHenry, rates only one line (line 50), but it is one of the sharpest in the poem: "To night we will assay what ev'n M'Henry sings." He was born in Ireland and came to Philadelphia in 1824 by way of Baltimore and Pittsburgh, where he spent seven years. The *Dictionary of American Biography* says that for eighteen years he was "prominent as a physician, merchant, political leader, magazine editor, poet, and critic" in Philadelphia. His

[17] P. 10.

[18] Dawes came to Baltimore in 1828 to establish a literary weekly called the *Emerald*. Within a year it was combined with another weekly edited by John H. Hewitt called the *Minerva* and continued as the Baltimore *Minerva and Emerald*.

[19] *The Complete Works of Edgar Allan Poe*, ed. James A. Harrison (New York, 1902), XV, 191. This edition will be referred to hereafter as *Works*.

[20] *Works*, XI, 131–147.

eighteenth-century bias and conservative reviews of poetry in the *American Quarterly Review* made him especially disliked by the younger American poets who admired Wordsworth and the other English Romantic poets. None of these were acceptable to McHenry except Byron, and he only because of his occasional antiromantic prejudices. McHenry probably wrote the review article with the running title "American Poetry" in the *American Quarterly Review*, September 1829, which has already been cited. One sentence in this article might have suggested the comment on McHenry in "The Musiad." The reviewer complains of the omission of Joseph Hopkinson, remembered now, if at all, only for his poem "Hail Columbia," from Kettell's *Specimens of American Poetry*, and adds: "Notwithstanding that our own doings in metre are obscure and anonymous, as the Irish gentleman said of the letter—we could . . . but feel a little jealous and resentful that *we* were omitted." He quotes with approval Byron's praise of Pope and his criticism of his own Romantic verse and that of his contemporaries.[21] McHenry was closely associated with prominent Irish families in Philadelphia, including the Careys, and he was an occasional contributor to their annual, the *Atlantic Souvenir*. Whether Poe knew him as early as 1830 I cannot say, but he must have read McHenry's contributions to the *Souvenir*. Years later Poe reviewed his epic, *The Antediluvians, or the World Destroyed*, in *Graham's Magazine* for February 1841. Here he is severe, saying, "Had Milton never written poetry, Dr. McHenry would never have published bombast." However, in "An Appendix of Autographs" in the same magazine for January 1842, he defends McHenry's poem against the "unjust" and "disgraceful pasquinade on the part of Professor Wilson," the editor of *Blackwood's*.[22] About the same time, in *The Quacks of Helicon* (Philadelphia, 1841), Lambert A. Wilmer, who probably knew McHenry in Philadelphia about 1829–30, condemns another poet's verse as "The veriest, vilest drivel, (such as drops, / In slimy lustre from M'H—y's chops)."[23]

[21] McHenry was undoubtedly also the author of the review-essay "American Lake Poetry," *American Quarterly Review*, March 1832. There he condemns Bryant and Willis as imitators of Wordsworth. The first sentence of this essay reads: "We have always considered it very unfortunate for the reputation of American poetry, that just about the time it began to be much cultivated, a false style was introduced into poetical composition, by what are called the 'Lake Poets' of England."

[22] *Works*, X, 105–109; XV, 258.

[23] The fact that Wilmer spells McHenry's name in *The Quacks of Helicon* as it is spelled in "The Musiad," whereas Poe, in 1841 and 1842, spells it in the usual

The Muses are described in lines 51–66 as sitting on books written by well-known American writers. *Hadad,* on which Melpomene, the tragic Muse, is seated, is a drama in blank verse by James Hillhouse based in part on the biblical story of Absalom's rebellion and in part on the apocryphal book of Tobit and the Talmud. Samuel Kettell calls it "a master-piece of its kind,"[24] and even the reviewer of Kettell's anthology in the *American Quarterly Review* names Hillhouse along with Bryant, Halleck, Percival, Dana, and Sprague as the best American poets. Willis praised the poem, which was published in 1825 while he was still a student at Yale.[25]

The "last new lie of Cooper" on which Polyhymnia "lolls" must be his *Notions of the Americans Picked Up by a Travelling Bachelor,* published in the summer of 1828, while Cooper was in Europe. This is also a travel book; the narrator is represented as an English gentleman traveling in America. It is not clear whether Cooper's "lie" is his praise or his censure of America in that book; certainly the praise outweighs the censure. It is possible that the poet of "The Musiad" had not read the book, and that he took his cue from an article entitled "National Literature" in Willis's *American Monthly Magazine,* September 1829. The article quotes from Cooper's book, referred to as *Travelling Bachelor,* a passage which includes the following: "Another obstacle against which American literature has to contend, is the poverty of materials. . . . There are no annals for the historian; no follies (beyond the most vulgar and commonplace) for the satirist; no manners for the dramatist; no obscure fictions for the writer of romance; no gross and hardy offences against decorum for the moralist; not any of the rich artificial auxiliaries of poetry." In this predicament, Cooper adds, "What cannot be found at home, may be sought abroad."

Poe reviewed a number of Cooper's later books, the first being *Sketches of Switzerland,* which appeared in two installments in the *Southern Literary Messenger,* May and October 1836, and some of his comments there relate to the unpopularity of Cooper following his publication of *A Letter to His Countrymen* in 1834.[26] For example, in the October installment he says, "We are a bull-headed and prejudiced people, and it were well if we had a few more of the stamp of

---

way, may be an argument, though not a great one, for Wilmer's authorship of "The Musiad."

[24] *Specimens of American Poetry* (Boston, 1829), II, 356.

[25] Henry A. Beers, *Nathaniel Parker Willis* (Boston, 1885), p. 70.

[26] For the October installment, see *Works,* IX, 162–164. Harrison does not include the May installment in his edition, though it seems surely to be Poe's.

Mr. Cooper who would feel themselves at liberty to tell us so to our teeth."

Why Erato, the Muse of erotic poetry, should be treating a tale of Irving so disgracefully is hard to understand. Even though this is an "old" tale—presumably from *The Sketch Book* (1819), *Bracebridge Hall* (1822), or *Tales of a Traveller* (1824), and certainly not from the *Life of Columbus* (1828) or *The Conquest of Granada* (1829)—it was not a poem and could hardly have been erotic. Of course, it might have been abused by Erato precisely because it was not. The poet may have aimed his barb at Erato rather than at Irving.[27]

Calliope is usually identified as the Muse of heroic poetry, but the *New English Dictionary* adds to that "eloquence," which makes her appropriate for either Patrick Henry or William Wirt, his biographer. Although Wirt's *Life of Patrick Henry* was first published in 1817, it was frequently reprinted and was still widely read in 1830. That being the case, it seems contradictory to say that Calliope is a lighter weight for Henry to uphold than Wirt's biography. This is one of the few passages in the poem which may be used as evidence that Poe did not write "The Musiad." It is well known that Poe owed a great deal to Wirt, admired him, and visited him for advice as soon as he arrived in Baltimore in May 1829; hence it is hard to see why he should write anything uncomplimentary about his book at this time. Still, Poe was usually an honest critic, and it may be that the reference is to the heaviness of Wirt's Southern eloquence. John Neal wrote of the biography in one of his *Blackwood* articles about 1825 that "the biographer has overlooked everything but himself, in his passion for rhetorical ornament."[28] Even so, line 66 is very severe to have been written by Poe.

The lines describing the manner and appearance of Nathaniel P. Willis are very accurate. This does not mean, however, that the poet was personally acquainted with him, for Willis was so popular and wrote so much about himself in the early issues of the *American Monthly Magazine* (1829–31) that his portrait and his idiosyncrasies were universally known. His biographer informs us that he had already won a national reputation before he left Yale in 1827; he also

[27] This is what we should expect if Poe was the poet, for he did not approve of erotic poetry, and he always afterward had high praise for Irving. See, for example, his review of *The Crayon Miscellany* in the *Messenger*, Dec. 1835 (*Works*, VIII, 91–92).

[28] *American Writers: A Series of Papers Contributed to "Blackwood's Magazine,"* ed. F. L. Pattee (Durham, N.C., 1937), p. 184.

says he wore "conspicuously good clothes." His first publisher, Samuel G. Goodrich, says of Willis that, "being possessed of an easy and
captivating address, he became the pet of society and especially of
the fairer portion of it."[29] His early portrait, used as the frontispiece of
Beers's biography and of several editions of his poems, shows Willis
wearing a high stock that leaves only the top edge of his shirt collar
visible. The high stock was fashionable at that time, before long
beards made it uncomfortable. His bow to the Muses is natural
enough, but it may also allude to the line "I seldom make a bow,"
which I take to be ironic, in the poem "I'm not a Lover now,"
published in the *Boston Statesman*, March 28, 1828. The parenthetical
phrase "I'm scarce of age" in line 73 may have been suggested by
Willis's poem "I'm twenty-two—I'm twenty-two," published in the
Atlantic Souvenir for 1829.[30] Willis edited the *Token,* which Goodrich
published, for 1828 only. The *Token* survived, but not under his
editorship. It is not clear what the poet intends by "a Gazette." It
might refer to George P. Morris's *Mirror,* which kept the full title *New
York Mirror and Ladies Literary Gazette* at least until July 1830.
Though a contributor to the *Mirror* as early as March 1828, Morris
was not associated with it as an editor until September 1831. I am
inclined to believe that it refers to Willis's *American Monthly Magazine,* which he founded in April 1829 and maintained for more than
two years. The term "Gazette" is used in its general sense of a
periodical as distinguished from a book. The *Token* was an annual
and therefore a book. The "unwritten things" that Willis writes (line
79) refer undoubtedly to his two prose sketches, "Unwritten Poetry"
and "Unwritten Philosophy," in the May and November volumes (the
only ones published) of *The Legendary,* which Willis edited and
largely wrote for Goodrich in 1828.[31] Willis also wrote an essay "Unwritten Music" for the first issue of the *American Monthly Magazine,*
April 1829.[32] Willis frequently praised Wordsworth's poetry, and later

[29] Beers, pp. 69, 73, 91. Beers also quotes O. W. Holmes (p. 75) as saying of
Willis: "He came very near being handsome."

[30] This poem was not reprinted by Willis in his collected verse. If it was written
on his twenty-second birthday it dates from January 20, 1828. The 1829 *Souvenir*
was actually published in September or October 1828.

[31] Both were included by Mary Russell Mitford in *Stories of American Life by
American Authors* (London, 1830).

[32] If "The Musiad" was not printed until after January 1830, its author might
have seen a lampoon in the *Boston Courier,* reprinted by Willis in the *American
Monthly* for January 1830, in which all three of these prose pieces are mentioned.

he called an imitator of Wordsworth;[33] hence it might have been the knowledge of this fact, in part, that induced the poet of "The Musiad" to introduce his name along with Moore's in the introductory lines. As an epigraph to the poem "Night Sketches" in his first book, *Sketches,* Willis quotes a dozen lines from "Lines Composed above Tintern Abbey," beginning "Therefore let the moon / Shine on thee in thy solitary walk"; and in the *American Monthly* for July 1829, in a review of the *Memoirs of Goethe,* Willis called Wordsworth "the noblest and purest mind that has shone upon the world since Milton," adding that the "majesty and harmony" of the intimations "Ode" are "unsurpassed in the whole compass of English poetry."

The Pickering mentioned in line 80 is Henry Pickering, the son of Colonel Timothy Pickering, who at the time of Henry's birth in Washington's Headquarters at Newburgh, New York, was Quarter-master-General of the Army. After the Revolutionary War, Colonel Pickering lived for a time in Philadelphia and also for several years in the country west of that city. Since Henry was born in 1781, it is probable that he knew Philadelphia as a boy and young man. His literary life, however, is associated with Salem and Boston. He published four volumes of verse, of which the most representative and probably the best is *Poems by an American* (1830). He is not in the *Dictionary of American Biography,* and his books are extremely rare, but many of his poems, which sometimes remind me of Bryant's, are excellent, and they deserve to be better known. He must have known Willis in Boston between 1827 and 1831, and he may have been a member of the supper club, described by Beers, which consisted of perhaps a dozen men, including Willis, Rufus Dawes, and Washing-ton Allston.[34] Two of his poems were printed in early issues of the *American Monthly,* "Niagara" in June 1829 and "The Moonbeam" the following August. Pickering is well represented in Kettell's *Specimens of American Poetry* with eleven poems, including four exquisite sonnets. Kettell liked these poems, but he believed they were "perhaps too much of the old school, to suit the taste of the day." If the reader is disposed to be critical he might, Kettell thought, "observe an occasional want of music in the versification." This last comment seems to me to reflect Kettell's insensitiveness rather than Pickering's to the more subtle cadences of poetry. These comments may help to explain

[33] See above, p. 78, note 21.

[34] P. 92. Allston painted a picture for Henry Pickering. See the footnote to Pickering's "On a Picture by Allston."

why the poet of "The Musiad" says Pickering is grieved to find in Willis another "sad example" of poets who "Will not write sense, and dare not sonnetize." I should guess, although I have no specific facts, that Pickering liked Willis personally but, like some other friends, found fault with his somewhat foppish manner and his free style of versification.[35] It may be supposed that Pickering had published somewhere a critical comment on Willis's poetry that was known to the poet of "The Musiad," but, if so, it has not come to my attention.[36]

The lines about Poe are naturally among the most interesting of the poem, since he is the only one of the young poets named who afterward achieved lasting fame. It is significant that though he and his poetry were then unknown, except to a few friends and acquaintances, he is given more lines in the poem than Fairfield, then well known, and almost as many as Willis, who was famous at that time, both as a person and as a poet. Since the general tone and import of the lines devoted to Poe are complimentary, the intent of the writer must have been friendly. The phrases "smil'd at reason" and "laugh'd at law," understood within their context, clearly refer not to Poe's public life but solely to his theory and practice of poetry. In the eyes of his older contemporaries especially, he "strain'd" the license generally allowed to the poetic imagination; and both older and younger critics complained of his irregular meters, where, no doubt, they thought he "crack'd a string." Nevertheless, these same critics found much of his verse pleasing, and they recognized his genius. I doubt if Poe was "beardless" at that time—he was twenty-one years old, or very near that age, when this poem was written—but he was in the habit then and later of asserting that his poems were written when he was a boy. Even as late as 1845, though he was being facetious no doubt, he asserted that he had written "Al Aaraaf" and published it in book form before he had completed his tenth year.[37]

The reference to Billy Gwynn (misspelled in "The Musiad") is

[35] It may be that Willis found the sonnet's "narrow bounds," as Wordsworth described them approvingly, too demanding for his talents. In any case he did not write many. I find only three in his collected works. Two, without titles, were published in *Sketches*, but these were not reprinted. None of them are very good, and all are inferior to Pickering's.

[36] The exclamation "fond youth!" in line 80, though seeming grammatically to refer to Pickering, must surely be meant for Willis, since Pickering was nearly fifty years old in 1830.

[37] See above, pp. 31–32. As to "Al Aaraaf," see Quinn, pp. 485–489, for an account of Poe's reading the poem in Boston, October 16, 1845, and the criticism of it which provoked Poe's ridiculous assertion in the *Broadway Journal*.

easily explained; that to Fielding Lucas, not so easily. William Gwynn
was a prominent lawyer and man of affairs in Baltimore during the
1820's and 1830's. He was a member of the Delphian Club, which met
regularly at his house, called Tusculum, just back of the offices of the
newspaper he edited, the *Federal Gazette and Baltimore Daily Advertiser*. In Poe's time it was usually called the Baltimore *Gazette and
Daily Advertiser*.[38] Even after the Delphian Club was officially discontinued, William Gwynn, who had been its last president, continued to
invite friends and former members to his house as before. Among
those invited were Fielding Lucas, Jr., William Wirt, and John P.
Kennedy. Latrobe described Gwynn in the early 1830's as very fat and
jolly, an epigrammatist and something of a versifier, acquainted not
only with all the important politicians, including Daniel Webster, but
also with the celebrities of the stage. Latrobe called him "one of the
kindest and most benevolent of men, loved by all who knew him."
Fielding Lucas, Jr., a prominent bookseller and publisher in Baltimore
between 1811 and 1831, was the publisher of William Wirt's *Letters of
the British Spy*. Latrobe called him "my old and best friend" and
described him as very large and one of the handsomest old men he
ever saw.[39] Actually he was only 48 years old in 1829.

The familiar "Billy" in the reference to William Gwynn is in keeping with the spirit of the poem, and he might have been called "the
great" either humorously because of his obesity or seriously because of
his genuine importance in Baltimore. Fielding Lucas is called "little"
almost certainly because he was very large, an irony Baltimoreans
would appreciate. But how did Gwynn and Lucas "combine" to "put
down" Poe's "line"? These words make sense only if Gwynn and Lucas
were instrumental in the publication of Poe's poems. On May 18, 1829,
William Gwynn had published 39 lines (194–201, 214–220, 237–260)
of Part II of "Al Aaraaf"—the first time any part of this poem had been
printed. It is also possible that Poe borrowed money, or credit, from
Gwynn to pay or guarantee payment for the printing of *Al Aaraaf,
Tamerlane, and Minor Poems* in November or December 1829. When
Poe returned from West Point and New York to Baltimore he wrote to

[38] Other prominent Delphians were John Neal, John Pierpont, and, during its
last years, J. H. B. Latrobe. See John Earle Uhler, "The Delphian Club,"
Maryland Historical Magazine, XX (Dec. 1925), 305–346. See also John E.
Semmes's *John H. B. Latrobe and His Times, 1803–1891* (Baltimore, 1917),
which is a mine of information.

[39] Semmes, pp. 185–187, 207–208, and *passim*.

Gwynn on May 6, 1831, requesting his "influence in obtaining some situation or employment in this city" and suggesting that Gwynn himself might give him employment since his cousin Neilson Poe, formerly employed by Gwynn, had left him. But a more significant portion of this letter is the first sentence: "I am almost ashamed to ask any favour at your hands after my foolish conduct upon a former occasion—but I trust to your good nature." Because Poe did not leave New York until after March 10, 1831, as his letter to Colonel Thayer of that date shows, the "former occasion" must surely have occurred before he went to West Point in June 1830, and probably before he left Baltimore for Richmond in December 1829 or January 1830. It is unlikely that he was seeking employment in 1829. He was busy then with his poems and was supported by John Allan pending his appointment to West Point.[40] I can think of no reason why his conduct could have been foolish in connection with the printing of the lines from "Al Aaraaf" in Gwynn's newspaper. Hence my conjecture—and it is no more than that, since there is no positive evidence—that Gwynn had contributed financially to the publication of Poe's book and had not been repaid.

Fielding Lucas's connection with the printing of Poe's verse is also conjectural. He was a friend of William Gwynn, and he had for many years been closely associated with Mathew Carey and his sons in the publishing and bookselling business. Of his publishing enterprises his biographer says: "Some of these were joint enterprises of Lucas and other publishers of Baltimore or of Philadelphia. In these cases his name is found on the title page in association with one or more others."[41] Lucas would want his name on all important publications issued jointly with others, but it is possible that in minor publications by obscure publishers like Hatch and Dunning he would prefer that his name not be shown. He was much in the public eye and was a member of the City Council from 1829 until 1843.[42] He was also one of the principal suppliers of textbooks for the schools. He published illustrated books for children, some of them done by Latrobe.[43] It is easy to believe that he would have helped a promising young poet like Poe, but it would have been no credit to him to advertise his associa-

[40] See Poe's letters to Allan in November 1829, and his letters to Colonel Thayer and William Gwynn (*Letters*, pp. 33–34, 44, and 45).

[41] James W. Foster, "Fielding Lucas, Jr., Early 19th Century Publisher of Fine Books and Maps," *Proceedings of the American Antiquarian Society*, LXV (1955), 171.

[42] *Ibid.*, p. 177.   [43] Semmes, p. 102.

tion with Poe's publishers. Eugene V. Didier says: "Hatch & Dunning were two young men from New York who started in Baltimore with a small capital. After a year or two they disappeared."[44] The printers of Poe's book were a newly organized firm, Matchett and Woods. R. J. Matchett had been a publisher as well as a printer for many years. He established a short-lived weekly paper about 1820, and later another paper, called the *Wanderer*, presumably a literary weekly, in the late 1820's or early 1830's.[45] For several years Matchett published a book called *Matchett's Baltimore Director*, which I presume was a guide to the city. An advertisement in the *American and Commercial Advertiser*, October 28, 1829, announced that R. J. Matchett had taken a partner, a practical printer named Woods (first name not given), and that the firm of Matchett and Woods would devote themselves exclusively to job and book printing. The printing of Poe's poems must have taken place after the date of this advertisement. I looked for an advertisement of *Al Aaraaf, Tamerlane, and Minor Poems*, but found no mention of it, nor for that matter of any other contemporary literary work except annuals. If Fielding Lucas did have anything to do with the publication of Poe's book it was as a silent partner of Hatch and Dunning. He might have been, along with William Gwynn, a guarantor of the costs of printing. His biographer says Lucas was regarded as a capitalist by 1830.[46]

There is good reason to believe that Gwynn had seen the entire manuscript of "Al Aaraaf," not just the excerpts he published in his newspaper. In an address in Baltimore on November 17, 1875, at ceremonies commemorating the unveiling of a monument at Poe's grave, John Latrobe made the following statement concerning the meeting of the committee that awarded the *Saturday Visiter's* prize for

---

[44] *The Life and Poems of Edgar Allan Poe* (rev. ed.; New York, 1879), p. 39 note. On the facts of Poe's life Didier is not always to be trusted, but in a matter of this kind he may be believed. He was a native Baltimorean, from an old and prominent family, and must have known a great deal of Baltimore history. I have examined the *American and Commercial Advertiser*, an important Baltimore newspaper, including the advertising sections, for 1829, and have confirmed my opinion that Hatch and Dunning were small operators, both in publishing and in bookselling. They advertised annuals for sale, but not, like the larger booksellers, medical books and classics imported from abroad. On November 28, they advertised *The Gentleman's Remembrancer* for the year 1830 (a sort of calendar with much useful information), representing themselves as "appointed Agents for the Work."

[45] J. T. Scharf, *The Chronicles of Baltimore* (Baltimore, 1874), pp. 90, 93.

[46] Foster, p. 175.

Poe's "MS. Found in a Bottle": "I believe that up to this time [October, 1833] not one of the committee had ever seen Mr. Poe, and it is my impression that I was the only one that had ever heard of him. When his name was read, I remembered that on one occasion, Mr. William Gwynn, a prominent member of the bar in Baltimore, had shown me the very neat manuscript of a poem called 'Al Aaraaf' which he spoke of as indicative of a tendency to anything but the business of matter of fact life. Those of my hearers who are familiar with the poet's work will recollect it as one of his earlier productions. Although Mr. Gwynn, besides being an admirable lawyer, was noted as the author of wise and witty epigrams, 'Al Aaraaf' was not in his vein, and what he said of the writer had not prepared me for the production before the Committee."[47] If we can trust Latrobe's memory, we must suppose that it was the entire manuscript of "Al Aaraaf," not merely the excerpts published in the *Gazette*. If so, Latrobe must have seen it after July 28, 1829, when Poe wrote to Carey, Lea and Carey saying he had "made a better disposition of his poems" than he had a right to expect and asking them to return his manuscript by mail.[48] I doubt whether Poe had had time to show the entire manuscript to Gwynn and allow him to select excerpts for printing on May 18 before he went to Philadelphia to offer it to Carey, Lea and Carey. He did this very soon after he arrived in Baltimore in May 1829. It seems probable, then, that Gwynn had the entire manuscript in his possession sometime between August 1 and November 1, 1829, and that Latrobe had seen it then. Poe told Allan in his letter of October 30 that he had not had the manuscripts in his possession since Carey, Lea and Carey took them.[49] The fact that Gwynn told Latrobe the poems did not indicate in the poet a tendency to the business of matter-of-fact life does not preclude his thinking them worth a small risk in the publication.

Returning now to lines 84–87 of "The Musiad," we may consider some critical comments on "Al Aaraaf" made about the time it was printed that might have suggested this passage. William Wirt wrote to Poe on May 11, 1829, after reading the poem, that it might please

---

[47] Semmes, p. 561. Probably Semmes quoted from a manuscript left by Latrobe, since his text differs slightly from the one printed by Sara Sigourney Rice in her *Memorial Volume* (Baltimore, 1877) recording the events of the occasion.

[48] *Letters*, p. 27.

[49] *Letters*, p. 31. Poe says, "they have been continually in the hands of some person or another" since he collected them.

modern readers but not old-fashioned people like himself.[50] As I have pointed out in the preceding essay (p. 34), an implied criticism of Poe's verse, not of "Al Aaraaf" but of "Fairy-Land," was made by N. P. Willis, to whom Poe had sent the poem with some complimentary lines to the editor, in the hope that it might be printed in the *American Monthly Magazine.* Willis mentions "some by-gone non-sense-verses of our own, inserted in brackets by the author to concili-ate our good will." One may well believe that Willis thought better of the poem than his comment would indicate, but this was the period of his most supercilious comments in "The Editor's Table." Poe had earlier sent the same poem, giving it then the title "Heaven," to John Neal, editor of the *Yankee and Boston Literary Gazette.* Neal quoted portions of it in his September issue, but he termed it "exquisite nonsense" and added that Poe if he "would but do himself justice might make a beautiful and perhaps a magnificent poem." Poe sent Neal a letter of thanks, undated but probably written in October, and also other poems, with selections from "Al Aaraaf" amounting to 41 lines. Neal printed the 41 lines and called them "genuine poetry."[51] Mrs. Sarah Josepha Hale, the editor of the *Ladies Magazine,* pub-lished a brief critical paragraph on Poe's 1829 volume in the January 1830 issue of her magazine which I quote in full: "It is very difficult to speak of these poems as they deserve. A part are exceedingly boyish, feeble, and altogether deficient in the common characteristics of po-etry; but then we have parts, and parts too of considerable length, which remind us of no less a poet than Shelly [sic]. The author, who appears to be very young, is evidently a fine genius, but he wants judgment, experience, tact." A much longer review was published by J. H. Hewitt early in 1830 in the *Baltimore Minerva and Emerald,* of which he was then editor. The issue containing this review seems not to have survived; hence its exact date cannot be determined. Among the Hewitt papers at Emory University there is a manuscript, recently published, that contains all or most of the review. Hewitt wrote: "There is something in these poems so original, that we cannot help introducing them to the public as a literary curiosity, full of burning thoughts, which so charm the reader that he forgets he is travelling over a pile of brick-bats, for such we must compare the measure to."[52]

[50] *Valentine Letters,* pp. 131–132.

[51] Four of the lines from "Al Aaraaf" printed in the *Yankee* do not appear in Poe's 1829 volume or any later text.

[52] "Recollections of Poe, by John Hill Hewitt," ed. Richard Barksdale Harwell,

The "pile of brick-bats" phrase might have suggested line 86 of "The Musiad," and "burning thoughts" might have suggested line 93, if these lines were written after the review was published.

The last eight lines of "The Musiad" refer to Sumner Lincoln Fairfield, who was born in Massachusetts, June 25, 1803, attended Brown University, was in England and France several months in 1825–26, and lived in or near Philadelphia about a year from the fall of 1828 to the fall of 1829. After that he lived in New York and Boston until his return to Philadelphia in 1832, where, beginning in November, he began publishing the *North American Quarterly,* which lasted several years.[53] The commas inserted between the names in line 95 may be a satiric thrust at a poet whose name has "two and twenty letters," and whose imagination, as his biographer reports (p. 48), aimed at "the *grand* and the *ideal."* He published half a dozen volumes of verse during the 1820's. The third edition of *The Cities of the Plain, with Other Poems* was published in Philadelphia in the fall of 1828 and was fairly successful.[54] A few months afterward he became headmaster of Newtown Academy, about thirty miles from Philadelphia, and he remained there until the late summer of 1829 when the school broke up after the drowning of a student who lived with the Fairfields. Whether he returned to Philadelphia for a time after that before going to Boston is not certain, but it seems probable that he did. At Newtown, Mrs. Fairfield says, "away from scenes of turmoil, strife, and scandal, that he had endured during his short stay in Philadelphia, he began to feel new aspirations." He began what is considered his best work, a long poem (anticipating Bulwer's novel) entitled *The Last Night of Pompeii* (New York, 1832). About the time he went to Philadelphia in 1828, a former friend with whom he had quarreled printed large handbills in retaliation and scattered them widely in public places with the intention of damaging Fairfield's

---

Emory University Publications, Sources and Reprints, Ser. V (Atlanta, 1949), pp. 22–24. Much of this is the same as portions printed by Hewitt himself in *Shadows on the Wall,* pp. 41–43. Poe is said to have attributed the review to Rufus Dawes and in revenge to have attacked Dawes in his own reviews of Dawes's work in later years (see Quinn, p. 165). For an anonymous review recently discovered, see "Poe in Search of a Career," p. 47 and note 41.

[53] See the *Dictionary of American Biography;* also *The Life of Sumner Lincoln Fairfield,* by his widow, Jane Fairfield (New York, 1848). Mrs. Fairfield is sometimes inaccurate, especially in her dates.

[54] The title poem and some of the others had been published in England, probably in 1826. An edition published in Boston in 1827 is called the second edition.

reputation—apparently with considerable success. Mrs. Fairfield reports that "this slander created a fearful revolution in the poor man's destiny."[55] Although he never lived in Baltimore, unless very briefly, these handbills, I suspect, and other circumstances of Fairfield's unfortunate career, if not the poet himself, were well known to the author of "The Musiad" and accounted for the tone of the lines about him.

III

This completes the analysis of the poem itself. As I said at the beginning of Section II of this paper, it may be assumed, on the basis of internal evidence, that "The Musiad" is incomplete as printed. Another reason for believing it incomplete is the existence of the numerals in parentheses prefixed to nineteen of the lines, which must have been intended as references to notes to be appended but which do not appear in the pamphlet as we have it. Mrs. Whitman thought the notes were torn off (see p. 66 above), but there seems to be no evidence that any pages have been removed unless the last part of the poem itself was taken with them.

The Preface seems to support the theory that the present pamphlet is but a fraction of the original manuscript as printed. The fact that the manuscript was "done up in a canvass envelope" suggests a heavier parcel than 101 lines would produce. Moreover, the Preface affirms unequivocally that the entire manuscript was printed and published, although the stranger who left it with the printer never returned to claim it or to pay the printer. If we take such statements as literal fact, we must believe that a much longer poem once existed and that 499 printed copies of it have been lost as well as the greater portion of the one copy remaining. But, of course, we are not to take the Preface seriously. The facetious tone, with its learned reference to Epictetus,[56] its punning on the term "printer's devil," and its general hocus-pocus, assures us that the editor is joking. In the last sentence,

---

[55] Pp. 33–34, 46.

[56] In the *Discourses* of Epictetus, Book II, chap. xxvi, we may read (in Elizabeth Carter's translation, 1758): "Every Error in Life implies a Contradiction: for, since he who errs, doth not mean to err, but to be in the Right, it is evident, that he acts contrary to his Meaning. . . . Now every rational Soul is naturally averse to Self-contradiction: but so long as any one is ignorant, that it is a Contradiction, nothing restrains him from acting contradictorily: but, whenever he discovers it, he must necessarily renounce and avoid it . . ."

which is in keeping with the humorous satire of the poem itself, the editor makes a perfect ending to his joke: "Still I would not have ventured to issue the books . . . were I not perfectly convinced that the satire is harmless, in as much as the persons satirized are, for the most part, as far beyond injury as my housekeeper's eggs."

Printing a manuscript left by a mysterious stranger is a time-worn literary device. The "editor" in such cases is usually the author, and there is good reason to believe that the editor of "The Musiad" was also the author of it. I confess at once that I cannot confidently identify that author. I believe, however, that by a process of elimination I can reduce the number of probable authors to two or three. I have drawn up a list of twenty-two names of literary men who are the only possible candidates: John P. Kennedy, J. H. B. Latrobe, William Gwynn, Fielding Lucas, Jr., Francis Scott Key, John N. McJilton, T. S. Arthur, Nathan C. Brooks, Edward C. Pinkney, Frederick Pinkney, John Lofland, Robert Walsh, James McHenry, John Neal, Henry Pickering, N. P. Willis, Sumner Lincoln Fairfield, Rufus Dawes, John H. Hewitt, Poe's brother William Henry Leonard Poe, Lambert A. Wilmer, and Edgar Poe himself. These I will consider in the order listed.

Several of them can be dismissed at once for one reason or another. Kennedy and Latrobe, two of the judges who awarded Poe a prize in the *Saturday Visiter* contest of 1833, did not know him in 1830. William Gwynn, who did know him, and Fielding Lucas, Jr., who might have known him, may be dismissed, Lucas because he was no poet, and Gwynn because he was only an epigrammatist and because he would probably not have called himself "the great." Francis Scott Key was no satirist; McJilton, a Methodist minister at this time or soon afterward, and T. S. Arthur, then only nineteen years old and afterward a member of the temperance society and writer of prose fiction, cannot easily be imagined as having written such a poem. Brooks, who was also only nineteen and at the time a teacher in a school for boys, knew Poe later but probably not in 1829. He wrote chiefly melancholy verse and religious poems. Edward Pinkney died in 1828, and his brother Frederick, even if he was competent, was too much the Southern gentleman and too little the bohemian to have written a humorous satire. John Lofland, the "Milford Bard," apparently knew Poe,[57] but he was a newspaper versifier and surely incapable of the

---

[57] Hewitt (p. 155), says Poe "often vented his spleen on poor Dr. Lofflin, who styled himself the 'Milford Bard,' and who outstripped Poe in the *quantity* of his

witty style of "The Musiad." Robert Walsh and James McHenry were residents of Philadelphia. Walsh, the editor of the *National Gazette* and the *American Quarterly Review,* had seen Poe, but he was too busy to amuse himself with a poem of this kind, even if he had the skill for it. McHenry, the principal book reviewer for the *Quarterly,* was a dull poet and critic, and he would hardly have satirized himself in any case. Neither of them would have gone to Baltimore to have a manuscript printed. John Neal was just the kind of man to have contrived a satire, but he wrote Mrs. Whitman in 1874 that he had never seen nor heard of the poem. Moreover, he had not lived in Baltimore since 1824. Henry Pickering had never lived in Baltimore, nor in Philadelphia since his early youth, and so he could not have been familiar with the literary scene in either city in 1829–30. His published verse reveals no gift or taste for satire. Willis did not know Poe personally, though he knew a little of his poetry, and he was in Boston at the time, quite busy with editorial duties. Fairfield had lived in Philadelphia in 1828–29, but I doubt if he knew either Poe or his poems. Finally, neither Willis nor Fairfield was likely to have said of himself what the poet of "The Musiad" said of him.

There remain five of the twenty-two who were familiar with the literary scene in Baltimore and who might have known Poe. Rufus Dawes came to Baltimore in 1828 and established a literary weekly called the *Emerald.* Later this was combined with the *Minerva* and edited by Hewitt. It is doubtful that Dawes knew Poe personally before 1831, though Miss Phillips relates, on doubtful authority how, at a place called The Seven Stars, Poe mingled jovially with Dawes, Hewitt, Wilmer, T. S. Arthur, and John Lofland. If such mingling occurred, it was probably after Poe returned from West Point.[58] So far as I can learn, Dawes never published any opinion of Poe or his poetry, and there is nothing in his verse that demonstrates a talent or taste for satire. He wrote no satiric poetry that has survived, but Hewitt recalls that about this time he published in his periodical a series of poems under the title of the "Times" which "gave clear proof of the author's satiric vein."[59] On the whole, it seems very unlikely that Dawes was the author of "The Musiad."

---

poetry, if not the *quality.*" Hewitt's memory failed him in the spelling of the Bard's name and maybe also in the matter of Poe's spleen. Hewitt was not without spleen himself.

[58] Mary E. Phillips, *Edgar Allan Poe, the Man* (Chicago, 1926), I, 461. For further comments on Dawes, see above, p. 77.

[59] Hewitt, pp. 9–11.

Hewitt is apparently a more likely candidate. He reviewed *Al Aaraaf, Tamerlane, and Minor Poems* in 1830, and he seemed to think that this review was the source of Poe's dislike of him. But it seems possible that Poe did not learn who wrote the review until his return to Baltimore in 1831. Certainly Poe and Hewitt quarreled in 1833 over Hewitt's having submitted a poem in the *Saturday Visiter* contest, though he was its editor at the time. It may be that his recollection of events many years afterward was faulty and that he confused the 1830 episode with that of 1833. In any case, he says he did not know Poe when he wrote the review, and if that statement is true, he could not have written "The Musiad."[60]

Poe's brother, William Henry Leonard Poe, should not be overlooked as a possible author of the poem. Henry, as he was called, was about two years older than Edgar; and except for periods of uncertain date and length when he was abroad, perhaps in maritime service, he lived all his life in Baltimore. He was probably in Baltimore in 1827, when he contributed a number of poems to a literary weekly called the *North American*. He is thought to have been the author of "The Pirate" published in that paper November 27, 1827. Part of this story seems to have been suggested by Edgar's "Tamerlane" and his youthful love affair with Sarah Elmira Royster. Henry Poe may have been employed, for a while at least, in the office of Henry Didier, who lived on Baltimore Street not far from the offices of the publishers Hatch and Dunning and the printers Matchett and Woods. Eugene L. Didier, an early biographer of Edgar A. Poe, says that Henry Didier was Henry Poe's godfather; he also says that Henry was in Russia in September 1829. The first of these statements by Didier is doubtful since it has not been authenticated. The second is certainly untrue, for Edgar wrote to John Allan on August 10, 1829, that Henry was in Baltimore, but "entirely given up to drink & unable to help himself, much less me."[61] All of Henry's poems that Allen and Mabbott collected and published in *Poe's Brother* were printed in 1827, and none

[60] Pp. 41, 154.

[61] *Letters*, p. 29. For Didier's account of Henry see his edition of the poems, p. 26. Eugene Didier was from an old Baltimore family and may have been related to Henry Didier, though he does not say so. Henry Didier came to Baltimore about 1790 and became fairly prominent. In 1829 he was one of the directors of the Baltimore and Susquehanna Railroad, according to Scharf (pp. 266, 432). There is little reliable information about Henry Poe. What there is may be found in Appendix IV, Hervey Allen's *Israfel*, pp. 874–879, and also in the introduction to *Poe's Brother: The Poems of William Henry Leonard Poe*, ed. Hervey Allen and T. O. Mabbott (New York, 1926).

are humorous or satirical. The reference in line 97 of "The Musiad" to the "two and twenty letters" in Fairfield's name could have been suggested by the fact that Henry's full name had twenty-two letters, but the parallel might have occurred to any one who knew both men. Henry knew Dawes, Hewitt, and Wilmer and probably other literary men in Baltimore in the late twenties. He might have contributed some bit to "The Musiad," but he would not have been as well acquainted with the literary scene as the writer of this poem obviously was. Moreover, if, as Poe wrote Allan, he was "given up to drink" in August 1829, he would no longer have been capable, if he ever had been, of such a clever satire. He died August 1, 1831.

There remain only Lambert A. Wilmer and Edgar Poe himself. Unfortunately there is no biography of Wilmer, and he is not included in any of the biographical dictionaries that I have seen. We must depend for information chiefly on the "Introductory Narrative" of his *Our Press Gang; or, a Complete Exposition of the Corruptions and Crimes of the American Newspapers* (Philadelphia, 1859), and that is not very dependable or informative. T. O. Mabbott says, "Wilmer was born in Maryland, about 1805," and he assumes that he was a native of Kent County, though he could find no record of his birth there.[62] I, too, have searched available records without much success for information about Wilmer. In *Our Press Gang* he calls Baltimore his native city, and I suspect he was, in fact, born there.[63]

In his "Introductory Narrative" Wilmer wrote: "For almost thirty years, I have been connected, in one way or another, with the public journalism of the United States . . . I began my career as a newspaper writer at the age of nineteen; having previously studied law and prepared myself for admission to the bar." But if he was born in 1805, he became nineteen in 1824, thirty-five years before he published *Our Press Gang*. Five years are not accounted for. He was about to begin the practice of law in Baltimore when he was invited to "take charge of a rural newspaper at Elkton, Md." He also seems to say that he remained with this rural newspaper until he went to Philadelphia to join the editorial staff of the *Saturday Evening Post*. I have examined

[62] See the Introduction in his facsimile edition of Wilmer's verse drama *Merlin* (New York, 1941), p. x.

[63] See p. 39. G. A. Hanson's *Old Kent* (Baltimore, 1876) names a large number of Wilmers in Kent County, dating back to the early eighteenth century. There are several Lambert Wilmers, but no Lambert A. Wilmer. The name Allison, assumed to be Wilmer's middle name, does not occur in the book at all.

all issues of the *Post* for the years 1828–30, and the first signed contribution by Wilmer that I found was in the issue of April 17, 1830. That does not mean he was not employed earlier, since his editorial contributions were not signed. It is not likely, however, that he would have remained on the staff many months before making a literary contribution. The best interpretation I can make of his account is that he wrote occasionally for papers in Baltimore until about 1829, when his full career as a newspaperman began in Elkton. This would be in accordance with a career of thirty years before 1859.

In his "Recollections of Edgar A. Poe" Wilmer says his acquaintance with Edgar Poe "commenced in Baltimore, soon after his return from St. Petersburg." Unless Wilmer is confused again, this must have been in 1829, after Poe was discharged from two years' service in the army. I presume Poe told Wilmer he had been in Russia (as Henry, apparently, really had been earlier) because he did not want people to know he had been an enlisted soldier.[64] This might have been as early as May 1829. It seems likely that he did not go to Philadelphia, and perhaps not to Elkton, until after the summer of that year. He wrote a series of humorous and satirical poems for the *Post* under the general title *Horace in Philadelphia,* the first of which appeared May 1, 1830. They continued each week until August 7; No. XIII appearing on that date. There were no more during the year 1830, but they were resumed the following spring, No. XIV appearing in May. I have not seen all the issues for that year, but I have seen the issue of August 13, which contains No. XXIV, bearing the title "To His Muse." The valedictory tone and general content of this poem suggest that it was meant to be the last of the series.[65] It is uncertain just when Wilmer left Philadelphia. He says that after he left he spent "some months" in the country and "took charge of a rural academy near the Catoctin mountains," which are about forty miles west of Baltimore. But he was not content and soon went to Washington, perhaps in November or early December 1831, where he was employed for four or five weeks by General Duff Green, the editor of an anti-Jackson newspaper. Then

[64] Wilmer's "Recollections" were originally printed in the Baltimore *Daily Commercial,* May 23, 1866; they were reprinted by Mabbott in his facsimile edition of *Merlin,* pp. 29–34.

[65] In his review of Wilmer's *Confessions of Emilia Harrington* (*Southern Literary Messenger,* Feb. 1836) Poe mentions these poems and remarks that they "attracted great attention, and have been deservedly admired." See *Works,* VIII, 234–237. Most or all of the "Odes" were reprinted in the Philadelphia *Casket,* No. XXIV in Dec. 1831.

he was called back to Baltimore to edit the *Saturday Visiter,* the first number of which was issued February 4, 1832.[66]

After a dispute with the owners of the *Visiter,* Wilmer returned to Elkton in the fall of 1832 to edit a Whig newspaper. He remained in that area more than two years and then returned to Baltimore, about the end of 1834 or early in 1835, with the design of founding a literary journal. "With reference to this design," he wrote, "Edgar A. Poe and I had had some correspondence. He proposed to join me in the publication of a monthly magazine of a superior intellectual character, and he had written a prospectus, which he transmitted to me for examination. While this project was under consideration, Poe was invited to assume the editorial duties of the *Southern Literary Messenger.*"[67] After four years of failure and poverty in Baltimore, Wilmer went to Philadelphia to reside permanently. In 1841 he published a verse satire on American poets, somewhat in the manner of the English eighteenth-century satirists, called *The Quacks of Helicon.* Poe reviewed it, on the whole favorably, in *Graham's Magazine,* August 1841, though he did complain of Wilmer's indiscriminate censure and his "gross obscenity."[68] Privately he also praised the poem, saying in a letter to J. E. Snodgrass, July 12, 1841: "You must get this satire & read it—it is really good—good in the old-fashioned Dryden style."[69] They remained friends, though they were not close, until 1843, while both were living in Philadelphia. Wilmer wrote to John Tomlin, a mutual friend, on May 20, 1843, that Poe was drinking and that he feared he was "going headlong to destruction, moral, physical, and intellectual." When Poe saw this letter he wrote to Tomlin on August 28: "In Philadelphia no one speaks to him. He is avoided by all as a reprobate of the lowest class. Feeling a deep pity for him, I endeavoured to befriend him, and you remember that I rendered myself liable to some censure by writing a review of his filthy pamphlet called the 'Quacks

[66] My authority for this date is Hewitt (p. 39), who followed Wilmer as editor after eight months.

[67] *Our Press Gang,* pp. 35–36. This prospectus, like the correspondence between the two friends, has been lost. The literary journal must have been a mere pipe dream, for neither of them had any money. When Poe was preparing to leave the *Messenger,* he suggested that Wilmer come to Richmond and apply for the editorship as his successor, but Wilmer says (p. 39) that he could not raise enough money to make the trip.

[68] *Works,* X, 182–195. *The Quacks of Helicon* was a paperbound pamphlet published in Philadelphia.

[69] *Letters,* pp. 175–177.

of Helicon.' He has returned my good offices by slander behind my back. *All* here are anxious to have him convicted—for there is scarcely a gentleman in Phil[a] whom he has not libelled, through the gross malignity of his nature."[70] It should be added that, after Poe's death, Wilmer was his staunchest defender. Probably Poe overstated in his anger the ill feeling of Philadelphia gentlemen for Wilmer, though it must be admitted that in *The Quacks* as well as in *Our Press Gang* Wilmer had little of good to say of anybody.

The evidence in favor of Wilmer as the author of "The Musiad" may be briefly summarized. He was in Baltimore in 1829, he was then an intimate associate of Poe, he was an effective though severe satirist in *The Quacks of Helicon* in 1841, and he was both humorist and mild satirist ten years earlier in *Horace in Philadelphia*. The *Quacks*, like "The Musiad," disparages American authors in comparison with British, while complaining of the uncontrolled influx of British books. Both satirize McHenry, Willis, and Fairfield, though *The Quacks* satirizes many not mentioned in "The Musiad," including Bryant, Pierpont, Neal, and—very bitterly—George P. Morris. Two lines of "The Musiad" (61–62) display something of the bad taste which Poe censured in his review of *The Quacks*. In his Preface to *The Quacks* Wilmer says that to propitiate "the blue-stockings and ultra-sentimentalists" he may have to publish "a volume of sonnets of the most musical construction and with as little meaning as possible." This is rather like some lines in "The Musiad," particularly line 83: "Will not write sense, and dare not sonnetize"—referring to Willis's poems. On the negative side, there is no definitive evidence. Wilmer might have written the poem in the early fall of 1829 and had it printed with an advance date of 1830, as often happened in the publishing of books. The mention of the firm name of Carey, Lea and Carey is good evidence the poem was written in 1829, perhaps as early as September, since that firm name was not used after that month.[71] However,

[70] Wilmer's letter may be seen in Woodberry's *Life of Poe*, II, 42; for Poe's letter, see *Letters*, pp. 235–236.

[71] The firm name became Carey, Lea and Carey about 1828 when Edward L. Carey joined his brother Henry C. Carey and his brother-in-law, Isaac Lea. In September 1829 the partnership broke up, and two firms were organized: Carey and Lea, consisting of Henry C. Carey and Isaac Lea, and Carey and Hart, consisting of Edward L. Carey and a new member, a young bookseller named Abraham Hart. The approximate date of this change can be determined from the advertisements in Baltimore newspapers of the time. See also *One Hundred and Fifty Years of Publishing* (Philadelphia, 1935), pp. 20–25, a history of the publishing firm founded by Mathew Carey. See also above, p. 33, note 33.

"The Musiad" is genuinely humorous and witty beyond the capacity of Lambert Wilmer, so far as I can judge from what I have seen of his verse.[72]

We have, finally, to weigh the evidence for Poe's authorship. While it may not be conclusive, it is considerable, and far more persuasive than what I have found in support of authorship by any other poet. Much of this evidence has already been pointed out or implied in the foregoing analysis and need only be briefly summarized here. Poe was in Baltimore at the time when it seems most probable that the poem was composed. The printing might also have been done then but dated 1830 in advance. It could even have been printed, of course, while he was in Baltimore during the late spring or early summer of 1830, before he left for West Point, though that is unlikely.

Introducing the Muses at dinner with Thomas Moore and William Wordsworth is in keeping with Poe's literary taste at the time. He was then a great admirer of Moore, and in "Al Aaraaf" had borrowed extensively from his *Lalla Rookh* and *The Loves of the Angels*.[73] There is reason to suppose he knew and admired Moore's satires, particularly *The Fudge Family*, and the comic opera *M. P., or, The Blue-Stocking*. In his Preface to *Poems* (1831), which is in the form of a letter to his publisher, Elam Bliss, Poe glibly criticizes Wordsworth's later poetry for being "metaphysical," but he asserts that the young Wordsworth "had the feelings of a poet" and that "there are glimpses of extreme delicacy in his writings."

He had talked with Isaac Lea and probably the other members of the firm of Carey, Lea and Carey, and since they had kept the manuscripts of his poems for possible publication through most of the summer, he must have had them much on his mind in the late months of 1829. In their popular annual, *The Atlantic Souvenir*, to which he was invited to submit poems, though apparently none were published in it, he must surely have read the verse of many contemporaries, including James McHenry, N. P. Willis, Henry Pickering, and Rufus Dawes. He had not met Willis at this time but he was interested in him and could hardly help reading of his appearance and his manner

[72] Since I have mentioned McHenry, Walsh, and Fairfield, of Philadelphia, it may be asked why no other poets of that city have been considered. The sad fact is that, according to E. P. Oberholtzer (*Literary History of Philadelphia*, Philadelphia, 1906, pp. 153, 268), there were none of consequence at that time. If there had been, there is no reason to suppose they would have known Poe.

[73] For a number of specific references see the notes on "Al Aaraaf" in Killis Campbell's *Poems of Edgar Allan Poe* (Boston, 1917), pp. 171–192.

in the *American Monthly Magazine* or elsewhere. That Poe continued
to be interested in Willis as a subject of satire is evident from his tale
"The Duc de L'Omelette," first published in the Philadelphia *Saturday
Courier,* March 3, 1832.[74] The Duke tells the Devil he has "just come
of age" and that he is the "author of the Mazurkiad." In "The Musiad"
Willis says (line 73) "(I'm scarce of age) an early devotee!" He is
made the author of the "Mazurkiad" appropriately since he says (in
line 75) "I dance—the Muses dance." Like all who read the newspapers and kept up with current events, Poe would have known of
Frances Wright, Captain Basil Hall, and Mrs. Anne Royall.

We should not expect to find many parallels in style between satire
and lyric or lofty narrative verse, but I have found a few. For example,
the word "loll" in various forms occurs in four poems published by Poe
between 1829 and 1833. In "Al Aaraaf" (I, 17) Nesace's "world lay
lolling on the golden air"; in "The Sleeper," in the 1831 and later
versions, "The lily lolls upon the wave"; in the 1831 version of "Fairy-
Land" but not in the 1829 version or any subsequent to 1831, we find
the line "My soul is lolling on thy sighs!"; and in "The Coliseum" we
read (line 22) that "the monarch lolled" on his throne.[75] The word
occurs also in line 59 of "The Musiad," where we are told that
"Polyhymnia lolls upon" a book by Cooper. About 20 per cent of the
lines of "The Musiad" are run-on lines. By comparison "Al Aaraaf,"
which is also written in pentameter couplets, has nearer 30 per cent,
and "The Coliseum," which is blank verse, has about 25 per cent.
About 20 per cent of the lines of "The Musiad" have feminine endings,
but there are only 10 or 12 per cent in "Al Aaraaf." Other early poems
of Poe's have relatively few feminine endings, whereas in the later
poems they become numerous: up to 25 or 30 per cent in some cases.

---

[74] It was called "The Duke de L'Omelette" in the *Courier.* The text is reprinted
in *Edgar Allan Poe and the Philadelphia Saturday Courier,* ed. J. G. Varner
(Charlottesville, Va., 1933), pp. 25–31. It was considerably revised afterward; see
Works, II, 197–202. For evidence that this was a satire on Willis, see "Poe's 'Quiz
on Willis,' " by K. L. Daughrity, *American Literature,* V (Mar. 1933), 55–62. The
phrase "quiz on Willis" is drawn from a letter from J. K. Paulding to T. W. White
of the *Southern Literary Messenger,* March 3, 1836. Paulding says Poe's "quiz on
Willis, and the burlesque of 'Blackwood' . . . will be understood by all" (*Works,*
XVII, 377–378). Daughrity assumes, correctly I think, that the "quiz on Willis"
refers to "The Duc de L'Omelette," though Paulding does not say so.

[75] "The Coliseum" was submitted in the *Saturday Visiter* prize contest, details of
which were announced June 15, 1833. The Byronic echoes in the verse may
suggest that it was composed somewhat earlier, but there is no certain way to
determine the date of its composition.

A comparison of the verse of "The Musiad" with that of "O, Tempora! O, Mores!"—an early satire which has been attributed to Poe on persuasive grounds—may be more significant.[76] Both are in rhymed couplets in the manner of Moore and Byron rather than that of Pope and Dryden. They have almost exactly the same proportion of run-on lines and feminine endings. Neither has many imperfect rhymes—two to four in each, depending upon one's criteria for perfection. By contrast, Wilmer's *The Quacks of Helicon* is conspicuously in the eighteenth-century manner. It has almost no run-on lines, only about 1 per cent of feminine endings, but with 20 per cent of the rhymes imperfect. What is perhaps more significant, lines 70–71 of "The Musiad" are almost identical with lines 71–72 of the earlier poem. In "The Musiad": "Willis! whose shirt-collar—whose look—whose tone is / The beau-ideal fancied for Adonis!" In "O, Tempora! O, Mores!" (describing the youth who is the object of the satire): "In short, his shirt-collar, his look, his tone is / The 'beau-ideal' fancied for Adonis."

In addition to what has been said of the Preface earlier, I should like to point out two or three features of its style and content that should be weighed in deciding its authorship. The style has been thought to resemble Poe's early prose style, particularly in his first humorous and satirical tales. I am not sure what Poe meant by the "large Italian hand" in which the envelope containing the manuscript was labeled, but the term is usually applied to handwriting that is clear. Sometimes it indicates a printlike writing.[77] Poe's own writing, especially in his early manuscripts, might possibly be designated an "Italian hand," though it was then small rather than large. The writing of Wilmer might have been intended in the description of the label. Poe, in the "Autography," includes a facsimile of Wilmer's signature, which is large and easily read, but he adds that "it does not convey the print-like appearance of the MS."[78] The idea that the label could not be deciphered precisely because it "was much too plain and self-evident" is very important as a clue to authorship of the Preface as well as the poem. The notion was a favorite of Poe's. It occurs in "The Bargain Lost," a tale originally published in the *Saturday Courier*, December

[76] See Jay B. Hubbell's "'O, Tempora! O, Mores!' A Juvenile Poem by Edgar Allan Poe," in *Elizabethan Studies and Other Essays in Honor of George F. Reynolds* (University of Colorado Studies, Ser. B, II; Boulder, Colo., 1945), 314–321.

[77] In his "Autography" (*Works*, XV, 180) Poe describes the writing of Professor Charles Anthon as "the most regularly beautiful of any in our collection," giving "to a casual glance, the appearance of Italic print."   [78] *Works*, XV, 228.

1, 1832, in the statement that the hero's philosophical doctrines were
not generally understood "although by no means difficult of comprehension." In the later revised version, called "Bon-Bon," the phrasing
is but slightly altered. The same idea is the basis of much of M.
Dupin's ridicule of the Parisian police and is very clearly stated in
"The Purloined Letter," where the letter is most securely concealed
when it is put in the most conspicuous place. This is illustrated further
in the same tale when Dupin points out that large-charactered words
on a map are harder to see than small ones.[79]

As I stated near the end of Section I of this paper, I am inclined to
believe Poe is the author of "The Musiad" and also of its Preface. I am
willing to concede that Lambert Wilmer may have had a hand in it,
and possibly also Poe's brother Henry, but I don't think they contributed anything particularly important. The evidence, such as it is, and
such as I have found it, points to Poe, and it is very persuasive.
Positive proof, I suspect, will never become available.

[79] In a brief note, Howard Haycraft quotes a conversation between Dupin and
the Prefect earlier in the story as "undeniably suggestive" of Poe's authorship, but
he does not cite the examples mentioned above ("Poe and 'The Musiad,'" *Papers
of the Bibliographical Society of America*, LIX [1965], 437–438).

IV. An Interpretation of "Al Aaraaf"

"AL AARAAF" is a notoriously obscure poem, but it is not, as some have supposed, unintelligible. It was certainly never intended by its author as a hoax.[1] On the contrary, it was a serious and ambitious attempt to produce a great poem. Its obscurity is partly due to imperfections of style. Fragmentary and rambling sentences, ambiguous punctuation, confusion of images, inadequate transitions, and seemingly irrelevant parentheses and allusions conspire to perplex the unwary reader. But imperfections of style obscure only the details. More serious are the defects in structure, because they obscure the whole conception of the poem. Unless sustained by patience and determination, therefore, the reader may conclude that Poe was not master of his own thoughts—that, literally, he did not know what he was talking about. Such a conclusion, however, if not altogether false, would surely be unjust. "Al Aaraaf" is not a masterpiece, to be sure, but rather a potpourri of undigested materials and purposes that converge to no focus; yet it requires no clairvoyance to discern, running through it in shadowy outline, the purposive vision projected uncertainly from the poet's mind.

Some of the difficulties of style have been eliminated by the diligence and insight of editors and other commentators. What remains to be explained is not of vital importance to the essential meaning of the poem. I do not intend here to deal specifically with such matters, believing, as I do, that the chief problem yet unsolved is one of structure. The primary aim of this essay, then, is to rediscover, as far as possible, the underlying plan or pattern of the poem, reduce this plan to its structural elements, and then analyze and refashion these

[1] Charles W. Kent suggests the possibility that the poem was not meant to be understood. A brief review of opinions is given by Killis Campbell in *The Poems of Edgar Allan Poe* (Boston, 1917), p. 173. All quotations from the poems in this essay follow Campbell's text; this work is cited as *Poems*.

elements in such a manner as to reveal their individual significance as well as their relation to one another and to the general plan.

The underlying plan of "Al Aaraaf" might be illustrated by a chart of the stellar universe, with three slight modifications: increasing the relative size of the Earth, adding a prominent star the movements of which are independent of the law of gravity, and localizing God and Heaven in the region without and above this material universe, visible but unapproachable. Through the added star, which is Al Aaraaf, rays of influence flow from God to all parts of the cosmos. The poem is thus a representation, mainly pictorial, of the relation of God to the whole universe, but to the inhabitants of Earth and Al Aaraaf in particular, expressed in terms of power and beauty. Killis Campbell has noted that its central idea is "the divineness of beauty."[2] George E. Woodberry thinks Poe's purpose was to show that "beauty is the direct revelation of the divine to mankind, and the protection of the soul against sin."[3] Similarly, Émile Lauvrière finds in the poem the doctrine of "la Beauté suffisant à l'homme pour l'eclairer et le sauver."[4] These interpretations, though excellent so far as they go, take no account of the fact, clearly revealed in the poem, that God sometimes manifests His deity in a show of power.[5] In its emphasis upon God's rule by power, and in many other ways, "Al Aaraaf" is not unlike *Paradise Lost;*[6] it is different, however, in being descriptive and fanciful, whereas Milton's poem is in quality dramatic and realistic.

Three separate threads, constituting the three structural elements of the poem, are confusedly interwoven to form this general pattern. Each element has its own theme or motif, separately conceived apparently, which the poet has attempted with but indifferent success to unite with its fellows in conformity with the general theme. The poem fails to impress the reader with the effect of totality because he loses his way where the threads cross, and finds himself in a maze with no definite goal in sight. Once having discovered its separate themes and elements, however, and disentangled its threads of thought, broken in places yet generally traceable, we shall find "Al Aaraaf" not only more

---

[2] *Poems*, p. 173.   [3] *Life of Poe* (Boston, 1909), I, 61–62.

[4] *Edgar Poe, sa vie et son oeuvre* (Paris, 1904), p. 333.

[5] Power is a form of beauty, too, but terrible rather than fair. See "Al Aaraaf," I, 84–85 (references to this poem are to parts and lines).

[6] Campbell has pointed out several resemblances in details in his notes (*Poems*, pp. 174 ff.).

intelligible than before, but more significant in the aesthetic development of its author.

I

The first structural element has a religious motif, being concerned with man in his relation to the authority of God, particularly as that authority is manifested in the fulfillment of Biblical prophecy. It also has a secondary astronomical motif designed to explain prophecy in terms of observed phenomena, thus supplementing the religious motif. As conceived in this part of the poem Al Aaraaf is a material star that becomes the instrument of God in the destruction of the world.

This religious-astronomical motif, if we may think of the two as one, had its origin in a curious interest in Biblical prophecy. The existence of God Poe never doubted, and he always believed in a life of the spirit in some form after death; but he despaired of ever understanding either by the processes of mere thought.[7] He was the more inclined, therefore, to have recourse, as he frequently did, to the imagination. He was an eager, if desultory, student of astronomy, being especially interested in such romantic problems as the existence of intelligent beings in other worlds than ours, or the possible collision of Earth with one of the heavenly spheres. Poe was willing to believe, with some reservations, that the events foretold in the Bible would occur literally as described.[8] Such a catastrophe, therefore, accomplishing the destruction of the world, might easily appear to him to be the expression of the Divine Will. But he held nature to be the outward expression of the law of God, single and infallible, yet providing for every possible contingency.[9] How, then, it may be asked, did he reconcile the wandering star with the law of gravity? Though he did not inform us, we may be sure that he could have done so by that specious mode of reasoning, doubtless sincere, to establish a favorite theory, in which subsequently, as in *Eureka*, he demonstrated his skill.

[7] "Marginalia," in the *Complete Works of Edgar Allan Poe*, ed. James A. Harrison (New York, 1902), XVI, 135. All references to Poe's prose are to this edition, hereinafter cited as *Works*.

[8] See the review of Stephens' *Arabia Petraea*, *New York Review*, Oct. 1837 (*Works*, X, 9); see also the review of Duncan's *Sacred Philosophy of the Seasons*, *Burton's Gentleman's Magazine*, March 1840 (*Works*, X, 81 ff).

[9] *Eureka* in *Works*, XVI, 254–255.

It is unnecessary to explain Poe's interest in the theory of the destruction of the world by collision with a star or a comet, for men have speculated upon that question for centuries. But his interest was quickened by his having somewhere in his early reading come across an account of the "new star" discovered by Tycho Brahe in the sixteenth century.[10] In a footnote on the title of his poem Poe makes the following statement: "A star was discovered by Tycho Brahe which burst forth, in a moment, with a splendor surpassing that of Jupiter—then gradually faded away and became invisible." In the edition of 1845 the note was changed to read: "A star was discovered by Tycho Brahe which appeared suddenly in the heavens—attained, in a few days, a brilliancy surpassing that of Jupiter—then as suddenly disappeared, and has never been seen since." Both statements are exaggerated. Tycho first saw the star November 11, 1572, when it was as bright as Venus. In December it began to grow fainter, but did not disappear altogether until sixteen months subsequent to its first appearance.[11] The star appeared not to move in the heavens; hence Tycho declared it to be a fixed star, in the eighth sphere.[12] In a note on "Al Aaraaf" in his edition of the *Selected Poems of Edgar Allan Poe* (New York, 1928) Mabbott suggests that the star of the poem is really a comet. That may be true; and yet Poe could not have derived such an idea from Tycho himself, who stoutly maintained that it could not be a comet because it had neither the appearance nor the motion of a comet.[13] As an astrologer, Tycho predicted dire disaster following the appearance of this strange star. A similar star was said to have appeared at the time of Hipparchus, about 125 B.C., with terrible consequences. As the star of Bethlehem foretold the birth of Christ, it was generally supposed that the new star heralded his second coming and the end of the world.[14]

I see no reason for supposing that Poe thought of Al Aaraaf as a comet, since he everywhere refers to it as a star; nevertheless, it may be of interest to introduce here from Poe's later writings an account of

[10] He might have read of Tycho's star in some odd corner of a newspaper, or else he might have come across the story in some book about the more famous Kepler, who was a friend and disciple of Tycho.

[11] J. L. E. Dreyer, *Tycho Brahe* (Edinburgh, 1890), pp. 41–42. The star seems to have been noticed by others four or five days earlier.

[12] *Ibid.*, p. 48. Tycho, it seems, adhered to the Ptolemaic system.

[13] *Ibid.*, p. 48.

[14] *Ibid.*, p. 68. What Tycho saw, of course, was what astronomers now call a "nova," but that is immaterial in this discussion.

what he imagined would happen if the Earth should pass through the tenuous substance of a comet. There would be an unnatural excess of oxygen in the Earth's atmosphere, the consequence of which must be immediate and omniprevalent combustion. He describes this event as one having experienced it:

> For a moment there was a wild lurid light alone, visiting and penetrating all things. Then—let us bow down, Charmion, before the excessive majesty of the great God!—then, there came a shouting and pervading sound, as if from the mouth itself of Him; while the whole incumbent mass of ether in which we existed, burst at once into a species of intense flame, for whose surpassing brilliancy and all-fervid heat even the angels in the high Heaven of pure knowledge have no name. Thus ended all.[15]

Poe is here evidently attempting to portray the fulfillment of the following prophecy of the New Testament:

> But the day of the Lord will come as a thief in the night: in the which the heavens shall pass away with a great noise, and the elements shall melt with fervent heat, the earth also and the works that are therein shall be burned up.[16]

Though he believed, as he said, in the literal fulfillment of Biblical prophecy, yet he did not understand the predicted destruction of the universe to involve more than the crust of the Earth. Concerning these prophecies he remarks:

> We believe there are few intelligent men of the present day—few, either laymen or divines—who are still willing to think that the prophecies here referred to have any further allusion than to the orb of the earth, or, more strictly, to the crust of this orb alone.[17]

Poe's account of the end of the world, therefore, tallies perfectly with the Biblical prophecy as he interpreted it.

Poe also believed in the promise of the millennium after the passing of the old world: "And I saw a new heaven and a new earth: for the first heaven and the first earth were passed away; and there was no more sea."[18] After its "purification" by fire, the Earth, he imagines, will "clothe itself anew in the verdure and the mountain-slopes and the smiling waters of Paradise, and be rendered at length a fit dwelling-

[15] "The Conversation of Eiros and Charmion" (1839), in Works, III, 8.

[16] Peter 4:10. Cf. also Luke, 17: 26–30, quoted on p. 108.

[17] In the review of Duncan's Sacred Philosophy of the Seasons, Burton's Gentleman's Magazine, March 1840 (Works, X, 81). See also "Marginalia II," Democratic Review, Dec. 1844 (Works, XVI, 11).

[18] Revelation, 21:1.

place for man:—for man the Death-purged—for man to whose now exalted intellect there should be poison in knowledge no more—for the redeemed, regenerated, blissful, and now immortal, but still for the *material,* man."[19]

These examples of Poe's subsequent speculations on the predicted destruction of the world throw some light upon the obscure allusions in "Al Aaraaf." The star has just paid a visit to Earth,[20] but is now anchored temporarily near four bright suns,[21] as near Heaven as it is allowed to go.[22] Its mission, here assumed to be the destruction of the world, has been accomplished; hence the poem is also itself a prophecy, not a history, and this visit of the star must not be confused with the earlier one recorded by Tycho Brahe.

This mission, though not explicitly stated, is implied in various ways. God is beautiful, of course, because He is harmony, self-consistency; but His beauty has two aspects, the terrible and the fair.[23] His power is terrible. We are informed that "the stars trembled at the Deity," and that the angel Nesace hid her face among lilies to escape the fervor of His eye.[24] Al Aaraaf has made this visit to Earth by His direction ("Beneath thy burning eye");[25] it is not strange, therefore, that our world trembled at its approach like "Beauty's bust beneath man's eye."[26] Angelo, a Greek, was living on Earth at the time of Al Aaraaf's approach, dying at sunset before the fateful night. He remembered how strangely the light affected him that evening:

> The sun-ray dropp'd, in Lemnos, with a spell
> On th' Arabesque carving of a gilded hall
> Wherein I sate, and on the draperied wall—
> And on my eyelids—O the heavy light!
> How drowsily it weigh'd them into night![27]

As his spirit, released from the body, soared up beyond "her airy bounds," the world

> was into chaos hurl'd—
> Sprang from her station, on the winds apart,
> And roll'd, a flame, the fiery Heaven athwart.[28]

[19] "The Colloquy of Monos and Una" (1841), in *Works*, III, 205.

[20] "Al Aaraaf," I, 24–25. Earth was the favored sphere of God, but not necessarily the most obedient one. Poe is Scriptural here.

[21] *Ibid.*, I, 18. Tycho's star appeared in the constellation Cassiopeia near four stars now called β, α, γ, and κ. See Dreyer, p. 39.

[22] "Al Aaraaf," I, 88–89.   [23] *Ibid.*, I, 82–85.

[24] *Ibid.*, I, 118–121.   [25] *Ibid.*, I, 107–109.

[26] *Ibid.*, II, 258–260. There is here a suggestion of shame as well as of terror.

[27] *Ibid.*, II, 203–207.   [28] *Ibid.*, II, 234–236.

Except for poetic exaggeration, this passage parallels the one already quoted from the "Conversation of Eiros and Charmion." The world was not literally hurled into chaos, because Angelo and Ianthe are gazing upon its light from Al Aaraaf at the moment he is speaking.[29] Significant, and yet puzzling, are the last two lines of Angelo's account of the world's end:

> Dread star! that came, amid a night of mirth,
> A red Daedalion on the timid Earth.[30]

Al Aaraaf was a "dread star" because of its mission of destruction. Its coming "amid a night of mirth" was in fulfillment of another Biblical prophecy:

And as it was in the days of Noe, so shall it be also in the days of the Son of man. They did eat, they drank, they married wives, they were given in marriage, until the day that Noe entered into the ark, and the flood came, and destroyed them all. Likewise also as it was in the days of Lot: they did eat, they drank, they bought, they sold, they planted, they builded; but the same day that Lot went out of Sodom it rained fire and brimstone from heaven, and destroyed them all. Even thus shall it be in the day when the son of man is revealed.[31]

The phrase "red Daedalion" is ambiguous. The adjective implies destructiveness; Mars, for example, gives off a red light. The astrologers of Tycho Brahe's time read disaster in the red light of the new star.[32] The noun, evidently derived from "Daedalus," was chosen, I suppose, to suggest the transforming power of Al Aaraaf, as seen in the marvelous change produced on Earth by its coming.

One may ask why man and his world should be destroyed. The poem answers the question fully, and in the same way that it is answered in the book of Genesis. God created man in His own image, but He formed him out of the dust of the Earth, and He withheld from him knowledge, which is of Heaven. Knowledge is bad for man because his intellect is incapable of mastering it; misused, it works confusion. The desire for knowledge on the part of our first parents brought sin into the world "and all our woe," and that sin requires expiation. In the Millennium, after the world has been purified by fire, knowledge will no longer be poison to man's intellect.[33] According to

[29] *Ibid.*, II, 194–197.   [30] *Ibid.*, II, 243–244.   [31] Luke, 17:26–30.

[32] Tycho's star was first white, then yellow, then red, and finally a lead color. See Dreyer, p. 42.

[33] See the passages quoted above, pp. 106–107, from the "Conversation of Eiros and Charmion" and the "Colloquy of Monos and Una."

"Al Aaraaf" man has sinned in three principal ways: (1) by miscon-
ceiving the true nature of God, (2) by perverting His love, and
(3) by misunderstanding the means of His communication with His
creatures. We know, says Nesace, that God exists, and we feel that He
is eternal, but His true nature has never been revealed.[34] Yet some of
His creatures (men, of course), seeking truth by reason alone, have
come to the false conclusion that God is a Being like themselves —

> Have dreamed for thy Infinity
> A model of their own.[35]

The divine is debased to the level of the human, and man is led astray
in his search for God.[36] The second sin, the perversion of God's love on
Earth ("where all my love is folly"[37]), is not as clearly defined as the
first. It may mean, on the one hand, that men hold love lightly,
whereas it should be the guiding principle of their lives, or, on the
other, that God's love is wasted upon the human race because they
have refused to obey the laws of life that love has dictated; it very
probably means both.[38] The third sin, as God informs Nesace, is the
misunderstanding of His way of revealing Himself —

> and the crowd
> Still think my terrors but the thunder cloud,
> The storm, the earthquake, and the ocean wrath
> (Ah! will they cross me in my angrier path?).[39]

The implication is that men have erred in interpreting God solely by
the phenomena of nature, which are inadequate. We are left to
deduce the conclusion that God may better be known through the
exaltation of the soul. The line in parentheses seems to contain a
threat. The words "angrier path" doubtless refer back to the last lines
of the preceding stanza, where God's voice is contrasted with the
voice of nature and of the merely ideal:

> A sound of silence on the startled ear
> Which dreamy poets name "the music of the sphere."
> Ours is a world of words: Quiet we call

[34] "Al Aaraaf," I, 98–101.

[35] *Ibid.*, I, 104–105. In his notes Poe quotes several early church authorities
respecting the doctrine of anthropomorphism.

[36] In "A Few Words about Brainard" (1842) we find: "It is needless to say,
moreover, that the bestowing upon Deity a human form, is at best a low and most
unideal conception." *Works*, XI, 21. The authorities on anthropomorphism quoted
in the note to "Al Aaraaf" are also quoted here.

[37] "Al Aaraaf," I, 135.   [38] For further discussion of love, see below.

[39] "Al Aaraaf," I, 135–138.

> "Silence"—which is the merest word of all.
> All Nature speaks, and ev'n ideal things
> Flap shadowy sounds from visionary wings—
> But ah! not so when, thus, in realms on high
> The eternal voice of God is passing by;
> And the red winds are withering in the sky![40]

The terrible effect of silence was a favorite theme of Poe's. In "Silence —A Fable" he reveals the fact that of all terrors by which the courage of man may be tried, silence alone is unendurable. He is there thinking apparently of the silence of the tomb. In "Sonnet—Silence," however, he hints at a silence more awful than that of the tomb—the silence of total annihilation, or the death of the soul. This silence may be referred to in the threat of an "angrier path" quoted above.

Although life on Earth has already been destroyed, if my interpretation is correct, yet there are beings dwelling in other worlds who should be warned. To Nesace and her subordinates God commits the charge of bearing His secrets through "the upper Heaven," endowing her for this purpose with something of His own resplendency. This time she is to leave her star at its anchorage. Through the new "light" she brings, with its revelation of more of the pure knowledge of Heaven, it is hoped that she may save these beings of other worlds from the guilt of man, and so from his condign punishment.[41]

II

The second structural element is built about the conception of Al Aaraaf as an Eden. I adopt the word *Eden* for lack of a more specific term to denote that abode for which Poe sometimes longed, where, apart from the passions of the heart and the excitements of the mind, the weary spirit may find rest in an eternity of dreams. The term seems the more appropriate because Poe employed it frequently, and because, unlike the word *Paradise,* it does not exclude the idea of "Lethean peace," which is associated with that abode.

Among the spirits of Al Aaraaf, which in the development of the second motif Poe describes as an immaterial world, Nesace, the queen, and Ligeia, her handmaiden, are of a superior order. Like the angels of Heaven they seem to be spirits of original creation, never having

[40] *Ibid.,* I, 124–132.   [41] *Ibid.,* I, 141–150.

had a physical existence. Only two others are specifically named, Angelo, a spirit from Earth, and Ianthe, a spirit coming presumably from one of the numerous worlds to which Nesace and her followers are commanded to bear the secrets of Heaven.[42] Among the "thousand seraphs"—which may mean many thousands—there are doubtless spirits whose material existences belonged to widely different worlds;[43] yet they all, like Angelo, arrive on Al Aaraaf through the common gateway of death,[44] and belong, like him, to an order inferior to Nesace and Ligeia.

In addition to these higher intelligences, there exist also on Al Aaraaf such immaterial things as fairy flowers and the spiritual essences of objects that have their material existence elsewhere. We find there, for example, a fairy flower that drives bees mad, the

> gemmy flower, of Trebizond misnam'd—
> Inmate of highest stars, where erst it sham'd
> All other loveliness;[45]

there, also, is

> that aspiring flower that sprang on Earth—
> And died, ere scarce exalted into birth,
> Bursting its odorous heart in spirit to wing
> Its way to Heaven, from garden of a king.[46]

These and other "fair flowers and fairy" have the function of bearing Nesace's song in odors up to Heaven.[47] Nesace's palace itself, with its "dome by linked light from Heaven let down,"[48] seems rather a spiritual emanation than a material edifice.[49] About its pillars and cornices seraphs have seen

> The dimness of this world: that greyish green
> That Nature loves the best for Beauty's grave.[50]

Its friezes and sculptured cherubs, which still seem earthly when obscured by shadows, have been transported there in spirit from such

[42] Some scholars differ with me on this point. Campbell says, in his note to II, 178: "'Ianthe, apparently, was native to Al Aaraaf" (*Poems*, p. 190).

[43] In *Eureka* (1848), he calls mankind "a member of the cosmical family of Intelligences" (*Works*, XVI, 187). See also "Mesmeric Revelation" (1844), *ibid.*, V, 252.

[44] "Al Aaraaf," II, 156–161.   [45] *Ibid.*, I, 50–52.   [46] *Ibid.*, I, 70–73.

[47] *Ibid.*, I, 42–81.   [48] *Ibid.*, II, 20.

[49] Campbell compares it to Pandemonium in *Paradise Lost*. See *Poems*, p. 182.

[50] "Al Aaraaf," II, 29–30.

treasuries of ancient art as Tadmor, Persepolis, Balbec, and Gomor-rah.[51]

The name of Poe's spirit world is identical, except in spelling, with that of the Mohammedan purgatory, al Arâf, but the two places have little else in common. In many respects the one is the exact antithesis of the other. Concerning al Arâf the Koran says in Chapter VII, entitled Al Arâf:

And between the blessed and the damned there shall be a veil; and men shall stand on al Arâf, who shall know every one of them by their marks; and shall call unto the inhabitants of paradise, saying, Peace be upon you: yet they shall not enter therein, although they earnestly desire it. And when they shall turn their eyes towards the companions of hell fire, they shall say, O Lord, place us not with the ungodly people!

This passage will be more easily understood if we quote a part of Sale's commentary:

Before we proceed to a description of the *Mohammedan* paradise, we must not forget to say something of the wall or partition which they imagine to be between that place and hell, and seems to be copied from the great gulph of separation mentioned in scripture [Luke, xvi, 26]. They call it *al Orf,* and more frequently in the plural, *al Arâf,* a word derived from the verb *arafa,* which signifies to *distinguish* between things, or to *part* them; tho' some commentators give another reason for the imposition of this name, because, say they, those who stand on this partition, will *know* and *distinguish* the blessed from the damned, by their respective marks or characteristics: and others say the word properly intends any thing that is *high raised* or *elevated,* as such a wall or separation must be supposed to be. The *Mohammedan* writers greatly differ as to the persons who are to be found on *al Arâf.* Some imagine it to be a sort of *limbo,* for the patriarchs and prophets, or for the martyrs and those who have been most eminent for sanctity, among whom they say there will be also angels in the form of men. Others place here such whose good and evil works are so equal that they exactly counterpoise each other, and therefore deserve neither reward nor punishment; and these they say, will on the last day be admitted into paradise, after they shall have performed an act of adoration, which will be imputed to them as a merit, and will make the scale of their

[51] It is said, as Poe tells us in a note, that the remains of Gomorrah and other cities engulfed by the waters of the Dead Sea "may be discovered by looking down into the transparent lake." In a letter to John Neal (December 1829) regarding "Al Aaraaf," Poe explains that he has "supposed many of the lost sculptures of our world to have flown (in spirit) to the star 'Al Aaraaf'—a delicate place more suited to their divinity" (Woodberry, I, 59).

good works to overbalance. Others suppose this intermediate space will be a receptacle for those who have gone to war, without their parents' leave, and therein suffered martyrdom; being excluded paradise for their disobedience, and escaping hell because they are martyrs."[52]

The differences between the Mohammedan al Arâf and Poe's Al Aaraaf may be summarized thus:

1. Al Arâf is a wall permanently fixed to separate Hell from Heaven; Al Aaraaf is a star free to wander at God's direction throughout the universe.

2. Al Arâf affords a view of both Heaven and Hell, and its inhabitants are able to distinguish both the good and the evil by their respective marks; Al Aaraaf cannot approach Heaven, and is remote from Hell, and its inhabitants know nothing of good and evil, being non-moral.

3. Al Arâf, according to Sale, is a sort of purgatory,[53] and according to the Koran, its inhabitants desire to enter Heaven but may not; Al Aaraaf is a place of happiness, and its inhabitants are content.

Of the wandering habits of Al Aaraaf enough has been said already. The second and third points of difference, however, the happiness of the spirits of Al Aaraaf and their ignorance of good and evil, require further discussion.

Happiness on Al Aaraaf is not the high felicity of Paradise, but a pleasurable contentment. It is like the sensuous luxuriance one might find on Earth

> In dreamy gardens, where do lie
> Dreamy maidens all the day.[54]

Nesace is the happiest creature on Al Aaraaf,[55] but Ligeia is the most joyous.[56] At its present anchorage the star is rolling in seas of splendor,[57] wherein even the flowers are happy.[58] The inferior spirits, though less happy, yet find contentment in dreams of beauty and in the milder delights of love.[59] Woodberry has said that they "choose, instead of that tranquility which makes the highest bliss, the sharper delights of love, wine, and pleasing melancholy, at the price of annihilation in the moment of their extremest joy."[60] It seems to me, however, that they choose it for its beauty, and that it is precisely the sharper delights, or passions, which are forbidden them, as the story of

[52] George Sale, tr., *The Koran* (London, 1734); *Preliminary Discourse*, sec. IV, pp. 94–95.

[53] He specifically calls it a purgatory in his note to chap. VII.

[54] "Al Aaraaf," I, 12–13 (1831 version). [55] *Ibid.*, p. 30.

[56] *Ibid.*, II, 104–110. [57] *Ibid.*, I, 20–21. [58] *Ibid.*, II, 60–61.

[59] *Ibid.*, II, 72–89. [60] I, 61–62.

Angelo and Ianthe is intended to emphasize.[61] But if their delights are mild, so are their pains. Their griefs are so softened that they seem almost pleasurable—

> Joy's voice so peacefully departed
> That, like the murmur in the shell
> Its echo dwelleth and will dwell.[62]

As Poe explains it in a note:

Sorrow is not excluded from "Al Aaraaf," but it is that sorrow which the living love to cherish for the dead, and which, in some minds, resembles the delirium of opium. The passionate excitement of Love and the buoyancy of spirit attendant upon intoxication are its less holy pleasures—the price of which, to those souls who make choice of "Al Aaraaf" as their residence after life, is final death and annihilation.[63]

Such happiness as the spirits of Al Aaraaf possess is possible only because they have no knowledge of good and evil, for such knowledge, as I have shown,[64] is disastrous to all except the angels of Heaven, whose knowledge is perfect. Nesace's followers are

> Seraphs in all but "Knowledge," the keen light
> That fell, refracted, thro' thy bounds, afar,
> O Death! from eye of God upon that star:
> Sweet was that error—sweeter still that death—
> Sweet was that error—ev'n with *us* the breath
> Of Science dims the mirror of our joy—
> To them 'twere the Simoom, and would destroy.[65]

Knowledge, then, is the pure light from Heaven, which it is the aim of science to understand. But its dazzling brightness cannot be reflected in mere human minds, which are clouded by the protective atmosphere of material nature. When this protective atmosphere is removed by death, the mind is unable to bear the light unless purified itself by the Divine Truth which produced it. Its pure white ray is refracted as it passes through death into the atmosphere of Al Aaraaf, which is apparently denser than that of Earth, and is there dispersed in its

---

[61] Passion belongs to the comets, or fallen angels, of Hell; it is the "red fire of their heart," which drives them ceaselessly. See "Al Aaraaf," I, 91–97.

[62] *Ibid.*, I, 8–10.

[63] *Poems*, p. 190. Poe's note to II, 173. The part of the note here quoted refers, I think, to Poe's star Al Aaraaf, not to the al Arâf of the Arabians, which is mentioned earlier in the same note, as Woodberry seems to take it.

[64] See above, p. 108.   [65] "Al Aaraaf," II, 159–165.

component colors. The "error" is the error of refraction, and it is sweet because it creates on Al Aaraaf a soothing influence that makes life there an unintellectual and unemotional state of dream. Hence, the spirits of this star know nothing of good and evil; they neither desire Heaven nor fear Hell, but find complete satisfaction in the tranquil pleasures of dreams and fantasies. With the intellect and the passions they properly have nothing to do.

> Beyond that death no immortality—
> But sleep that pondereth and is not "to be"—
> And there—oh! may my weary spirit dwell—
> Apart from Heaven's Eternity—and yet how far from Hell![66]

"To be" here implies "to think"; hence there can be no immortality without intellectual activity. To ponder, on the other hand, as Poe uses the word, is to engage in reverie or daydreaming,[67] which is an activity of the imagination rather than of the intellect. Thus the spirits of Al Aaraaf may be said to have no immortality.

Not even in Al Aaraaf, however, is the spirit exempt from duty. Nesace, as we have seen, calls upon her subject spirits to aid her in carrying God's messages to all parts of the universe. They do not themselves reflect, but obey Nesace's commands, or else suffer just punishment; to quote Ianthe's phrase—

> not to us
> Be given our lady's bidding to discuss.[68]

Not even love can excuse disobedience,

> for Heaven no grace imparts
> To those who hear not for their beating hearts.[69]

The fate of Ianthe and Angelo is the fate of all on Al Aaraaf who fail in the performance of their duty. This does not mean that love is wholly forbidden, but it must not interfere with duty, as it probably will if it is passionate.

> O! where (and ye may seek the wide skies over)
> Was Love, the blind, near sober Duty known?
> Unguided Love hath fallen.[70]

Thought alone can make us partners of God's throne,[71] but we may approach it through beauty sufficiently near to find in the effluence of

[66] Ibid., II, 170–173. [67] Ibid., II, 72–75. [68] Ibid., II, 245–246.
[69] Ibid., II, 176–177. [70] Ibid., II, 179–181. [71] Ibid., I, 110–113.

divinity the fulfillment of our soul's highest aspirations. In Poe's earliest poems we find evidence of this conception of beauty as a means, independent of thought, by which we may communicate with God. In "Stanzas" (1827) he speaks of a "wild light" that had strange power over his spirit; it was perhaps the "unembodied essence" of thought, given in beauty to those whose passion would otherwise draw them down to Hell. Beauty, or the love of beauty, is consequently of especial value to those in whom the reasoning faculty is weak, because it is a bar to the degrading pull of the passions. Contrary to the general opinion, however, Poe did not set beauty above truth, but wished to demonstrate that each in its own way draws us toward God, the one exalting the soul, the other strengthening the mind. Al Aaraaf, the birthplace of the Idea of Beauty,[72] is reserved for the spiritual abode of all lovers of beauty, apart from the enthusiasm of Heaven, yet safe from the misery of Hell.

III

Of the earlier interpretations of "Al Aaraaf" the fullest is that of W. B. Cairns.[73] He agrees with Woodberry and others in finding in the poem the doctrine that through devotion to the higher beauty one may avoid sin, which, being a passion or the fruit of passion, is antagonistic to beauty. He also points out the fact that both knowledge and passion are denied to the spirits of Al Aaraaf. But his most interesting suggestion is that "the idea of beauty indefinitely bodied forth in 'Al Aaraaf' seems to foreshadow the critical theory of poetry" later formulated by Poe. He thinks, however, that such foreshadowing was not consciously planned. "That 'Al Aaraaf' was intended as a presentation of Poe's view of poetry," he concludes, "or that he had consciously formulated his critical theories in 1829, is hardly to be believed."

It is my own opinion, notwithstanding the difficulty of establishing it, that "Al Aaraaf" was written by Poe with the conscious purpose of presenting allegorically his theory of poetry, and that this theory, as then conceived, was substantially the same as later enunciated. The development of this purpose, with its aesthetic motif, constitutes the third structural element of the poem.

[72] *Ibid.*, I, 31.
[73] "Some Notes on Poe's 'Al Aaraaf,'" *Modern Philology*, XIII (May 1915), 35–44.

Poe was himself by no means averse to the use of an undercurrent of allegory, though he was strongly opposed to pure allegory, and went so far as to remark in one of his essays that "all allegories are contemptible";[74] he was provoked to the statement, however, by a poor example of allegorical writing. He read with much interest and partial approval the *Kunstromane,* or Art Novels of Germany,[75] which, he explains, are

books written not so much in immediate defence, or in illustration, as in personification of individual portions of the Fine Arts—books which, in the guise of Romance, labor to the sole end of reasoning men into admiration and study of the beautiful, by a tissue of *bizarre* fiction, partly allegorical, and partly metaphysical. In Germany alone could so mad—or perhaps so profound—an idea have originated.[76]

His own "Al Aaraaf" is something like a personification of his theory of art; that is, it is pictorial rather than expository. As allegory it is impressionistic, not formal. All of his allegorical poems and tales—and most of the poems are allegorical to some extent—are of the impressionistic type with a few exceptions, such as "The Conqueror Worm" and "William Wilson."

Such allegories are of necessity indefinite, and their indefiniteness illustrates a theory that was early formulated and invariably adhered to by Poe throughout his career; namely, that the poem, unlike the romance, has "for its object an *indefinite* instead of a *definite* pleasure."[77] This theory does not require, of course, that the poem be incoherent or obscure, but an unskillful artist may by attempting to follow it produce an obscure poem. That, apparently, is what happened in the case of "Al Aaraaf."

In one of his later critical essays Poe has said that all that we can understand or feel to be poetic has grown out of the struggle of the soul "to apprehend the supernal Loveliness."[78] This desire to apprehend supernal beauty he calls the poetic sentiment, and its expression

[74] Review of H. B. Hirst's poems, *Broadway Journal,* July 12, 1845 (*Works,* XII, 174).

[75] Carlyle says Goethe's *Wilhelm Meister's Apprenticeship* is the earliest *Kunstroman,* and is considered by the Germans "greatly the first in excellence." *Carlyle's Works,* Centenary Edition (London, 1896), XXI, 4.

[76] From the review of H. F. Chorley's *Conti the Discarded, Southern Literary Messenger,* Feb. 1836 (*Works,* VIII, 231).

[77] "Letter to B———" (originally the preface to the volume of 1831), reprinted in *Poems,* pp. 317–318.

[78] "The Poetic Principle," in *Works,* XIV, 274.

is poetry. As thus used, the term "poetry," including painting, sculpture, architecture, and music as well as the poetry of words, is equivalent to the term "art," and Poe has often employed it in this general sense.

It is no mere appreciation of the Beauty before us—but a wild effort to reach the Beauty above. Inspired by an ecstatic prescience of the glories beyond the grave, we struggle, by multiform combinations among the things and thoughts of Time, to attain a portion of that Loveliness whose very elements perhaps, appertain to eternity alone.[79]

The poet, then, is an inspired artist who seeks to reproduce in Earthly forms the Heavenly beauty revealed to him in visions. By the poet's reproductions, others are led to a contemplation of the beautiful, in which, Poe says, is found that elevation of soul—not of intellect or of heart—from which is derived the purest and most intense pleasure.[80] The soul is elevated, or excited, in being made to harmonize more perfectly with divine beauty; hence poets become the means of drawing men closer to God.

Poe declared beauty to be the sole province of the poem;[81] that is, of art. In our allegory, the star Al Aaraaf is the realm of beauty, and the spirits who dwell there are artists, lovers of beauty, whose duty it is to reveal to men the true nature of God. Nesace is the personification of beauty itself, while Ligeia is the personification of harmony, which is the quality of beauty that induces or stimulates in the artist the poetic sentiment. So it is that through Ligeia, Nesace arouses the spirits of Al Aaraaf to a sense of their duty, and urges them to the performance of it. In conventional poetry the Muse bears the same relation to the poet as Nesace bears to her subjects. The divine harmony, which Poe calls beauty, but which others have named truth, descends from God to men not in its original purity, but as made intelligible to terrestrial senses in perceptible forms of beauty, just as the absolute silence of God's voice is first translated into the material silence of Nesace's spiritual song, and then further translated into the audible music of Ligeia.[82]

God can be apprehended in only two ways: intellectually, by process of reason, and spiritually, by ecstasy or exaltation of soul. The

---

[79] *Ibid.*, XIV, pp. 273–274.   [80] *Ibid.*, XIV, p. 275.
[81] "The Philosophy of Composition," in *Works*, XIV, 198. Most of Poe's principles of criticism may be found in several different places and in varying forms among his critical essays.
[82] See "Al Aaraaf," I, 124 ff., II, 64 ff., II, 144 ff.

former is closed to man because his knowledge is yet imperfect. By the latter, therefore, that is, through feeling instead of thought, he must correct his misconceptions of God.[83] The poet arranges the forms of terrestrial beauty in a semblance of the celestial pattern, in the contemplation of which man's soul is exalted to ecstasy and made one with the divine. Thus the poets, like the spirits of Al Aaraaf, are the messengers chosen of God to divulge the secrets of Heaven.

Nesace, who, it will be remembered, receives her commission from God by communication of thought, transfers it in music to her followers. But communication to men must be by other means, and that means is fantasy, or the imagination. As Nesace says,

> By winged Fantasy,
>   My embassy is given,
> Till secrecy shall knowledge be
> In the environs of Heaven.[84]

Reason sees the pure white light of truth; fantasy sees the same light after it has been broken up into its component colors, that is, after refraction. On Al Aaraaf, it will be observed, the dominant colors are purple, opal, and gold—never pure white, except in the lily, where other symbolic values intrude. The philosopher is concerned with the pure ray, the artist with the component colors; and whereas the instrument of the one is reason, the instrument of the other is imagination. Images are created in the mind, then by the technical skill of the artist *personified* in forms of beauty.[85] "Imagination is, possibly in man," says Poe, "a lesser degree of the creative power in God. What the Deity imagines *is,* but *was not* before. What man imagines, *is,* but *was* also. The mind of man cannot imagine what *is not.*"[86] It is, in fact, a kind of "chemistry of the intellect," its "sole object and inevitable

---

[83] See above, p. 109.   [84] "Al Aaraaf," I, 114–117.

[85] Every one is familiar with Poe's definition of the poetry of words as "the rhythmical creation of beauty." In a review of Griswold's *Poets and Poetry of America* (*Philadelphia Saturday Museum,* 1843) he comments thus upon this definition: "Poetry . . . may be more properly defined as *the rhythmical personification of existing or real beauty.* One defines it as the 'rhythmical *creation* of beauty'; but though it certainly is a 'creation of beauty' in itself, it is more properly a personification, for the poet only personifies the image previously created by his mind" (*Works,* XI, 225–226). On the question of the authorship of this review, see below, "Mood, Meaning, and Form in Poe's Poetry," note 11 (p. 192).

[86] Review of the poems of Drake and Halleck, *Southern Literary Messenger,* April 1836 (*Works,* VIII, 283, note 2).

test" being the fabrication of beauty.[87] Poe identified the human
instinct of veneration with the faculty of ideality, which, in turn, he
defined as the sentiment of poesy. "This sentiment is the sense of the
beautiful, of the sublime, and of the mystical. . . . Imagination is its
soul."[88]

But this faculty of ideality, this sense of the beautiful, has nothing
to do with the passions of mankind.[89] Even love, if it is passionate,
hinders the poet in his devotion to beauty. Nesace, on this account,
calls upon her spirits to forego love for duty:

> And true love caresses —
> O! leave them apart:
> They are light on the tresses,
> But lead on the heart.[90]

The story of Angelo and Ianthe is an illustration of how the passion of
love may cause the ruin of artists by distracting them from their
proper work, the creation and dissemination of beauty.

> They fell: for Heaven to them no hope imparts
> Who hear not for the beating of their hearts.[91]

The artist who, for whatever reason, perverts his art by devoting it to
the delineation of passion instead of beauty will "fall"; that is, he will
cease to be a true artist. If passion is to be made the subject of poetry,
it must be softened, for otherwise it is best suited to prose:

True passion is prosaic—homely. Any strong mental emotion stimulates
all the mental faculties; thus grief the imagination:—but in proportion as
the effect is strengthened, the cause surceases. The excited fancy triumphs
—the grief is subdued—chastened,—is no longer grief. In this mood we
are poetic, and it is clear that a poem now written will be poetic in the
exact ratio of its dispassion. A passionate poem is a contradiction in terms.[92]

The sorrow of Al Aaraaf is precisely that softened grief "which the
living love to cherish for the dead" that is here described as poetic.[93]
Sometimes a writer, as Tennyson in "Locksley Hall," brings to the aid
of passion the "terseness and pungency which are derivable from
rhythm and from rhyme." But the effect produced is passionate, that
of a "magnificent philippic," not poetic. The same poet's "Oenone," on

[87] Review of N. P. Willis, *Broadway Journal,* Jan. 18, 1845 (*Works*, XII, pp.
38–39).
[88] Review of the poems of Drake and Halleck, *op. cit.,* VIII, 282–283.
[89] *Ibid.,* p. 283.   [90] "Al Aaraaf," II, 96–99.   [91]*Ibid.,* II, 263–264.
[92] "Marginalia II," from the *Democratic Review,* Dec. 1844 (*Works*, XVI, 56).
[93] See the quotation on p. 114 above.

the other hand, exalts the soul to a conception of pure beauty, which "as far transcends earthly passion as the holy radiance of the sun does the glimmering and feeble phosphorescence of the glowworm." Poe admits that the majority of mankind are perhaps "more susceptible of the impulses of passion than of the impressions of beauty"; nevertheless he believes the sentiment of the beautiful to be a "divine sixth sense" which is yet little understood.[94] This sixth sense brings intimations of divine Love, transcending all human love, and especially passionate love, which is suited to the highest poetry. It is perhaps this divine Love without which the spirits of Al Aaraaf could not be happy—

> O, how, without you, Love!
> Could angels be blest?[95]

The distinction between passionate love and divine Love is clearly made by Poe in his essay on "The Poetic Principle":

> It has been my purpose to suggest that, while this Principle itself is, strictly and simply, the Human Aspiration for Supernal Beauty, the manifestation of the Principle is always found in *an elevating excitement of the Soul,* quite independent of that passion which is the intoxication of the Heart, or of that Truth which is the satisfaction of the Reason. For, in regard to Passion, alas! its tendency is to degrade rather than elevate the Soul. Love, on the contrary—Love, the true, the divine Eros, the Uranian, as distinguished from the Dionaean Venus—is unquestionably the purest and truest of all poetical themes.[96]

Divine Love exalts the soul because it is akin to the instinct of veneration and the faculty of ideality, which Poe identified with the sentiment of poesy. It is this Uranian Eros who in Israfel's heaven is a "grown-up God."[97]

The sonnet "To Science," which was intended as a proem to "Al Aaraaf," condemns science for destroying the world of romance and imagination.

> Hast thou not dragged Diana from her car,
> And driven the Hamadryad from the wood
> To seek a shelter in some happier star?
> Hast thou not torn the Naiad from her flood,

---

[94] Review of R. H. Horne's *Orion, Graham's Magazine,* March 1844 (*Works,* XI, 255).

[95] "Al Aaraaf," II, 88–89.   [96] "The Poetic Principle" in *Works,* XIV, 290.

[97] See "Israfel," line 25.

The Elfin from the green grass, and from me
The summer dream beneath the tamarind tree?[98]

Al Aaraaf is doubtless the happier star, where, in place of the summer dream, we have the "sleep that pondereth and is not 'to be.'"[99] Science, the enemy of the poetic sentiment, would destroy these dreaming spirits of Al Aaraaf—

To them 'twere the Simoom, and would destroy—
For what (to them) availeth it to know
That Truth is Falsehood—or that Bliss is Woe?[100]

It would destroy them by dissipating their illusions, the product of imagination, by which their existence is made calm and happy. In his critical essays Poe often assumes truth to be identical with knowledge and science as here used, opposing it to beauty and imagination. In this sense truth is inimical to art because it destroys the artist's illusions, thereby impairing his imagination and upsetting his values.

It is not the function of art, therefore, to give instruction. If the artist must concern himself with morality, it should be only through suggestion. In a review of Lowell's poems, he complains of the "error of *didacticism*" in the "Legend of Brittany." "The story," he adds, "might have been rendered more *unique*, and altogether more in consonance with the true poetic sentiment, by suffering the morality to be *suggested*."[101] Elsewhere he says that "didactic subjects are utterly *beyond*, or rather beneath, the province of true poesy."[102] But truth may be properly employed to arouse the poetic sentiment; Coleridge, for example, wished in the "Ancient Mariner" "to infuse the *Poetic Sentiment* through channels suggested by mental analysis."[103] Knowledge

[98] Lines 9–14. In the mention of the tamarind tree, and in the "sleep that pondereth and is not 'to be,'" there is a suggestion of the Buddhist Nirvana, where the soul is released from karma.

[99] See p. 115 above.

[100] "Al Aaraaf," II, 162–165.

[101] In *Graham's Magazine*, March 1844 (*Works*, XI, 247).

[102] In his review of *Twice-Told Tales* (*Graham's Magazine*, May 1842) Poe makes the point that prose is a more suitable medium for the inculcation of truth than is poetry. "In fact, while the *rhythm* of this latter is an essential aid in the development of the poet's highest idea—the idea of the Beautiful—the artificialities of this rhythm are an inseparable bar to the development of all points of thought or expression which have their basis in Truth" (*Works*, XI, 108).

[103] Review of *The Book of Gems*, *Southern Literary Messenger*, Aug. 1836 (*Works*, IX, 95). See also the discussion of poetic effect through the harmony of truth in "The Poetic Principle," in *Works*, XIV, 290.

(truth as above defined) leads to death,[104] and it is the artist's duty to save man by leading him "gently back to Beauty, to Nature, and to Life." After the destruction of the world, this fact will be known. In the "Colloquy of Monos and Una" one of the characters says:

> Occasionally the poetic intellect—that intellect which we now feel to have been the most exalted of all—since those truths which to us were of the most enduring importance could only be reached by that *analogy* which speaks in proof-tones to the imagination alone, and to the unaided reason bears no weight—occasionally did this poetic intellect proceed a step farther in the evolving of the vague idea of the philosophic, and find in the mystic parable that tells of the tree of knowledge, and of its forbidden fruit, death-producing, a distinct intimation that knowledge was not meet for man in the infant condition of his soul.[105]

Here Poe is making an important distinction between the truth that is reached through reason and the truth that is attained by imagination. The former is conformity to the reality of Earth, the latter is conformity to the reality of Heaven, and hence supernal, ideal.

Imagination, by which this divine truth is revealed, is the soul or active principle of the sentiment of poesy, or sense of the beautiful.[106] It is a more certain means to truth than reason.

> Truth is, in its own essence, sublime—but her loftiest sublimity, as derived from man's clouded and erratic reason, is valueless—is pulseless—is utterly ineffective when brought into comparison with the unerring *sense* of which we speak.[107]

Poe goes so far as to express the belief that "all *very* profound knowledge" originates in a highly stimulated imagination.[108] At its highest, the imagination becomes a function of the soul. Kepler "guessed" the laws from which Newton deduced the fact of gravitation; that is, "he *imagined* them," grasped them with his soul "through mere dint of intuition."[109] But it is in the artist that imagination is strongest; his glimpses of the supernal are clearest, and his knowledge of the great secrets is most profound. Through him chiefly must be revealed the divine truths now hidden from man and beyond the power of reason ever to attain. Yet this benefactor of the human race is little esteemed.

> When *shall* the artist assume his proper situation in society? . . . How long shall the veriest vermin of the Earth, who crawl around the altar of

---

[104] See p. 108 above.   [105] *Works*, III, 202.   [106] See p. 120 above.
[107] Review of R. H. Horne's *Orion* (*Works*, XI, 257).
[108] "Fifty Suggestions" in *Works*, XIV, 187.
[109] *Eureka* in *Works*, XVI, 196–197.

Mammon, be more esteemed of men than they, the gifted ministers to those exalted emotions which link us with the mysteries of Heaven?[110]

His answer is, "Not long." The poem "Al Aaraaf," written several years before the words just quoted, was, I am convinced, an attempt to improve the status of the artist in the opinion of the world.

No argument is necessary to establish the fact that the poem exalts beauty, or that, in keeping with the sonnet, "To Science," originally printed as a head-piece, it condemns knowledge, or science. Does it thereby condemn truth? I think not; for Poe had in mind precisely that ideal truth, the truth of Heaven rather than the truth of Earth, which, as we have just seen, he later associated with poetry and imagination. This divine truth he identified with supernal beauty. He offered *Eureka*, as he explains in the Preface, to those who feel, not think; "not in its character of Truth-Teller, but for the Beauty that abounds in its Truth, constituting it true." In the poem itself—for he calls it a poem, an "Art-Product"—he asserts that "a perfect consistency can be nothing but an absolute truth."[111] Of the Nebular Theory of Laplace, for example, he says, "It is by far too beautiful, indeed, *not* to possess Truth as its essentiality."[112] Symmetry he calls "the poetical essence of the Universe"; but "symmetry and consistency are convertible terms:—thus Poetry and Truth are one." Hence the conclusion: "Man cannot long or widely err, if he suffer himself to be guided by his poetical, which I have maintained to be his truthful, in being his symmetrical, instinct."[113]

The spirits of Al Aaraaf, the artists of our human world, reveal through beauty the truth of Heaven. When this truth shall become known—when

> secrecy shall knowledge be
> In the environs of Heaven—

then man may rise in thought towards God and become a partner of His throne.[114]

If this study has made Poe's "Al Aaraaf" more intelligible, my main purpose is accomplished. I should like to think, however, that it has also helped to give significance to a poem often unappreciated. By way of conclusion, I should like to bring two suggestions to the

[110] Review of Chorley's *Conti the Discarded* (*Works*, VIII, 230).
[111] *Eureka* in *Works*, XVI, 196.   [112] *Eureka* in *Works*, XVI, 252.
[113] *Ibid.*, 302.   [114] See "Al Aaraaf," I, 110–117.

attention of students of Poe. In the first place, I believe we misjudge Poe when we class him as a worshipper of beauty for its own sake. On the contrary, he loved beauty as a revealer of truth beyond the scope of reason. In the second place, I wish to point out what I hope has already become evident; namely, that Poe developed his theory of poetry at the very beginning of his career, and that to the end of his life it remained substantially as originally conceived.

V.   Poe's Debt to Coleridge

I

THE object of this essay is to collect and present as clearly as possible the evidence of Poe's debt to Coleridge in poetry and prose fiction, in criticism, and in speculative thought. In seeking to do this, I have necessarily to take account of what has already been accomplished by others; but I hope to add something of my own, and to treat the subject more fully and systematically than has heretofore been done. I shall endeavor to avoid arbitrary or unsupported judgments; indeed I should like to eschew judgments altogether, but I find that impossible without incurring the serious risk of ambiguity. If sometimes I seem to deal in trivialities, let my desire for thoroughness be an excuse. I shall do my best not to exaggerate or subject myself to the charge of attacking Poe's reputation for originality.

Before proceeding to the consideration of influences, however, it is well to know what Poe at various times said of Coleridge. He mentions Coleridge four times in his earliest work of criticism, the "Letter to B__," which he used as a Preface to the third edition of his poems, published in 1831.[1] In the first passage mentioning Coleridge, after a disparaging remark about the Lake Poets, he adds: "The wise must bow to the wisdom of such men as Coleridge and Southey, but being wise, have laughed at poetical theories so prosaically exemplified." In the second passage he calls Coleridge "a giant in intellect and learning," yet with diffidence ventures to dispute his authority. In the third passage he says: "We see an instance of Coleridge's liability to err, in his *Biographia Literaria*—professedly his literary life and opinions, but, in fact, a treatise *de omni scibili et quibusdam aliis.* He goes wrong by reason of his very profundity. . . ." In the fourth passage he writes:

[1] This Preface is reproduced in Vol. VII of *The Complete Works of Edgar Allan Poe,* edited by James A. Harrison (New York, 1902). This edition is hereafter referred to as *Works*.

Of Coleridge I cannot speak but with reverence. His towering intellect! his gigantic power: To use an author quoted by himself, "J'ai trouvé souvent que la plupart des sectes ont raison dans une bonne partie de ce qu'elles avancent, mais non pas en ce qu'elles nient," and to employ his own language, he has imprisoned his own conceptions by the barrier he has erected against those of others.[2]

We next hear from Poe as editor of the *Southern Literary Messenger*. In December 1835, he refers to Coleridge's "appreciation of the value of words" and to his power to "discriminate closely approximating meanings."[3] The following January he praises a poem by a contemporary as, "like the Christabelle [*sic*] of Coleridge, entitled to be called *great* from its power of creating intense emotion in the minds of great men."[4] He affirmed his belief that Coleridge had written "the purest of all poems,"[5] and named him among those poets whom he chose to call "spiritual."[6] In a review of Allsop's *Letters, Conversations and Recollections of S. T. Coleridge*, June 1836, he writes: "But with us (we are not ashamed to confess it) the most trivial memorial of Coleridge is a treasure of inestimable price. He was indeed a 'myriad-minded man,' and ah, how little understood, and how pitifully vilified!"[7] He wonders why the *Biographia Literaria* has not been published in America; if it were he thinks it would "do away with the generally received impression here entertained of the mysticism of the writer."

Between 1837 and 1842 he expresses no opinion. When he finally speaks, he seems to have modified his former opinion. Coleridge, he

[2] So reads Poe's original text. The quotation is to be found in the *Biographia Literaria* (London, 1817), p. 121. Coleridge names no source. When Poe reprinted the "Letter to B ___," in 1836, he struck out the phrases "to use an author quoted by himself," and "to employ his own language," and so worded his sentence that the reader would not know he had borrowed from Coleridge at all. In both places Poe misquotes by omitting the word "tant" which in the *Biographia Literaria* stands after "pas." The quotation appears in "Marginalia" in *Works*, XVI, 98, with the same omission, and with no mention of Coleridge.

[3] Review of Godwin's *Lives of the Necromancers* (*Works*, VIII, 93).

[4] Review of the poems of Mrs. Sigourney, Miss Gould, and Mrs. Ellet (*Works*, VIII, 123).

[5] Review of the poems of Drake and Halleck, April 1836 (*Works*, VIII, 284).

[6] Review of Bryant's poems, Jan. 1837 (*Works*, IX, 304).

[7] *Works*, IX, 51. The epithet "myriad-minded" is borrowed from the *Biographia Literaria*, p. 151, where Coleridge applies it to Shakespeare. Poe's last phrase has reference to the activities of Coleridge's detractors, who did not hesitate to attack him after his death.

now thinks, "should be regarded as one who might have done much, had he been satisfied with attempting but little."[8] Consequently, as he remarks some time later, he should be judged, not by what he has done, but "by what he evinces a capability of doing."[9] In 1845 he refers to Coleridge's "preposterously anomalous metaphysicianism."[10] Having occasion to mention Coleridge as the author of *Aids to Reflection*, Poe remarks parenthetically that he "aided reflection to much better purpose in his 'Genevieve.' "[11] Finally, he refers contemptuously to Leigh Hunt's "absurd eulogies on Coleridge's 'Pains of Sleep.' "[12]

To comment at length on these opinions is unnecessary. It is fairly obvious that Poe composed the "Letter to B——" with enthusiasm. He had been reading Coleridge and Wordsworth. His enthusiasm arose, I surmise, in part from real pleasure in what he read, and in part from a vain and boyish delight in confuting persons of respect and authority. He belittles their poetry in order to persuade the reader that it has not influenced his own. Perhaps, too, he has not fully recovered from the spell of Byron and Moore. He is much impressed with the erudition of the *Biographia Literaria*. His praise of its author is spontaneous and genuine; his occasional strictures, on the other hand, which seem mild enough when compared with his flippant ridicule of Wordsworth, may be charged to the conceit of youth. His references to Coleridge are most favorable around 1836; after that they are mostly noncommital or derogatory. Corresponding to this change there is perceptible in his work an increasing reluctance to acknowledge his obligations to Coleridge. His passion for originality made him suspicious of others and

[8] Printed among the "Marginalia," in Stedman and Woodberry's edition, VII, 238. See also Poe's article in *Graham's Magazine*, March 1842 (*Works*, XI, 99).

[9] Review of Hawthorne in *Godey's Lady's Book*, Nov. 1847 (*Works*, XIII, 149).

[10] Review of Mrs. Browning's *Drama of Exile*, *Broadway Journal*, Jan. 4 (*Works*, XII, 33). See also "Marginalia" (*Works*, XVI, 150), where the word "preposterously" is omitted. In the *Biographia Literaria*, pp. 7–8, Coleridge calls metaphysics "this preposterous pursuit," and thinks it a "mental disease" injurious to his natural powers.

[11] Review of Willis's *American Prose Writers*, *Broadway Journal*, Jan. 18, 1845 (*Works*, XII, 37). I suppose Poe alludes not to the juvenile poem "Genevieve," but to the later poem "Love," in which the name of the heroine is Genevieve.

[12] Review of Hunt's *Indicator and Companion, Part II*, *Broadway Journal*, Aug. 30, 1845 (*Works*, XII, 238). For other references to Coleridge, see the following: "Marginalia" in *Works*, XVI, pp. 61, 72, 128; "Fifty Suggestions," XIV, 172; "Mystification," III, 106; and an article on Robert Conrad in *Graham's Magazine*, republished with the *Doings of Gotham*, ed. T. O. Mabbott (Pottsville, Pa., 1929), p. 96.

inordinately apprehensive lest unwittingly he should lay himself open to the charge of imitation.

II

In poetry the effort to be original, or at least to eradicate all traces of influence, produced extraordinary results. It is not my purpose to consider Poe's indebtedness to poets in general. Broadly speaking, he gained in originality as he grew older. The poems of 1827 are decidedly Byronic, although in one or two a Shelleyan flavor may be detected. Moore's influence is strong in the poems of 1829, where, also, echoes of Coleridge first appear. But the witchery of Coleridge is most potently felt in the poems written between 1829 and 1831. Poe must not have been altogether sincere, therefore, or else he confused Coleridge's theories with Wordsworth's, when he said in the "Letter to B——" that Coleridge's theories of poetry are "prosaically exemplified." A little farther on in the same essay he speaks as we should expect the author of the poems of 1831 to speak of the author of "Christabel"; that is, as one who apprehends vaguely the mood and manner of Coleridge without understanding thoroughly his meaning and purpose. Thus Poe: "In reading that man's poetry I tremble—like one who stands upon a volcano, conscious, from the very darkness bursting from the crater, of the fire and the light that are weltering below."

Only four poems—"The Ancient Mariner," "Christabel," "Kubla Khan," and "Youth and Age"—have been prominently mentioned as having influenced Poe's verse. Harry T. Baker[13] finds in the albatross, the angel's song that "makes the heavens be mute," and the calm of the sea in "The Ancient Mariner" the originals of the albatross of "Al Aaraaf," the song of Israfel at which the stars are mute, and the sea's hideous serenity in "The City in the Sea." He thinks "The Sleeper" is "most definitely influenced," finding in it an atmosphere "delicately redolent of Coleridge," besides the following particulars that suggest "Christabel": tetrameter verse (chiefly iambic), midnight, moonlight, and a strange lady from afar. He believes there is more than "coincidence" in the likeness between these lines from "Christabel,"

[13] "Coleridge's Influence on Poe's Poetry," *Modern Language Notes*, XXV (March 1910), 94–95.

> That saints will aid if men will call,
> For the blue sky bends over all—

and the following from "The Raven":

> "Prophet," said I, "thing of evil!—prophet still, if bird or devil!
> By that Heaven that bends above us—by that God we both adore—
> Tell his soul with sorrow laden . . ."

Finally, he reiterates the theory that the repetends of "Ulalume," "Lenore," and "The Raven" were suggested by Coleridge in "Christabel" and other poems. Even "The Haunted Palace," he thinks, has "certain faint mist-wreaths of 'Kubla Khan' hanging about it." It is his conclusion, therefore, that "in the light of such evidence it becomes questionable whether Poe's originality as a poet has not been at least a trifle overestimated."

James Routh points out the similarity between the dome of Nesace's palace in "Al Aaraaf" and Kubla Khan's "dome in air," and adds that Poe must have written with Coleridge's poem in mind.[14] He holds that "Fairy-Land," especially in its latter part, is a satire on "Kubla Khan," and calls attention to the following similarities in setting: in the one a "deep romantic chasm" and a "waning moon" in association with enchantment, and in the other "dim vales" and sleep-inducing moons that wax and wane. He also alludes to Poe's yellow albatross, which of course suggests "The Ancient Mariner" rather than "Kubla Khan."

Killis Campbell sees an "unconscious reproduction" of Coleridge's style in "The City in the Sea" and other poems.[15] Poe's line in the earlier "To Helen,"

> Like those Nicéan barks of yore,

bears, as he points out, a "manifest resemblance" to the line,

> Like those trim skiffs, unknown of yore,

of Coleridge's "Youth and Age."

I have only a few items of my own to add to these particulars. They are far from being conclusive, and I merely mention them for what they are worth. First I desire to point out the vague but unmistakable likeness between two passages in "The Sleeper" hitherto unnoticed

---

[14] "Notes on the Sources of Poe's Poetry: Coleridge, Keats, Shelley" (*Modern Language Notes*, XXIX, March 1914, pp. 72–75).

[15] *The Poems of Edgar Allan Poe* (Boston, 1917), p. xlviii.

and corresponding passages in "Christabel." In the early (1831) version of "The Sleeper" there are two lines—

> Lady, awake! lady awake!
> For the holy Jesus' sake!—

which produce in the mind of the reader the same effect as two similar lines in "Christabel"—

> Hush, beating heart of Christabel!
> Jesu, Maria, shield her well! (Lines 53–54)

Compare, also, the following passages:

> Oh, lady bright! can it be right—
> This window open to the night?
> The wanton airs, from the tree-top,
> Laughingly through the lattice drop—
> The bodiless airs, a wizard rout,
> Flit through thy chamber in and out,
> And wave the curtain canopy
> So fitfully—so fearfully—
> Above the closed and fringéd lid
> 'Neath which thy slumb'ring soul lies hid,
> That, o'er the floor and down the wall,
> Like ghosts the shadows rise and fall!
> Oh, lady dear, hast thou no fear?
> Why and what art thou dreaming here?
> ("The Sleeper," lines 18–31)

> With open eyes (ah woe is me!)
> Asleep, and dreaming fearfully,
> Fearfully dreaming, yet, I wis,
> Dreaming that alone, which is—
> O sorrow and shame! Can this be she,
> The lady, who knelt at the old oak tree?
> ("Christabel," lines 292–297)

The name "Lalage," which occurs in *Politian*, may have been suggested by one of Lessing's poems translated by Coleridge, the first stanza of which is as follows:

> I ask'd my fair one happy day
> What I should call her in my lay;
> By what sweet name from Rome or Greece;
> Lalage, Neaera, Chloris,

Sappho, Lesbia, or Doris,
Arethusa or Lucrece.[16]

Finally, let me quote two passages from Coleridge's "Limbo":

The sole true Something—This, in Limbo's Den.
It frightens Ghosts, as here Ghosts frighten men.
Thence cross'd unseized—and shall some fated hour
Be pulverized by Demogorgon's power
And given as poison to annihilate souls—

.   .   .   .   .

'Tis a strange place, this Limbo!—not a Place
Yet name it so;—where Time and weary Space
Fettered from flight, with night-mare sense of fleeing,
Strive for their last crepuscular half-being.

The Something described in the first passage, with its power to annihilate souls, is suggestive of the incorporate Silence of Poe's "Sonnet—Silence," which is more terrible than the corporate silence, Death. The second passage, describing Limbo, is not unlike Poe's description in "Dream-Land" of that

wild weird clime that lieth, sublime,
Out of SPACE—out of TIME.

It seems proper to consider here, also, certain traces of the influence of Coleridge's poetry on Poe's imaginative tales.

In the Introduction (p. 12) to her edition of the *Tales of Edgar Allan Poe* (1928) Blanche Colton Williams has suggested that the "MS. Found in a Bottle" "probably grew from appreciation of Coleridge's 'Rime of the Ancient Mariner' and its marginalia," but has not set forth in detail the data on which she bases her suggestion. I have arranged below a few of these details in parallel columns.

"The Ancient Mariner"	"MS Found in a Bottle"
And ice, mast high, came floating by, As green as emerald. (I.53–54) The ice was here, the ice was there, The ice was all around. (I.59–60)	". . . ramparts of ice . . . looking like the walls of the universe." (II.13)

[16] Perhaps, however, as Campbell points out (*Poems*, p. 230), the suggestion of the name came from Horace, *Odes*, I, xxii.

"The Ancient Mariner"	"MS Found in a Bottle"
We were the first that ever burst Into that silent sea. (II.105–106)	"We were . . . farther to the southward than any previous navigators." (II.6)
About, about, in reel and rout The death-fires danced at night; The water, like a witch's oils, Burnt green, and blue and white. (II.127–130)	"Eternal night continued to envelope us, all unrelieved by the phosphoric sea-brilliancy to which we had been accustomed in the tropics." (II.6)
The Mariner's ship meets a "spectre-bark," which, as well as the mariner's ship itself at times, is carried on without a wind or against the wind. (II.202; V.335, 390)	The narrator's ship meets a strange ship, which "bore up under a press of sail in the very teeth of that supernatural sea, and of that ungovernable hurricane." (II.7)
First the Mariner's ship is driven by a hurricane (I.41), and later it is moved by a supernatural wind that does not touch the sails yet makes a roaring noise (V. 309 ff.). Again the ship is carried forward with "a sudden bound" yet is not overturned.	The narrator hears a "loud, humming noise," and a moment later a terrific blast of wind strikes the ship and sweeps it on, yet miraculously it does not sink. (II.3)
The gloss states that the ship was "driven by a storm toward the south pole." (I.41)	"Perhaps this current leads us to the southern pole itself." The ship is actually carried down by a whirlpool, presumably at the pole. (II.14)
The albatross figures prominently in the poem. (Passim)	"At times we gasped for breath at an elevation beyond the albatross." (II.6)

Two other tales bear some evidence, I think, of Coleridge's influence. "Silence—A Fable" may owe something in style, atmosphere, and content to Coleridge's "Wanderings of Cain," which was first printed in the *Bijou* of 1828 and reprinted with his poetical works in 1828, 1829, and 1834. In both the style is poetic and evidently modeled on the language of the Bible. Both deal with the supernatural, and the atmosphere of silence, desolation, and terror is common to both. In the "Wanderings of Cain" an unhappy man stands under a rock, then flees away in terror, but returns; in "Silence—A Fable" an unhappy man sits on a rock, then flees away in terror, but does not return. Coleridge speaks of a God of the dead who is antagonistic to the God of the living; Poe hears his story, not indeed from the God of the dead, but from a daemon who sits in the shadow of the tomb, and who is the enemy of living man. The other tale that may owe something to Coleridge is the "Masque of the Red Death." The Prince in this story, it will be remembered, had retired to a magnificent abbey to escape the plague, and had taken with him his courtiers, musicians, buffoons, and ballet-dancers. In the seven voluptuous chambers of the abbey the Prince has arranged an elaborate masquerade. Poe describes them thus:

To the right and left, in the middle of each wall, a tall and narrow Gothic window looked out upon a closed corridor which pursued the windings of the suite. These windows were of stained glass whose color varied in accordance with the prevailing hue of the decorations of the chamber into which it opened. . . . Now in no one of the seven apartments was there any lamp or candelabrum, amid the profusion of golden ornaments that lay scattered to and fro or depended from the roof. There was no light of any kind emanating from lamp or candle within the suite of chambers. But in the corridors that followed the suite, there stood, opposite to each window, a heavy tripod, bearing a brazier of fire that projected its rays through the tinted glass and so glaringly illumined the room. And thus were produced a multitude of gaudy and fantastic appearances.

There is in Coleridge's description of the Temple of Superstition in his "Allegoric Vision," which was printed as a part of the introduction to the *Lay Sermon Addressed to the Higher and Middle Classes* and appended to the *Biographia Literaria,* but included with the poetical works in 1829 and 1834, a passage very similar to the description just quoted from Poe's tale. I quote only the most pertinent part of the description:

Every part of the building was crowded with tawdry ornaments and fantastic deformity. On every window was portrayed, in glaring and inelegant colours, some horrible tale or preternatural incident, so that not a ray of light could enter, untinged by the medium through which it passed. The body of the building was full of people, some of them dancing in and out, in unintelligible figures, with strange ceremonies and antic merriment, while others seemed convulsed with horror, or pining in mad melancholy.

These may in themselves, be trifles; but if taken in conjunction with the more weighty evidence of Coleridge's influence on Poe to be found in the essays and reviews, they acquire an added significance. I turn now to an examination of these essays and reviews with a view to ascertaining the extent of Poe's indebtedness to Coleridge in criticism.

III

Poe was ambitious to establish himself as a critic and a literary leader in America, but he realized that to do so he must be familiar with the literature and thought of other times than his own. He was a journalist, however, with the journalist's bias for all that is contemporary, and, besides, had scant time for general reading in the literature of the past. In his search for the knowledge he needed he was therefore constrained to make the most of such handbooks, encyclopedias, and other similar short cuts as he could lay his hands on. Coleridge's *Biographia Literaria* was to him a treasure, for it not only contained a digest of an entire school of philosophy and criticism, but also made reference to a variety of sources to which he might not otherwise have been introduced. After a careful reading of this book he could discourse with some assurance on A. W. Schlegel's theories of criticism, for instance, or on Schelling's system of identity with but little firsthand acquaintance with the writings of these authors. The question arises, then, whether an idea which Poe held in common with both Coleridge and Schlegel was borrowed, if borrowed at all, from one or the other.

The question would be simple if we knew which he read first. Schlegel's *Lectures on Dramatic Art and Literature,* which was the only work of Schlegel's which materially influenced Poe, was translated into English in 1815. F. C. Prescott thinks that Poe had read this book before writing the "Letter to B——," basing his opinion on the fact that Poe uses the phrase "the bee Sophocles," and that Schlegel "refers to the fact that Sophocles was called the 'Attic Bee.' "[17] But is it not a fact that Sophocles was known generally among the ancients as the "Attic Bee"? And could not Poe have come across the epithet in numerous other places? Since Poe does not name Schlegel nor otherwise allude to him in this essay, I much doubt whether he had read

[17] *Selections from the Critical Writings of Edgar Allan Poe* (New York, 1909), pp. xxx, 325.

the *Lectures on Dramatic Art and Literature* at this time. His earliest reference to Schlegel occurs in a review of the poems of Mrs. Sigourney, Miss Gould, and Mrs. Ellet, published in January, 1836.[18] That Poe had read the *Biographia Literaria* (1817) before writing the "Letter to B___" goes without saying, for the critical theories there mentioned were unquestionably borrowed from Coleridge's book. These same theories, moreover, as I have tried to show elsewhere,[19] were conceived at least as early as 1829, the date of the publication of "Al Aaraaf." It is highly probable, therefore, that Poe had read the *Biographia Literaria* at that date or earlier. The very fact that Coleridge was one of the most famous and influential poets and critics living at the time would have led the young American poet and critic to read his literary autobiography at the first opportunity.

In view of these facts, it seems to me probable that Poe owed most to Coleridge for such ideas as he held in common with Coleridge and Schlegel, even though in the development of those ideas he ultimately had recourse to the latter. The same is true of Schelling. Some of Poe's philosophical ideas that came to him through Coleridge are to be found most fully developed in the writings of Schelling. Poe had no opportunity to read Schelling unless he read him in the original German, for practically nothing of Schelling's work was translated until long after Poe's death.[20] It may be, as one writer has said,[21] that Coleridge is indebted to Schlegel for most of his principles of criticism; and he himself readily admitted that his philosophical principles were largely identical with Schelling's, though he denied that he had borrowed, explaining that their theories were the same because they learned them from the same masters.[22] It will thus be practically impossible to prove that in a given case Poe was influenced by Coleridge to the exclusion of others whose ideas corresponded so closely to his, nor shall I attempt to offer such proof. I wish merely to make my own position clear. Poe's first and chief debt was to Cole-

[18] *Works*, VIII, 126.

[19] See above, "An Interpretation of 'Al Aaraaf,'" pp. 116–125.

[20] According to Bayard Quincy Morgan, *A Bibliography of German Literature in English Translation*, University of Wisconsin *Studies in Language and Literature*, No. 16, 1922. In seeking in Coleridge's writing the source of Poe's ideas, I take no account of those works which were not published until after Poe's death.

[21] Anna Augusta Helmholtz, *The Indebtedness of Samuel Taylor Coleridge to August Wilhelm von Schlegel*, Bulletin of the University of Wisconsin, Philology and Literature Series, III, No. 4, 1907.

[22] *Biographia Literaria*, ed. J. Shawcross (2 vols.; London, 1907), I, 102–103. All citations of *Biographia Literaria* are made to this edition.

ridge; to Schlegel and Schelling he probably owed little directly, having been drawn to them through Coleridge. If he appeared sometimes to give credit to Schlegel and Schelling that might have belonged to Coleridge, it was because of a desire to appear and to be a man of erudition; and if as he grew older he became less enthusiastic in his admiration of Coleridge, it was because of an abnormal desire to appear and to be an original critic, and, consequently, a growing reluctance to admit, even to himself, perhaps, his obligation to the author of the *Biographia Literaria*.

Let me say at the very beginning that the theories which Poe and Coleridge held in common—or perhaps it would be more correct to say the theories which Poe developed from suggestions found in the writings of Coleridge—are almost wholly concerned with poetry. Poe's criticism of the short story derives from Coleridge only in so far as it embodies the same general principles that constitute his theory of poetry. What, then, is Poe's theory of poetry, and what evidence is there that it was derived, in part at least, from Coleridge? I believe I might assume that most readers of this essay are familiar with the elements of Poe's theory; but I hope I may be allowed, in the interest of clearness and brevity, to enumerate here what I consider to be the most characteristic and hence the most important constituent ideas in that theory. I find the following:

1. The immediate object of poetry is pleasure, not truth.
2. The pleasure derived from the poem differs from that derived from the romance in being indefinite, not definite.
3. Music is an essential element in poetry.
4. Beauty is the sole province of the poem.
5. Poetic Beauty has the quality of strangeness or novelty.
6. The poem must have unity or totality of effect or interest (the terms are variously combined).
7. The true poem must be brief.
8. Passion and poetry are discordant.
9. The tone of the poem should be sadness or melancholy.

Other ideas closely related to poetic theory are reserved for the next section of this essay because they are philosophical as well as critical in their import. There may be others yet; I do not pretend to have exhausted the list even of important ideas. The grounds on which my analysis rests should appear as the examination of the individual items proceeds.

The first three of these nine characteristic ideas are announced in the "Letter to B——," and the first, respecting the immediate object of poetry, is particularly emphasized. He pretends to oppose the poetic theory of the Lake School, which he calls "the most singular heresy" in the history of modern poetry. This heresy, which he defines rather incoherently, is what afterwards in "The Poetic Principle" and elsewhere he condemned as the "heresy of the didactic," though in his later references he refrained from naming the heretics so explicitly. He attacks the supposed didacticism of Wordsworth with the naïve argument that since the end of existence is happiness, the end of all instruction must be happiness; and that since happiness is but another word for pleasure, so the aim of instruction should be pleasure. It is amusing to observe how freely he borrows the ideas and even the very words of Coleridge and Wordsworth in venturing, with diffidence as he says, "to dispute their authority," "Aristotle," wisely asserts the young critic, "with singular assurance, has declared poetry the most philosophical of all writing—but it required a Wordsworth to pronounce it the most metaphysical." In a footnote to the phrase "most philosophical of all writing" he adds the following words in Latin characters: "spoudiotaton kai philosophikotaton genos." The phrase is perhaps borrowed from Coleridge, who objects to Wordsworth's occasional matter-of-factness "as contravening the essence of poetry, which Aristotle pronounces to be σπουδαιότατον καὶ φιλοσοφώτατο γένος, the most intense, weighty, and philosophical product of human art."[23] I presume Coleridge was quoting the *Poetics* from memory, altering it to suit his purpose; for he not only inverts the order of the original, but changes the form of the adjectives from the comparative to the superlative. Poe faithfully repeats Coleridge's errors and introduces a new one besides, using a late form of the adjective, *philosophikotaton*, instead of the classical *philosophotaton*. The entire quotation, all errors included, was repeated years later.[24] In a single paragraph near the end of the essay he formulates his theory of poetry, thus:

[23] *Biographia Literaria*, II, 101. In his note on Poe's quotation Prescott (p. 324), quotes the entire sentence from the *Poetics*, IX, 3: διo κℵι φιλοσοφώτερον και σπουδαιότερον ποιησις ιστοριας εστιν, which he translates, "Poetry, therefore, is a more philosophical and a higher thing than history." He adds the conjecture that Poe got the phrase from Wordsworth, who in the *Preface to the Lyrical Ballads* (1800) says: "Aristotle, I have been told, has said, that Poetry is the most philosophic of all writing. . . ."

[24] Review of Cockton's *Stanley Thorn, Graham's Magazine*, Jan. 1842 (*Works*, XI, 12). See also XII, 15, where he quotes the phrase in Greek characters without a translation, and denies its truth.

A poem, in my opinion, is opposed to a work of science by having, for its *immediate* object, pleasure, not truth; to romance, by having for its object an *indefinite* instead of a definite pleasure, being a poem only so far as this object is attained; romance presenting perceptible images with definite, poetry with *indefinite* sensations, to which end music is an essential, since the comprehension of sweet sound is our most indefinite conception. Music, when combined with a pleasureable idea, is poetry; music without the idea is simply music; the idea without the music is prose from its very definitiveness.

What was meant by the invective against him who had no music in his soul?

Now with this should be compared the following passage from the *Biographia Literaria:*

A poem is that species of composition, which is opposed to works of science, by proposing for its *immediate* object pleasure, not truth; and from all other species (having *this* object in common with it) it is discriminated by proposing to itself such delight from the *whole,* as is compatible with a distinct gratification from each component part.[25]

Obviously Poe's first clause is borrowed, almost word for word from Coleridge's first clause. Their opinion of the object of poetry is absolutely identical. Yet, as I have already shown, Poe's expressed purpose in writing the "Letter to B___" was to dispute the alleged doctrine of Coleridge and the other Lake Poets that the object of poetry is truth, or instruction.

Poe's second idea is that the pleasure to be derived from a poem is indefinite, whereas that derived from a prose romance is definite. Coleridge, too, makes a distinction between the pleasure derived from the poem and the romance; for we learn by the context that the "other species" referred to as having an object common with poetry are the novel and the romance. The mere "superaddition of metre, with or without rhyme," does not make a poem of a prose romance.

If metre be superadded, all other parts must be made consonant with it. They must be such as to justify the perpetual and distinct attention to each part, which an exact correspondent recurrence of accent and sound are calculated to excite.[26]

Such attention to sound and accent does not imply definite conceptions nor involve the reasoning faculty at all. The reader is "carried forward, not merely or chiefly by the mechanical impulse of curiosity,

[25] *Biographia Literaria,* II, 10.   [26] *Ibid.,* II, 9–10.

or by a restless desire to arrive at the final solution; but by the
pleasurable activity of mind excited by the attractions of the journey
itself."[27] The pleasure derived from sound and accent is of necessity
indefinite, and since the effect of the whole poem must be consonant
with that of each component part, that too is indefinite. But what does
Poe mean by the word "indefinite" as here used? In speaking of
Tennyson, he says:

> There are passages in his works which rivet a conviction I had long
> entertained, that the *indefinite* is an element in the true ποιησις. Why do
> some persons fatigue themselves in attempts to unravel such phantasy-
> pieces as the "Lady of Shalot?" . . . If the author did not deliberately
> propose to himself a suggestive indefinitiveness of meaning, with the view
> of bringing about a definitiveness of vague and therefore of spiritual *effect*
> —this, at least, arose from the silent analytical promptings of that poetic
> genius which, in its supreme development, embodies all orders of intellec-
> tual capacity. I *know* that indefinitiveness is an element of the true
> music—I mean the true musical expression.[28]

This spiritual effect is, of course, akin to that elevation of soul which
Poe called the sentiment of poesy, and which he believed to be allied
to that "instinct or primitive sentiment of worship" that phrenologists
call Veneration.[29] Coleridge likewise associates indefiniteness with
deep feelings. He urges his readers to habituate

> the intellect to clear, distinct, and adequate conceptions concerning all
> things that are the possible objects of clear conception, and thus to reserve
> the deep feelings which belong, as by a natural right to those obscure ideas
> that are necessary to the moral perfection of the human being, notwith-
> standing, yes, even in consequence, of their obscurity—to reserve these
> feelings, I repeat, for objects, which their very sublimity renders indefinite,
> no less than their indefiniteness renders them sublime: namely, to the ideas
> of being, form, life, the reason, and the law of conscience, freedom,
> immortality, God![30]

Elsewhere Coleridge says that he agrees with Aristotle that poetry is
"the most catholic and abstract" of arts.[31] This identification of the

---

[27] *Ibid.*, p. 149.   [28] "Marginalia," in *Works*, XVI, 28–29.

[29] Review of the poems of Drake and Halleck, *Southern Literary Messenger*,
April 1836 (*Works*, X, 282).

[30] *The Friend* (London, 1865; a reprint of the 2d ed. of 1818), p. 63.

[31] *Biographia Literaria*, II, 101. Prescott thinks Poe may have got the idea of the
indefinite from Wordsworth, who, in the preface to the 1815 edition of his poems,
informs us that the poetic imagination "recoils from everything but the plastic, the
pliant, and the indefinite." See Prescott, pp. 325, 328, notes.

indefinite and the infinite or sublime is an important part of Poe's
theory of poetry. From Norman Foerster it elicits the following comment: "Does it follow that, since the infinite is indefinite, the indefinite
is also the infinite, the spiritual? To argue so is to commit one of the
grossest logical blunders, as Poe, with his analytical mind, might have
been expected to demonstrate."[32] Perhaps Poe may be excused on the
ground that he was led to commit this logical blunder by a too
implicit faith in the logic of Coleridge, who first committed it.

Poe's third idea, that music is essential to poetry, is implicit in
Coleridge's requirement that poetry should have "an exact correspondent recurrence of accent and sound." Poe means the same thing when
he says that "verse originates in the human enjoyment of equality."[33]
The idea of equality, he explains, "embraces those of similarity, proportion, identity, repetition, and adaptation or fitness." Rhythm,
rhyme, meter, and the line are but modes of equality.[34] "The perception of pleasure in the equality of *sounds* is the principle of *music*," he
thinks; and he designates verse as "an inferior or less capable music."[35]
I do not think Coleridge would have agreed that poetry is a less
capable music, though he did say that the "sense of musical delight,
with the power of producing it," is one of the proofs of poetic genius.[36]
And, he adds, " 'the man that hath not music in his soul' can never be
a genuine poet." This quotation may have suggested Poe's question in
the "Letter to B——" as to the meaning of the invective against him who
had no music in his soul. Late in life Coleridge said of himself: "I
could write as good verses now as ever I did, if I were perfectly free
from vexations, and were in the *ad libitum* hearing of fine music,
which has a sensible effect in harmonising my thoughts, and in
animating and, as it were, lubricating my inventive faculty." With this
confession may be compared Poe's statement that music is "one of the
moods of poetical development," and that in music "the soul most
nearly attains the end upon which we have commented—the creation
of supernal beauty."[37]

This brings us to the central idea in Poe's theory of poetry, the idea
that Beauty is the sole province of the poem. It is hardly necessary to
repeat his famous definition of the poetry of words as "The Rhythmi-

---

[32] *American Criticism* (Boston, 1928), p. 39.
[33] "The Rationale of Verse" in *Works*, XIV, 218–219.
[34] *Ibid.*, pp. 225–226, 247.   [35] *Ibid.*, pp. 219–220.
[36] *Biographia Literaria*, II, 14.
[37] Review of Longfellow's *Ballads and Other Poems*, *Graham's Magazine*, April
1842 (*Works*, XI, 74). Cf. a similar remark in "The Poetic Principle."

cal Creation of Beauty." If pleasure, then, is the immediate object of the poet, Beauty is the means by which he is enabled to produce it.

"That pleasure," says Poe, "which is at once the most pure, the most elevating, and the most intense, is derived, I maintain, from the contemplation of the Beautiful. In the contemplation of Beauty we alone find it possible to attain that pleasurable elevation, or excitement, *of the soul,* which we recognize as the Poetic Sentiment."[38]

The poetic sentiment, or sense of the beautiful, is, like veneration, an immortal instinct inherent in each individual;[39] but of course poets are more highly endowed with it than others, and it is by awaking or stimulating this sense in others by the creation of beauty that the poet gives pleasure. But what is Beauty? Poe thinks of Beauty as order, proportion, harmony.[40] This is in accord with his statement in "The Rationale of Verse," already referred to, that verse originates in the human enjoyment of equality. Coleridge, too, makes harmony, proportion, the essential virtue of a poem.

But if the definition sought for be that of a *legitimate* poem, I answer, it must be one, the parts of which mutually support and explain each other; all in their proportion harmonizing with, and supporting the purpose and known influences of metrical arrangement.[41]

He goes on to say in this connection that a "harmonious whole" can only be obtained by a "studied selection and artificial arrangement" of the component parts. He does not insist on this point so much as Poe, however, nor does he use the word "Beauty" so frequently or so pointedly. He does say, though, that in reading a poem the reader should be excited "by the attractions of the journey." Again in distinguishing between the language of prose and the language of poetry, he asserts that in prose words must "express the intended meaning, and no more . . . But in verse you must do more;—there the words, the *media,* must be beautiful."[42] Coleridge's "legitimate poem" corresponds to Poe's "poetry of words"; and if we agree with Poe that beauty and harmony are synonymous terms, then the two definitions

---

[38] "The Poetic Principle," in *Works,* XIV, 275.   [39] *Ibid.,* p. 273.

[40] Review of Longfellow's *Ballads and Other Poems, Graham's Magazine,* April 1842 (*Works,* XI, 73). In the "Marginalia" (*Works,* XVI, 137) he says the "mathematical recognition of *equality* . . . seems to be *the root of all Beauty."* Cf. also *ibid.,* p. 85.

[41] *Biographia Literaria,* II, 10.

[42] *The Table Talk and Omniana of Samuel Taylor Coleridge,* arranged by T. Ashe (Bohn's Standard Library, London, 1884), p. 238. All citations of *Table Talk* and *Omniana* refer to this edition.

are approximately equivalent. I do not assert, however, that Poe's definition was suggested by Coleridge's.[43]

Akin to the idea that beauty is the sole province of the poem is the further idea, also characteristic of Poe's theory, that poetic beauty must have the quality of strangeness, or novelty. He was fond of quoting Bacon as an authority on the subject. In his essay on "Anastatic Printing" Poe writes:

> "There is no exquisite beauty," says Bacon, "without some strangeness in the proportions." The philosopher had reference, here, to beauty in its common acceptation; but the remark is equally applicable to all the forms of beauty—that is to say, to everything which arouses profound interest in the heart or intellect of man. In every such thing, strangeness—in other words, *novelty*—will be found a principal element. . . . Nothing, unless it be novel—*not even novelty itself*—will be the source of very intense excitement among men.[44]

The poet creates beauty by producing novel combinations of materials and forms which individually may be familiar enough.[45] Bacon's was a name to conjure with; consequently Poe used it at every opportunity. He seemed to avoid mentioning Coleridge, on the other hand, to whom I think he was really indebted for the idea—or perhaps, more accurately, to Coleridge and Wordsworth as interpreted in the *Biographia Literaria*. It is the "character and privilege of genius," says Coleridge, to "carry on the feelings of childhood into the powers of manhood; to combine the child's sense of wonder and novelty with the appearances which every day for perhaps forty years had rendered familiar." In the same connection he adds: "In poems, equally as in philosophic disquisitions, genius produces the strongest impressions of novelty, while it rescues the most admitted truths from the impotence caused by the very circumstance of their universal admission."[46] In explaining the occasion and plan of the *Lyrical Ballads* Coleridge writes: "During the first year that Mr. Wordsworth and I were neigh-

---

[43] Poe's definition was formulated probably ten years after the publication of "The Letter to B ____," and though I agree with Prescott that, in all likelihood, Schlegel's theory of beauty greatly influenced Poe's, I cannot believe that this influence was felt until long after Poe had become familiar with Coleridge's critical writings. See Prescott, p. xxxi.

[44] "Essays and Miscellanies," in *Works*, XIV, 153.

[45] Review of Longfellow's *Ballads and Other Poems*, *Graham's Magazine*, April 1842 (*Works*, XI, 73).

[46] *Biographia Literaria*, I, 59–60. These quotations are quoted in *Biographia Literaria* from *The Friend*, Essay 5; see note by Shawcross, I, 205.

bors, our conversations turned frequently on the two cardinal points
of poetry, the power of exciting the sympathy of the reader by a
faithful adherence to the truth of nature, and the power of giving the
interest of novelty by the modifying colours of imagination."[47] They
agreed that Coleridge was to write of the supernatural, things in
themselves strange, whereas Wordsworth proposed "to give the charm
of novelty to things of every day, and to excite a feeling analogous to
the supernatural, by awakening the mind's attention from the lethargy
of custom, and directing it to the loveliness and the wonders of the
world before us." This agreement was made in 1797; but that Coleridge did not change his opinion is evidenced by the statement in the
Biographia Literaria, written nearly a score of years later, that one of
the promises of genius in a young writer is "the choice of subjects very
remote from the private interests and circumstances of the writer
himself."[48]

Not only must a poem have the quality of novelty, but its materials
and forms must be so arranged as to produce an effect of totality or
unity. In the short poem, Poe explains,

the understanding is employed, without difficulty, in the contemplation of
the picture *as a whole;* and thus its effect will depend, in great measure,
upon the perfection of its finish, upon the nice adaptation of its constituent
parts, and especially, upon what is rightly termed by Schlegel *the unity or
totality of interest.*[49]

The italicized phrase seems to have been borrowed from Schlegel, but
I am inclined to think the idea involved had been previously adopted
by Poe as a part of his theory of poetry.[50] "Tamerlane" and "Al
Aaraaf," Poe's only two long poems, unless we include the dramatic
fragment, *Politian,* were published in 1827 and 1829 respectively. He

---

[47] *Ibid.,* II, 5.   [48] *Ibid.,* II, 14.

[49] Review of Longfellow's *Ballads and Other Poems, Graham's Magazine,* April
1842 (*Works,* XI, p. 79). A similar statement appears in a review of the poems of
Mrs. Sigourney, Miss Gould, and Mrs. Ellet in the *Southern Literary Messenger,*
Jan. 1836 (*Works,* VIII, 126), and the idea recurs frequently in Poe's reviews and
essays.

[50] Prescott says (p. xxxi), "He undoubtedly got from Schlegel the principle of
'unity' or totality of interest." But in another place (p. xxxiii) he modifies the force
of this statement by saying, "He doubtless found in Coleridge, as in Schlegel,
authority for his principle of unity,—as for example in Coleridge's 'tone and spirit
of unity,'—'reducing multitude into unity of effect.'" It is not improbable that
Coleridge was influenced by Schlegel to adopt the idea, and Schlegel, as Prescott
points out, had found the idea, or the source of the idea, in reading de la Motte
Fouqué (see Prescott's note, p. 331).

never afterwards wrote a poem of more than approximately one hundred lines, which he conceived to be the maximum length of a true poem.[51] If the effect to be produced is increased in intensity, the length must be shortened correspondingly. The chief new poems published in 1831 were about fifty lines in length. I have already shown that his interest in Coleridge was very great about this time. I am persuaded that both his poetry and his theory were profoundly influenced at this time by his study of the *Biographia Literaria*. He eventually abandoned Schlegel's phrase "unity of interest" and adopted in its place the phrase "unity of effect" or "unity of impression," which so much better expresses the idea in his mind and the character of his poems. Sometimes he varies the phrase to "totality of effect or impression."[52] In the passage above quoted, where Poe refers to Schlegel, he mentions as a quality of the poem coördinate with unity of interest "the nice adaptation of its constituent parts." With this we may compare Coleridge's definition, already quoted, requiring that the component parts of the poem shall "mutually support and explain each other; all in their proportion harmonizing, etc." The poet, says Coleridge, "diffuses a tone and spirit of unity, that blends, and (as it were) fuses, each to each, by that synthetic and magical power to which we have exclusively appropriated the name of imagination."[53] Among the evidences of poetic genius in a young poet he includes "the power of reducing multitude into unity of effect, and modifying a series of thoughts by some one predominant thought or feeling."[54] In poetry, he says again, the words ought to attract attention, "yet not so much and so perpetually as to destroy the unity which ought to result from the whole poem." But, he goes on to say, —

the great thing in poetry is, *quocunque modo*, to effect a unity of impression upon the whole; and a too great fulness and profusion of point in the parts will prevent this. Who can read with pleasure more than a hundred lines or so of Hudibras at one time? Each couplet or quatrain is so whole in itself, that you can't connect them. There is no fusion, — just as it is in Seneca.[55]

This entire passage, with its phrase "unity of impression" and its mention of "a hundred lines or so," might have been extremely sugges-

---

[51] "The Philosophy of Composition," in *Works,* XIV, 197.
[52] "A Chapter of Suggestions" (1845), in *Works,* XIV, 188, and "The Poetic Principle" and "The Philosophy of Composition," *passim.*
[53] *Biographia Literaria,* II, 12.   [54] *Ibid.,* II, 14.   [55] *Table Talk,* p. 238.

tive to Poe, who would have felt a natural disposition to agree with all that it contains. It seems to me highly probable, therefore, that Poe got from Coleridge rather than from Schlegel the phrase "unity of effect" as well as the principle it embodies.

Associated with the idea of unity of effect is the further idea, already touched upon, that a true poem must of necessity be short.[56] Poe's best poems excellently illustrate this theory, and most of them were doubtless written with it as a conscious guide. Among his critical works the theory is often stated, in "The Poetic Principle" somewhat elaborately.

> I hold that a long poem does not exist. I maintain that the phrase, "a long poem," is simply a flat contradiction in terms.
>
> I need scarcely observe that a poem deserves its title only inasmuch as it excites, by elevating the soul. The value of the poem is in the ratio of this elevating excitement. But all excitements are, through a physical necessity, transient. That degree of excitement which would entitle a poem to be so called at all, cannot be sustained throughout a composition of any great length. After the lapse of half an hour, at the very utmost, it flags—fails—a revulsion ensues—and then the poem is, in effect, and in fact, no longer such.[57]

Paradise Lost, he maintains, "is to be regarded as poetical, only when, losing sight of that vital requisite of all works of Art, Unity, we view it merely as a series of minor poems. If, to preserve its Unity—its totality of effect or impression—we read it (as would be necessary) at a single sitting, the result is but a constant alternation of excitement and depression."[58] A poem must not be too long to be read at a single sitting, else it loses "the immensely important effect derivable from unity of impression."[59] I have already referred to the limitation of one hundred lines. One passage from Coleridge will suffice for purposes of comparison:

> In short, whatever specific import we attach to the word poetry, there will be found involved in it, as a necessary consequence, that a poem of any length neither can be, nor ought to be, all poetry. Yet if a harmonious whole is produced, the remaining parts must be preserved in keeping with the poetry; and this can be no otherwise effected than by such a studied selection and artificial arrangement as will partake of one, though not a

---

[56] Prescott (p. xxxiii) thinks "perhaps" Poe got the idea from Coleridge.
[57] *Works*, XIV, 266.   [58] *Ibid.*, 267.
[59] "The Philosophy of Composition," in *Works*, XIV, 196.

peculiar, property of poetry. And this again can be no other than the property of exciting a more continuous and equal attention than the language of prose aims at, whether colloquial or written.[60]

Here Coleridge agrees with Poe that a long poem, so called, is really poetry only in parts. Yet, unlike Poe, he sanctions the writing of such long compositions; but to minimize their inconsistency, the language and form of the non-poetical portions should be made to conform as nearly as possible to the spirit of the parts that are poetical. In his statement that it is the property of poetry to excite "a more continuous and equal attention than the language of prose aims at," he approximates Poe's meaning in the statement that a poem deserves its title only "inasmuch as it excites, by elevating the soul."

The poet, writing in a mood of exaltation, excites and elevates the soul of the reader by the power of his art; that is, by the creation of beauty. This excitement is spiritual rather than physical. Poetry has "no inevitable, and indeed no necessary co-existence" with the passions of mankind, "although it may exalt, or inflame, or purify, or control them."[61] This was Poe's opinion in 1836. Later he came to consider passion antagonistic to the poetic mood. He was influenced in this by Coleridge,[62] with whom he was, or supposed himself to be, in agreement. First I wish to establish precisely what Poe meant by "passion," and then to show how he may have found authority for his opinion in certain statements of Coleridge's.

Commenting on Tennyson, Poe writes:

Although we agree, for example, with Coleridge, that poetry and *passion* are discordant, yet we are willing to permit Tennyson to bring, to the intense *passion* which prompted his "Locksley Hall," the aid of that terseness and pungency which are derivable from rhythm and from rhyme. The effect he produces, however, is a purely passionate, and not, unless in detached passages of this magnificent philippic, a properly poetic effect. His "Oenone," on the other hand, exalts the soul not into passion, but into a conception of pure *beauty*, which in its elevation—its calm and intense rapture—has in it a foreshadowing of the future and spiritual life, and as

[60] *Biographia Literaria*, II, 11.

[61] Review of the poems of Drake and Halleck, *Southern Literary Messenger*, April 1836 (*Works*, VIII, 283).

[62] Prescott says (notes, p. 345): "Poe regularly attributes to Coleridge the doctrine that 'poetry and passion are discordant,'—apparently without authority. Coleridge, like the other early nineteenth century critics, considered passion 'the all in all in poetry.'"

far transcends earthly passion as the holy radiance of the sun does the glimmering and feeble phosphorescence of the glow-worm.[63]

We see from these remarks that Poe found poetry and passion discordant, not because passion is a state of emotional excitement, but because it is ugly. As he puts it in "The Poetic Principle":

In the contemplation of Beauty we alone find it possible to attain that pleasurable elevation, or excitement, *of the soul,* which we recognise as the Poetic Sentiment, and which is so easily distinguished from Truth, which is the satisfaction of the Reason, or from Passion, which is the excitement of the heart.[64]

The distinction Poe makes between the excitement of the soul and the excitement of the heart will, I believe, throw much light on this problem. Of the two kinds of love, human and divine, Poe admits one as a proper subject for poetry and excludes the other. In praising one of Moore's poems, he says:

There are two of the lines in which a sentiment is conveyed that embodies the *all in all* of the divine passion of love—a sentiment which, perhaps, has found its echo in more, and in more passionate human hearts than any other single sentiment ever embodied in words.[65]

The poem in question is the melody beginning, "Come, rest in this bosom, my own stricken deer." The choice is significant in that it is a poem of love, and yet has no sexual interest whatever. It is, in fact, sexual desire and not true love that Poe calls passion:

For in regard to Passion, alas! its tendency is to degrade, rather than to elevate the Soul. Love, on the contrary—Love—the true, the divine Eros —the Uranian, as distinguished from the Dionaean Venus—is unquestionably the purest and truest of all poetical themes.[66]

Now observe what to the casual reader might appear to be a contradiction. He is explaining that the mood suited to the presentation of truth is not the poetical mood:

We must be perspicuous, precise, terse. We need concentration rather than expansion of mind. We must be calm, unimpassioned, unexcited—in a word, we must be in that peculiar mood which, as nearly as possible, is the exact converse of the poetical.[67]

[63] Review of R. H. Horne's *Orion, Graham's Magazine,* March 1844 (*Works,* XI, 255).
[64] *Works,* XIV, 275.   [65] *Ibid.,* 282.   [66] *Ibid.,* 290.
[67] Review of Longfellow's *Ballads and Other Poems, Graham's Magazine,* April 1842 (*Works,* XI, 70).

The poetic mood, then, is one in which the poet is impassioned and excited and has expansion of mind. This "impassioned" mood corresponds to the excitement or elevation of soul which he ordinarily identifies with the poetic mood. Thus there is really no contradiction. Poe made a difference between the softened emotion succeeding an outburst of passion and the outburst itself. He would probably not have quarreled with Wordsworth's stipulation that the poet's emotion must be induced by memory, emotion "recollected in tranquility."[68] The true poetic mood, as Poe conceived it, grows out of passion frequently, but composition never begins until the passion is tranquilized or transmuted into a spiritual exaltation.

> True passion is prosaic—homely. Any strong mental emotion stimulates *all* the mental faculties; thus grief the imagination:—but in proportion as the effect is strengthened, the cause surceases. The excited fancy triumphs —the grief is subdued—chastened,—is no longer grief. In this mood we are poetic, and it is clear that a poem now written will be poetic in the exact ratio of its dispassion. . . . When I say, then, that Mrs. Welby's stanzas are good among the class *passionate* (using the term commonly and falsely applied), I mean that her tone is properly subdued, and is not so much the tone of passion, as of a gentle and melancholy regret. . . .[69]

He refers to the "unpassionate emotion" of Bryant's poems as "the limit of true poetical art," and in the same connection he reiterates his theory that "poetry, in elevating, tranquilizes the *soul*."[70]

Coleridge does not exclude passion from poetry; yet there is much in his criticism which might have gone to the making of Poe's theory. Beautiful images, says Coleridge, "become proofs of original genius only as far as they are modified by a predominant passion; or by associated thoughts or images awakened by that passion. . . ."[71] But he is like Poe in denying to passion the creative function: "For the property of passion is not to create, but to set in increased activity."[72] There must be "an interpenetration of passion and of will, of spontaneous impulse and of voluntary purpose."[73] In fact he traces the origin of meter "to the balance in the mind effected by that spontaneous effort which strives to hold in check the workings of passion."[74] Thus a "more than usual state of emotion" is made to harmonize with "more

---

[68] Preface to the second edition of the *Lyrical Ballads* (1800).

[69] Notice of Amelia Welby, *Democratic Review,* Dec. 1844 (*Works,* XI, 277–278).

[70] Notice of William Cullen Bryant, *Godey's Lady's Book,* April 1846 (*Works,* XIII, 131).

[71] *Biographia Literaria,* II, 16.   [72] *Ibid.,* II, 42.

[73] *Ibid.,* II, 50.   [74] *Ibid.,* II, 49.

than usual order."[75] This is what Poe means when he says that poetry may exalt, purify, or control passion so that it is no longer passion, but a mood of spiritual exaltation, a mood in which the soul is excited yet at the same time somehow tranquilized. Coleridge sometimes calls this state spiritual fervor. In discussing Shakespeare's *Venus and Adonis* and the *Lucrece,* he says that the poet "himself unparticipating in the passions" of his characters, is "actuated only by that pleasurable excitement which had resulted from the energetic fervour of his own spirit."[76] Again Coleridge qualifies, somewhat as does Poe, the ordinary meaning of passion: "Now poetry, Mr. Wordsworth truly affirms, does always imply passion: which word must be here understood, in its most general sense, as an excited state of the feelings and faculties."[77] In *Satyrane's Letters* (No. 3) Coleridge gives a transcript of Wordsworth's notes on his conversations with Klopstock, in which we find Wordsworth objecting to passion in Wieland's *Oberon,* saying

> it was unworthy of a man of genius to make the interest of a long poem turn entirely upon animal gratification. He seemed at first disposed to excuse this by saying, that there are different subjects for poetry, and that poets are not willing to be restricted in their choice. I answered, that I thought the *passion* of love as well suited to the purposes of poetry as any other passion; but that it was a cheap way of pleasing to fix the attention of the reader through a long poem on the mere *appetite.*[78]

Wordsworth's distinction here between true passion and base appetite is somewhat suggestive of Poe's distinction between human and divine love. Compare with Poe's remarks on poetry and passion the following comment by Coleridge:

> I think nothing can be added to Milton's definition or rule of poetry,— that it ought to be simple, sensuous, and impassioned; that is to say, single in conception, abounding in sensible images, and informing them all with the spirit of the mind.[79]

It is significant that Coleridge represents Milton as having used the word "impassioned," whereas in fact the word he used was "passionate." He probably avoided the word "passionate," though not consciously, as being too suggestive of those violent emotions which are not suited to poetry. His phrase "spirit of the mind" means here something not very different from what Poe means by the phrase "excitement or elevation of the soul." Thus we not only find a close

---

[75] *Ibid.,* II, 12.   [76] *Ibid.,* II, 15.   [77] *Ibid.,* II, 55–56.
[78] Published with *Biographia Literaria,* II, 177.   [79] *Table Talk,* p. 38.

correspondence between the theories of Poe and Coleridge, but we are further enabled by the comparison to understand more clearly the distinction which Poe undoubtedly made between the "impassioned mood," which is essential to poetical creation, and the "passions," with which poetry has nothing whatever to do.

The other and final idea characteristic of Poe's theory of poetry — that the tone of a poem should be sadness or melancholy—I may dismiss with a word, because there is no reason, so far as I know, to suppose that in it he was influenced by Coleridge. The idea was one, however, common enough among the romantic poets of the day in all countries. If I omit it, I do so not because it is unimportant in Poe's criticism, but merely because it is not pertinent to my immediate purpose.

IV

It seems desirable to consider in a separate section certain ideas and principles which belong to the body of Poe's criticism, but less particularly to his theory of poetry than those already considered. Here his views will be found to diverge more widely from those of Coleridge, and yet there is no sufficient reason to suppose on this account that Poe was not influenced by the opinion of Coleridge. These ideas relate to the function of the critic, the supposed irritability of men of genius, the nature of imagination, and the extent to which poetry may deal with truth.

First, as to the function of the critic. Poe believed that critics were too much inclined to generalize and to praise, whereas they ought to establish certain principles and then apply those principles particularly to the work under survey. Thus he writes:

It appears to us, indeed, that in excessive *generalization* lies one of the leading errors of a criticism employed upon a poetical literature so immature as our own. We rhapsodize rather than discriminate; delighting more in the dictation or discussion of principle, than in its particular and methodical application.[80]

At the very beginning of his career as a reviewer he determined not to deal in generalities and not to advance unsupported assertions.[81] He

[80] Review of the poetry of Rufus Dawes, *Graham's Magazine*, Oct. 1842 (*Works*, XI, 133).

[81] Review of the poems of Drake and Halleck, *Southern Literary Messenger*, April 1836 (*Works*, VIII, 280).

severely condemned the critics who sneer at greatness and make
unsupported censures as "a set of *homunculi,* eager to grow notorious
by the pertinacity of their yelpings at the heels of the distinguished."[82]
He was not averse to censure where censure was due. "When," he
says, "we attend less to 'authority' and more to principles, when we
look *less* at merit and *more* at demerit, (instead of the converse, as
some persons suggest,) we shall then be better critics than we are."[83]
Excellence he considered an axiom, capable of self-manifestation, and
so requiring no elucidation; consequently,

it but remains for the critic to show when, where, and how it fails in
becoming manifest; and, in this showing, it will be the fault of the book
itself if what of beauty it contains be not, at least, placed in the fairest
light. In a word, we may assume . . . that in pointing out frankly the errors
of a work, we do nearly all that is critically necessary in displaying its
merits.[84]

The critic should avoid bias or prejudice; for "the province of a critic
is not that of the state advocate, who argues only on one side, but
rather that of the judge who sums up the case, and of the jury who are
sworn 'a true verdict to give according to the evidence.' "[85]

Coleridge differed with Poe in that he believed the critic should
dwell on the beauties rather than the defects of the work criticized.
Yet he would not omit the defects, for when characteristic they
become the basis for judging the merits of the author. He also agreed
with Poe in demanding that the critic adhere to fixed principles of
criticism in dealing with particular beauties and defects. These opinions are announced in the two following passages:

I know of nothing that surpasses the vileness of deciding on the merits of
a poet or painter—not by characteristic defects, for where there is genius,
these always point to his characteristic beauties—but by accidental failures
or faulty passages. . . .
He who tells me that there are defects in a new work, tells me nothing
which I should not have taken for granted without his information. But he
who points out and elucidates the *beauties* of the original work, does

[82] "A Chapter of Suggestions," in *Works,* XIV, 189.
[83] "Marginalia," in *Works,* XVI, 81.
[84] Review of Dickens' *Barnaby Rudge, Graham's Magazine,* Feb. 1842 (*Works,*
XI, 41).
[85] Review of Bulwer's *Zanoni, Graham's Magazine,* May 1842 (*Works,* XI,
123).

indeed give me interesting information, such as experience would not have authorized me in anticipating.[86]

But I should call that investigation fair and philosophical, in which the critic announces and endeavors to establish the principles, which he holds for the foundation of poetry in general, with the specification of these in their application to the different *classes* of poetry. Having thus prepared his canons of criticism for praise and condemnation, we would proceed to particularize the most striking passages to which he deems them applicable, faithfully noticing the frequent or infrequent recurrence of similar merits or defects, and as faithfully distinguishing what is characteristic from what is accidental or a mere flagging of the wing.[87]

He does not object to censure if it is directed at the work and not at the author.

Every censure, every sarcasm respecting a publication which the critic, with the criticized work before him, can make good, is the critic's right. The writer is authorized to reply, but not to complain.[88]

But if the critic brings in knowledge of the author gained elsewhere, his censure becomes personal injury and is without license.[89] Coleridge believes a review would succeed which should be started "upon a published code of principles, critical, moral, political, and religious"; which should be devoted exclusively to literature; "and which should really give a fair account of what the author *intended* to do, and in his own words, if possible, and in addition, afford one or two fair specimens of the execution. . . ."[90]

It appears that Poe differed from Coleridge in only one important point regarding the function of the critic; namely, his opinion that if the critic points out the defects of a work, its beauties will appear of themselves, which is just the opposite of Coleridge's opinion that we may take the defects for granted, but need to be apprised of the beauties. In the first passage quoted from Coleridge, however, the statement that characteristic defects always point to characteristic beauties virtually corroborates Poe's opinion. Their difference, such as it is, may perhaps be accounted for by the fact that Poe spoke as editor as well as critic, and as one who felt himself responsible for protecting a relatively uncultured public from imposition by weak but presumptuous writers.

[86] *Biographia Literaria*, I, 44.   [87] *Ibid.*, II, 85.   [88] *Ibid.*, II, 86–87.
[89] *Ibid.*, II, 87.   [90] *Table Talk*, p. 95.

Both Poe and Coleridge have a good deal to say about the irritability, real or supposed, of men of genius, particularly poets. Thus Poe:

That poets (using the word comprehensively, as including artists in general) are a *genus irritabile,* is well understood; but the *why,* seems not to be commonly seen. An artist *is* an artist only by dint of his exquisite sense of Beauty—a sense affording him rapturous enjoyment, but at the same time implying, or involving, an equally exquisite sense of deformity or disproportion. Thus a wrong—an injustice—done a poet, excites him to a degree which, to ordinary apprehension, appears disproportionate with the wrong. Poets *see* injustice—*never* where it does not exist—but very often where the unpoetical see no injustice whatever. Thus the poetical irritability has no reference to "temper" in the vulgar sense, but merely to a more than usual clear-sightedness in respect to Wrong:—this clear-sightedness being nothing more than a corollary from the vivid perception of Right— of justice—of proportion—in a word, of το καλον. But one thing is clear —that the man who is not "irritable," (to the ordinary apprehension,) is *no poet.*[91]

Poets, then, are irritable because of their extraordinary sensitiveness to deformity and injustice. The reason for this hypersensitiveness, Poe goes on to explain, lies in the inordinate power of their mental faculties existing in absolute proportion. The abnormal predominance of one faculty over all others is not an evidence of genius, but "a result of mental disease or rather, of organic malformation of mind." He continues thus:

Not only will such "genius" fail, if turned aside from the path indicated by its predominant faculty; but, even when pursuing this path—when producing those works in which, certainly, it is *best* calculated to succeed —will give unmistakable indications of *unsoundness,* in respect to general intellect. Hence, indeed, arises the just idea that "great wit to madness nearly is allied."

I say "just idea"; for by "great wit," in this case, the poet intends precisely the pseudo-genius to which I refer. The true genius, on the other hand, is necessarily, if not universal in its manifestations, at least capable of universality.[92]

Further, he says that the

absolute proportion spoken of, when applied to inordinate mental power, gives, as a result, the appreciation of Beauty and a horror of Deformity which we call sensibility, together with that intense vitality, which is implied when we speak of "Energy" or "Passion."[93]

[91] "Fifty Suggestions," in *Works,* XIV, 175–176.   [92] *Ibid.,* 176–177.
[93] *Ibid.,* 178.

Coleridge, who wrote an entire chapter on the subject, attempts to prove the injustice of the tendency of the public to "apply to all poets the old sarcasm of Horace upon the scribblers of his time: '*Genus irritabile vatum.*' "[94] The supposed men of genius whose actions provoke the just charge of irritability, he thinks, are really men of inferior talent disappointed in their ambition to acquire the reputation of genius. These are not men of sensibility, however; for—and in this he agrees with Poe—"sensibility, indeed, both quick and deep, is not only a characteristic feature, but may be deemed a component part, of genius."[95] But Coleridge differs from Poe in that he does not believe this quick sensibility makes men of genius more than others resentful of personal injustice; for "men of the greatest genius, as far as we can judge from their own works or from the accounts of their contemporaries, appear to have been of calm and tranquil temper, in all that related to themselves."[96] He remarks on Chaucer's cheerfulness and on Shakespeare's "evenness and sweetness of temper."[97] Nowhere in Spenser does he find "the least trace of irritability," and "the same calmness, and even greater self-possession, may be affirmed of Milton, as far as his poems and poetic character are concerned."[98] He considers it a characteristic of the sensibility of genius that it "is excited by any other cause more powerfully than by its own personal interests," the reason being that the man of genius lives most in the ideal world.[99] "And yet, should he perchance have occasion to repel some false charge, or to rectify some erroneous censure, nothing is more common than for the many to mistake the general liveliness of his manner and language, whatever is the subject, for the effects of peculiar irritation from its accidental relation to himself."[100] To this passage he appends the following interesting footnote:

This is one instance, among many, of deception by the telling the half of a fact, and omitting the other half, when it is from their mutual counteraction and neutralization that the whole truth arises, as a *tertium aliquid* different from either. Thus in Dryden's famous line "Great wit" (which here means genius) "to madness sure is near allied." Now as far as the profound sensibility, which is doubtless one of the components of genius, were alone considered, single and unbalanced, it might be fairly described as exposing the individual to a greater chance of mental derangement; but then a more than usual rapidity of association, a more than usual power of passing from thought to thought, and image to image, is a component

[94] *Biographia Literaria*, I, 19.   [95] *Ibid.*, I, 30.   [96] *Ibid.*, I, 21.
[97] *Ibid.*, I, 21.   [98] *Ibid.*, I, 23.   [99] *Ibid.*, I, 30.   [100] *Ibid.*, I, 30.

equally essential; and in the due modification of each by the other the genius itself consists . . .

It looks as if Poe had read Coleridge's chapter on the supposed irritability of genius, and had accepted it all except that part which states that men of great genius are never irritable. He then sought to find a justifiable basis for the poet's irritability, and he found it in the characteristic of sensibility. The only important difference between the two critics, therefore, is that whereas Coleridge considered sensibility a component part of genius, Poe held it to be synonymous with genius itself. They agree in the theory that the faculties of true genius are balanced, or proportionate, but are not wholly at one as to what these faculties are. They also agree in the corollary, that the inordinate development of a single faculty is mental disease or derangement, not genius.

Prescott points out that Poe derived from Coleridge the distinction between fancy and imagination, and "attempted to analyze and clarify it."[101] I agree with the first part of this opinion, but not altogether with the last part, which implies that Poe approved Coleridge's distinction. As a matter of fact, he opposed it, sought to refute it, and set up various theories in its place. In the end, however, he agreed substantially with Coleridge in all except a few terms.

In an early definition of "poesy," Poe includes this sentence, making it a separate paragraph for emphasis: "Imagination is its soul."[102] As a footnote to this statement, he adds:

> Imagination is, possibly in man, a lesser degree of the creative power in God. What the Deity imagines *is*, but *was not* before. What man imagines, *is*, but *was* also. The mind of man cannot imagine what *is not*.

He defines "the Poetic Sentiment" as "Ideality, Imagination, or the creative ability."[103] The first open disagreement with Coleridge occurs four years afterwards in a lengthy discussion of the poems of Moore, of which the following passage must be quoted at length:

> "The fancy," says the author of the "Ancient Mariner," in his *Biographia Literaria*, "the fancy combines, the imagination creates." And this was intended, and has been received, as a distinction. If so at all, it is one without a difference; without even a difference of *degree*. The fancy as

---

[101] P. xxxii.
[102] Review of the poems of Drake and Halleck, *Southern Literary Messenger*, April 1836 (*Works*, VIII, 283).
[103] *Ibid.*, 295.

nearly creates as the imagination; and neither creates in any respect. All novel conceptions are merely unusual combinations. The mind of man can imagine nothing which has not really existed. . . . It will be said, perhaps, that we can imagine a *griffin*, and that a griffin does not exist. Not the griffin certainly, but its component parts. It is a mere compendium of known limbs and features—of known qualities. Thus with all which seems to be *new*—which appears to be a *creation* of intellect. It is resoluble into the old. The wildest and most vigorous effort of mind cannot stand the test of this analysis.[104]

He then attempts a distinction of his own, according to which an imaginative work, unlike a work of the fancy, is one in which "the main conception springs immediately, *or thus apparently springs*, from the brain of the poet, enveloped in the moral sentiments of grace, of colour, of motion—of the beautiful, of the mystical, of the august— in short, of the ideal." He continues by way of conclusion:

> The truth is that the just distinction between the fancy and the imagina- tion (and which is still but a distinction *of degree*) is involved in the consideration of the *mystic*. We give this as an idea of our own, altogether. We have no authority for our opinion—but do not the less firmly hold it. The term *mystic* is here employed in the sense of Augustus William Schlegel, and of most other German critics. It is applied by them to that class of composition in which there lies beneath the transparent upper current of meaning an under or *suggestive* one. What we vaguely term the *moral* of any sentiment is its mystic or secondary expression.[105]

This new opinion in which the "mystic" was made to explain the imagination was apparently soon abandoned, for he does not insist on it afterwards, but continues to use Coleridge's terms. He calls the characters of Dickens' *Old Curiosity Shop* true *creations*, not carica- tures; they belong "to the most august regions of the *Ideal*." And then he adds: "In truth, the great feature of the 'Curiosity Shop' is its chaste, vigorous, and glorious *imagination*."[106] In another place he says that "in respect to compositions which have been really received as poems, the *imaginative*, or, more popularly, the creative portions *alone* have ensured them to be so received."[107] In the same connection, after

[104] Review of Moore's *Alciphron: A Poem, Burton's Gentleman's Magazine*, Jan. 1840 (*Works*, X, 61–62).

[105] *Ibid.*, 65.

[106] Review of *The Old Curiosity Shop, Graham's Magazine*, May 1841 (*Works*, X, 153).

[107] Review of Longfellow's *Ballads and Other Poems, Graham's Magazine*, April 1842 (*Works*, XI, 72).

explaining that the first element of poesy is the thirst for supernal beauty, he says:

Its second element is the attempt to satisfy this thirst by *novel* combinations, *of those combinations which our predecessors, toiling in chase of the same phantom, have already set in order.* We thus clearly deduce the *novelty,* the *originality,* the *invention,* the *imagination,* or lastly the *creation* of Beauty, (for the terms as here employed are synonymous) as the essence of all poesy. . . .

"Invention," however, or "imagination," is by far more commonly insisted upon. The word ποιησις itself (creation) speaks volumes upon the point.[108]

Poe's next attempt to formulate a distinction between fancy and imagination appears in a long comparison and analysis of imagination, fancy, fantasy, and humor, which, he says, "have in common the elements Combination and Novelty." He continues thus:

The imagination is the artist of the four. From novel arrangements of old forms which present themselves to it, it selects only such as are harmonious;—the result, of course, is *beauty* itself—using the term in its most extended sense, as inclusive of the sublime. The pure Imagination chooses, *from either beauty or deformity,* only the most combinable things hitherto uncombined; the compound as a general rule, partaking (in character) of sublimity or beauty, in the ratio of the respective sublimity or beauty of the things combined—which are themselves still to be considered as atomic— that is to say, as previous combinations. But, as often analogously happens in physical chemistry, so not unfrequently does it occur in this chemistry of the intellect, that the admixture of two elements will result in a something that shall have nothing of the quality of one of them—or even nothing of the qualities of either. The range of Imagination is therefore, unlimited. Its materials extend throughout the Universe. Even out of deformities it fabricates that Beauty which is at once its sole object and its inevitable test. . . . It is this thorough harmony of an imaginative work which so often causes it to be undervalued by the undiscriminating, through the character of *obviousness* which is superinduced. We are apt to find ourselves asking *"why is it* that these combinations have never been imagined before?"[109]

In the "Marginalia" Poe repeats this passage with minor verbal changes.[110]

For the sake of a fair comparison it will be necessary to quote

[108] *Ibid.,* 73–74.

[109] Review of Willis's *American Prose Writers, Broadway Journal,* Jan. 18, 1845 (*Works,* XII, 37–39).

[110] "Marginalia," XII, *Southern Literary Messenger,* April 1849 (*Works,* XVI, 155–156).

several passages from the writings of Coleridge. In an article first published with Southey's *Omniana* (1812) he names among the human faculties "the imagination, or shaping and modifying power; the fancy, or the aggregative and associative power."[111] The statement of Coleridge's theory which Poe alluded to is probably the following:

The imagination then I consider either as primary, or secondary. The primary imagination I hold to be the living power and prime agent of all human perception, and as a repetition in the finite mind of the eternal act of creation in the infinite I Am. The secondary I consider as an echo of the former, co-existing with the conscious will, yet still as identical with the primary in the kind of its agency, and differing only in degree, and in the mode of its operation. It dissolves, diffuses, dissipates, in order to recreate; or where this process is rendered impossible, yet still, at all events, it struggles to idealize and to unify. It is essentially *vital,* even as all objects (as objects) are essentially fixed and dead.

Fancy, on the contrary, has no other counters to play with, but fixities and definites. The Fancy is indeed no other than a mode of memory emancipated from the order of time and space; and blended with, and modified by that empirical phenomenon of the will, which we express by the word choice. But equally with the ordinary memory, it must receive all its materials ready made from the law of association.[112]

The distinction here made between the primary and the secondary imagination occurs nowhere else in Coleridge's writings; it may therefore be concluded, I think, that it was not very important. Most of his other definitions conform to the definition here made of the secondary imagination. He further describes the imagination as a "synthetic" power.

This power, first put in action by the will and understanding, and retained under their irremissive, though gentle and unnoticed, control (*laxis effertur habenis*) reveals itself in the balance or reconciliation of opposite or discordant qualities: of sameness, with difference; of the general, with the concrete; the idea, with the image; the individual, with the representative; the sense of novelty and freshness, with old and familiar objects; a more than usual state of emotion, with more than usual order; judgment ever awake and steady self-possession, with enthusiasm and feeling profound or vehement; and while it blends and harmonizes the natural and the artificial, still subordinates art to nature; the manner to the matter; and our admiration of the poet to our sympathy with the poetry.[113]

[111] *Omniana* (bound with *Table Talk*), p. 383. The passage is repeated in *Biographia Literaria,* I, 193.
[112] *Biographia Literaria,* I, 202.   [113] *Ibid.,* II, 12.

Summing up this part of his discussion, he says:

Finally, good sense is the body of poetic genius, fancy its drapery, motion its life, and imagination the soul that is every where, and in each; and forms all into one graceful and intelligent whole.[114]

Elsewhere he calls imagination "that reconciling and mediatory power, which incorporating the reason in images of the sense . . . gives birth to a system of symbols, harmonious in themselves, and consubstantial with the truths of which they are the conductors."[115] To understand this definition we must know that his distinction between reason and understanding is somewhat like that between imagination and fancy. The understanding he calls "the science of phenomena"; the reason, "the science of the universal, having the ideas of oneness and allness as its two elements or primary factors."[116] Finally he says:

The Fancy brings together images which have no connection natural or moral, but are yoked together by the poet by means of some accidental coincidence. . . . The Imagination modifies images, and gives unity to variety; it sees all things in one, *il piu nell' uno*.[117]

A casual examination of these passages reveals that Poe and Coleridge are agreed on the following points at least:

1. Imagination is the soul of poetry.
2. It harmonizes diverse matters and gives unity to variety.
3. It is analogous to the creative power of God.
4. Of two elements known and unlike it can create a third element different from either.

They differ, or seem to differ, in one point only: the meaning of the word "create." Coleridge says the imagination dissolves and diffuses in order to recreate; it creates, therefore, in the sense of bringing order out of chaos. Poe says creation by the imagination is merely the combination of whole parts of known objects in a new way. But in reality Poe means by combination exactly what Coleridge means by creation. For if one asks how small these combinable parts may be, the reply is obviously that they may be as small in their world, the ideal, as the atom in the physical world. He actually mentions physical chemistry as an aid to the understanding of imaginative creation, which he calls the "chemistry of the intellect." In the light of this

---

[114] *Ibid.*, II, 13.
[115] *The Statesman's Manual: A Lay Sermon* (London, 1816), p. 35.
[116] *Ibid.*, Appendix C, pp. v–vi.   [117] *Table Talk*, p. 291.

analogy his example of the griffin as an object created imaginatively is absurd. As a matter of fact, I feel confident that he agreed with Coleridge in every respect; but, impelled by the desire to be original, and painfully conscious of his obligation to Coleridge, he sought to avoid the obligation by opposing him. To this end he first conceived the theory that the idea of the mystic is involved in that of the imagination, but gave that up. It was only then that he began to quibble over the words "creation" and "combination." He often used the word "create" in Coleridge's sense, and undoubtedly applied Coleridge's theory, not his own, in all his best poems.

Poe was vigorously and consistently opposed to didacticism in poetry. His love of sweeping generalization and of striking metaphor sometimes betrayed him, however, into saying more than he really intended, as it did, for example, in the famous phrase about "the obstinate oils and waters of Poetry and Truth," often repeated. His ambiguity consists in his using the word "truth" in a special sense, yet permitting the reader to suppose it used in a general sense. In the "Letter to B__" he opposes "the heresy of what is called very foolishly, the Lake School," but thinks it would be a work of supererogation to refute their doctrine. This doctrine is doubtless the same that afterwards in "The Poetic Principle" he attacks as "the heresy of *The Didactic*," which he identifies with the doctrine that "the ultimate object of all Poetry is Truth."[118] He makes no clear distinction between philosophical poetry, such as that of Wordsworth, and poetry that is frankly didactic. Hence in the same essay he adopts Coleridge's definition of the *immediate* object of poetry as pleasure, but condemns him (as a member of the Lake School) as a philosophical poet. Sooner or later he must have understood the significance of the word "immediate" in Coleridge's sentence, as apparently he did not in 1831, for Coleridge, and Wordsworth too, for that matter, found no difficulty in making truth an ultimate object in poetry while admitting that the immediate aim is pleasure. One of the evidences of poetic genius mentioned in the *Biographia Literaria* is "depth and energy of thought." "No man," Coleridge says, "was ever yet a great poet, without being at the same time a profound philosopher. For poetry is the blossom and the fragrancy of all human knowledge, human thoughts, human passions, emotions, language."[119] But the poet's way of presenting truth is not the way of the scientist or mathematician.

[118] *Works*, XIV, 271.   [119] P. 155.

Comparing poetry with geometry in its relation to truth, he says, "The chief differences are, that in geometry it is the universal truth itself which is uppermost in the consciousness, in poetry the individual form in which the Truth is clothed."[120] In other words, poetry conveys truth by clothing it in forms or images, not by abstract precepts and principles.

Poe's view, rightly understood, is essentially the same. On the very page with the phrase referred to above about "the obstinate oils and waters of Poetry and Truth," we find the following:

Just as conscience, or the moral sense, recognizes duty; just as the intellect deals with truth; so is it the part of taste alone to inform us of BEAUTY. And Poesy is the handmaiden but of Taste. Yet we would not be misunderstood. This handmaiden is not forbidden to moralize—in her own fashion. She is not forbidden to depict—but to reason and preach, of virtue. As, of this latter, conscience recognizes the obligation, so intellect teaches the expediency, while taste contents herself with displaying the beauty: waging war with vice merely on the ground of its inconsistency with fitness, harmony, proportion—in a word with το καλον.[121]

Thus poetry becomes didactic, and so objectionable, only when it seeks to convey truth by preaching or reasoning. Not only may poetry depict truth; it may also insinuate or suggest truth. Poe objects to Hawthorne's story "The Minister's Black Veil" because "the *obvious* meaning of this article will be found to smother its insinuated one."[122] In the following passage he distinguishes between pure didacticism and poetic suggestion:

The defects observable in the "Legend of Brittany" are, chiefly, conse-quent upon the error of *didacticism*. After every few words of narration, comes a page of morality. Not that the morality, *here*—not that the reflections deduced from the incidents, are peculiarly exceptionable, but that they are too obviously, intrusively, and artificially introduced. The story might have been rendered more *unique*, and altogether more in consonance with the true poetic sentiment, by suffering the morality to be *suggested*; as it is, for example, in the "Old Curiosity Shop," of Dickens— or in that superb *poem*, the "Undine" of De la Motte Fouqué.[123]

[120] *Satyrane's Letters*, No. 2; *Biographia Literaria*, II, 159.
[121] Review of Longfellow's *Ballads and Other Poems*, *Graham's Magazine*, April 1842 (*Works*, XII, 70).
[122] Review of *Twice-Told Tales*, *Graham's Magazine*, May 1842 (*Works*, XI, 111).
[123] Review of Lowell's *Poems*, *Graham's Magazine*, March 1844 (*Works*, XI, 247).

Other references to *Undine* will further explain Poe's meaning. "How thoroughly—how radically—how wonderfully," he exclaims, "has 'Undine' been misunderstood! Beneath its obvious meaning there runs an under-current, simple, quite intelligible, artistically managed, and richly philosophical."[124] Again he writes:

> Of allegory properly handled, judiciously subdued, seen only as a shadow or by suggestive glimpses, and making its nearest approach to truth in a not obtrusive and therefore not unpleasant *appositeness*, the "Undine" of De La Motte Fouqué is the best, and undoubtedly a very remarkable specimen.[125]

Poe would agree with Coleridge that depth and energy of thought are an aid to the poet, and if not antagonized he would admit, too, I believe, that truth in the higher, ideal sense of the word, is of concern to the poet. But he would perhaps limit more strictly than Coleridge the means to be used in conveying truth in poetry. Both would exclude any method which would jeopardize the immediate aim of poetry, which is to give pleasure.

V

I ought not to bring this discussion to an end without taking some notice of Poe's speculative thought and its relation to that of Coleridge. They were alike in the variety of their interests, which included astronomy, electricity, mesmerism, phrenology, and other subjects from the field of science and pseudo-science. I cannot say how much Poe's interest in such subjects was influenced especially by that of Coleridge, because they were commented on everywhere in the public prints of the time. Poe was more enthusiastic and sought optimistically to find practical uses for these new aids to knowledge, whereas Coleridge's interest·was merely that of the philosopher. "Phrenology,"

---

[124] *Marginalia, Democratic Review,* Dec. 1844 (*Works,* XVI, 48).

[125] Notice of Nathaniel Hawthorne, *Godey's Lady's Book,* Nov. 1847 (*Works,* XIII, 148–149).

In a review of *Undine: A Miniature Romance,* in *Burton's Gentleman's Magazine,* Sept. 1839, he calls it "the finest romance in existence"; he also says, "What can be more divine than the character of the soulless Undine?" (*Works,* X, 37–39). See also "Marginalia," XVI, 51, for a repetition of this question. Poe may have been influenced here by Coleridge's opinion. "Undine," says Coleridge, "is a most exquisite work. . . . Undine's character, before she receives a soul, is marvellously beautiful" (*Table Talk,* p. 88).

Poe asserts, "is no longer to be laughed at . . . It has assumed the majesty of a science; and, as a science, ranks among the most important which can engage the attention of thinking beings."[126] He thinks it unaccountable that "a scholar and editor (who should be, if he be not, a man of metaphysical science)" should attempt to ridicule phrenology.[127] "Not the least service," he says, "which hereafter, mankind will owe to *Phrenology*, may, perhaps, be recognized in an analysis of the real principles, and a digest of the resulting laws of taste."[128] He defines the "sentiment of the beautiful" as "that sense which phrenology has attempted to embody in its organ of ideality."[129] Coleridge's head, according to Poe, "gave no great phrenological tokens of Ideality, while the organs of Causality and Comparison were singularly developed."[130] Perhaps Poe was influenced by the opinion of the phrenologist Spurzheim, who, as Coleridge's nephew records, "denied any *Ideality*, and awarded an unusual share of *Locality*, to the majestic silver-haired head of my dear uncle and father-in-law."[131]

Coleridge was interested in phrenology, but was never deceived into accepting it as a true science. He says:

Craniology is worth some consideration, although it is merely in its rudiments and guesses yet. But all the coincidences which have been observed could scarcely be by accident. The confusion and absurdity, however, will be endless until some names or proper terms are discovered for the organs, which are not taken from their mental application or significancy. The forepart of the head is generally given up to the higher intellectual powers; the hinder part to the sensual emotions.[132]

Again he says:

Spurzheim is a good man, and I like him; but he is dense, and the most ignorant German I ever knew. If he had been content with stating certain remarkable coincidences between the moral qualities and the configuration of the skull, it would have been well; but when he began to map out the cranium dogmatically, he fell into infinite absurdities.[133]

[126] Review of *Phrenology, and the Moral Influence of Phrenology*, by Mrs. L. Miles, *Southern Literary Messenger*, March 1836 (*Works*, VIII, 252).

[127] Review of *Didactics—Social, Literary, and Political*, by Robert Walsh, *Southern Literary Messenger*, May 1836 (*Works*, VIII, 329).

[128] Review of Longfellow's *Ballads and Other Poems*, *Graham's Magazine*, April 1842 (*Works*, XI, 65).

[129] Review of Horne's *Orion*, *Graham's Magazine*, March 1844 (*Works*, XI, 256).

[130] Review of the poems of Drake and Halleck, *Southern Literary Messenger*, April 1836 (*Works*, VIII, 285).

[131] *Table Talk*, p. 50 (note).   [132] *Ibid.*, p. 50.   [133] *Ibid.*, p. 104.

Yet he speaks of certain phrenological peculiarities of an acquaintance as having inclined him "to suspect, for the first time, that there may be some truth in the Spurzheimian scheme."[134]

Poe was fond of speculating upon the "power of words," and the effect of death on the mind of man. In some of his speculative tales he develops the idea that, since "no thought can perish," since "all motion, of whatever nature, creates," and since "the source of all motion is thought"—therefore thought is the great creative power, whether in God or man. Agathos points to a star which by the power of passionate words he had created.[135] When death releases the mind from the limitations of earth he imagined that it would approach in knowledge the perfection of God, and be able to perceive "the speculative Future merged in the august and certain Present."[136] Poe might have been influenced by an incident recorded in the *Biographia Literaria*. After relating the history of an illiterate young German woman who in a nervous fever had repeated numerous Latin, Greek, and Hebrew sentences which years before she had casually overheard as they were read by a Protestant minister in whose home she was working, Coleridge remarks that it is probable

that all thoughts are in themselves imperishable; and, that if the intelligent faculty should be rendered more comprehensive, it would require only a different and apportioned organization, *the body celestial* instead of *the body terrestrial*, to bring before every human soul the collective experience of its whole past existence.[137]

The characters in the two stories of Poe's just referred to were spiritual beings released from their terrestrial bodies and moving through starry space as celestial bodies, in accordance with Coleridge's hypothesis.

Although Poe was not a philosopher, and sometimes spoke with contempt of metaphysics, particularly that aspect of metaphysics known in New England as Transcendentalism, yet he has written passages here and there which have a decided transcendental flavor. His early opposition to Wordsworth because of the metaphysical nature of his poetry is not representative of his mature opinion. Five years afterwards he wrote the following passage:

We do not hesitate to say that a man highly endowed with the powers of Causality—that is to say, a man of metaphysical acumen—will, even with a

---

[134] *Ibid.*, p. 105 (note).
[135] "The Power of Words" (1844), in *Works*, VI, 144.
[136] "The Conversation of Eiros and Charmion" (1839), in *Works*, IV, 2.
[137] I, 79–80.

very deficient share of Ideality, compose a finer poem (if we test it, as we should, by its measure of exciting the Poetic Sentiment) than one who, without such metaphysical acumen, shall be gifted, in the most extraordinary degree, with the faculty of Ideality.[138]

He mentions Coleridge as such a man. He denies that "the calculating faculties are at war with the ideal."[139] Contrasting the metaphysics of Donne and Cowley with the metaphysics of Wordsworth and Coleridge, he says:

With the two former ethics were the end—with the two latter the means. The poet of the "Creation" wished by highly artificial verse, to inculcate what he supposed to be moral truth—the poet of the "Ancient Mariner" to infuse the Poetic Sentiment through channels suggested by analysis.[140]

Poe uses the word "metaphysics" here, as often elsewhere, to mean an analytical and logical process—the process by which he composed "The Raven." But there was in him, also, something of the transcendentalism which he so disliked in the New England philosophy. He was led into it, perhaps unaware, by the exalted conception of the imaginative power that he had derived from Coleridge. Thus he writes:

That the imagination has not been unjustly ranked as supreme among the mental faculties, appears from the intense consciousness, on the part of the imaginative man, that the faculty in question brings his soul often to a glimpse of things supernal and eternal—to the very verge of the *great secrets*. There are moments, indeed, in which he perceives the faint perfumes, and hears the melodies of a happier world. Some of the most profound knowledge—perhaps all *very* profound knowledge—has originated from a highly stimulated imagination. Great intellects *guess* well. The laws of Kepler were, professedly, *guesses*.[141]

I understand Poe to mean simply that the poet makes use of two complementary faculties: the intuitional or imaginative faculty, through which he is made aware of the beauty latent in nature

---

[138] Review of the poems of Drake and Halleck, *Southern Literary Messenger*, April 1836 (*Works*, VIII, 284).

[139] "Mr. Griswold and the Poets," *Boston Miscellany*, Nov. 1842 (*Works*, XI, 148).

[140] Review of *The Book of Gems*, *Broadway Journal*, May 17, 1845 (*Works*, XII, 140).

[141] "A Chapter of Suggestions," *The Opal*, 1845, published among the "Essays and Miscellanies" (*Works*, XIV, 187).

because it harmonizes with the beauty inherent in his own soul; and
the logical or metaphysical faculty, by means of which he is enabled
to render objective the beauty which he feels, and so to awake in
others a sentiment akin to his own. Conversely, when "through the
attainment of a truth, we are led to perceive a harmony where none
was apparent before, we experience, at once, the true poetical effect. . . ."[142] Thus he arrives ultimately to the full acceptance of truth
as a proper and even a necessary correlative of poetry. His final word
on the subject appears in *Eureka:*

And, in fact, the sense of the symmetrical is an instinct which may be
depended upon with an almost blindfold reliance. It is the poetical essence
of the Universe—*of the Universe* which, in the supremeness of its symmetry, is but the most sublime of poems. Now symmetry and consistency are
convertible terms:—thus Poetry and Truth are one. A thing is consistent in
the ratio of its truth—true in the ratio of its consistency. *A perfect
consistency, I repeat, can be nothing but an absolute truth.* We may take
for granted, then, that man cannot long or widely err, if he suffer himself to
be guided by his poetical, which I have maintained to be his truthful, in
being his symmetrical, instinct.[143]

This intuitional or imaginative faculty is not peculiar to poets, but is
the evidence of great intellect of whatever kind. This is what Poe
meant by saying "great intellects *guess* well." The combination of the
imaginative and logical faculties functioning in different minds is
illustrated in the discoveries of Kepler and Newton. The laws of
planetary movement, he says, were "*guessed* by the imaginative Kepler, and but subsequently demonstrated and accounted for by the
patient and mathematical Newton."[144]

   Coleridge connected the imagination with the reasoning faculty. He
defines imagination as

that reconciling and mediatory power, which incorporating the reason in
images of the sense, and organizing (as it were) the flux of the senses by
the permanence and self-circling energies of the reason, gives birth to a
system of symbols, harmonious in themselves, and consubstantial with the
truths of which they are the conductors.[145]

Coleridge's estimate of the relative functions of Kepler and Newton in
the discovery of gravitation and related laws is so nearly identical

---

[142] "The Poetic Principle," in *Works*, XIV, 290.   [143] *Works*, XVI, 302.
[144] *Ibid.*, 279.   [145] *The Statesman's Manual: A Lay Sermon*, p. 38.

with Poe's that I suspect Poe of having been intimately acquainted with it. Coleridge says in one place:

Galileo was a great genius, and so was Newton; but it would take two or three Galileos and Newtons to make one Kepler. It is in the order of Providence, that the inventive, generative, constitutive mind—the Kepler —should come first; and then that the patient and collective mind—the Newton—should follow, and elaborate the pregnant queries and illumining guesses of the former. The laws of the planetary system are, in fact, due to Kepler. There is not a more glorious achievement of scientific genius upon record, than Kepler's guesses, prophecies, and ultimate apprehension of the law of the mean distances of the planets as connected with the periods of their revolutions round the sun.[146]

From what has been already said it is evident that both Poe and Coleridge were attached to the transcendental doctrine that intuition is a means to truth, associating it with imagination. In a facetious letter at the beginning of *Eureka,* purporting "to have been written in the year *two* thousand eight hundred and forty-eight," Poe ridicules the idea that deductive and inductive reasoning, "the Aristotelian and Baconian roads are, and of right ought to be, the sole possible avenues to knowledge."[147] Again, he complains that these are "two narrow and crooked paths—the one of creeping and the other of crawling—to which, in their ignorant perversity, they have dared to confine the Soul—the Soul which loves nothing so well as to soar in those regions of illimitable intuition which are utterly incognizant of *'path'*."[148] In a Foreword Poe dedicates *Eureka* "to the dreamers and those who put faith in dreams as in the only realities," with the confident statement, *"What I here propound is true."*

I do not propose to go into Coleridge's "Dynamic Philosophy," which doubtless was largely borrowed. If it had any influence on Poe, and I think it had, the influence was Coleridge's, however, and not Schelling's or Plato's. The following ideas will suggest how it is related to Poe's fragmentary ideas. According to Coleridge, "truth is the correlative to being." Truth may be mediate (derived from other truths), or immediate and original. We must seek for "some absolute

---

[146] *Table Talk,* pp. 114–115. For other references to Kepler, see *The Friend* (London, 1865), p. 321; *Letters, Conversations, and Recollections of S. T. Coleridge,* ed. Thos. Allsop (New York, 1836), p. 81; and *Hints Towards the Formation of a More Comprehensive Theory of Life* (Philadelphia, 1848), p. 31. Poe mentions Kepler frequently. Tycho Brahe is also mentioned by Coleridge in *The Friend,* p. 363, and of course figures prominently in Poe's "Al Aaraaf."
[147] *Eureka,* in *Works,* XVI, 189.   [148] *Ibid.,* p. 195.

truth . . . self-grounded, unconditional," to which other truths may be referred. He finds this in the identity of subject and object, which is the self, or self-consciousness. His argument is, "*Sum*, I am; *sum quia sum; sum quia Deus est,* or *sum quia in Deo sum.*" Continuing, he says: "If therefore this be the one only immediate truth, in the certainty of which the reality of our collective knowledge is grounded, it must follow that the spirit in all the objects which it views, views only itself. If this could be proved, the immediate reality of all intuitive knowledge would be assured."[149] He arrives finally at the conclusion that "intelligence is a self-development," and reduces it, for philosophic construction, to "the idea of an indestructible power with two opposite and counteracting forces, which by a metaphor borrowed from astronomy, we may call the centrifugal and centripedal [*sic*]." He then adds: "It will be hereafter my business to construct by a series of intuitions the progressive schemes that must follow from such a power with such forces, till I arrive at the fulness of the human intelligence."[150] From this point he goes on to discuss the nature of imagination, which, as he says, is the creative power of the human mind which corresponds to the creative power of God. The promise of a work based on intuition was fulfilled in an essay, published in 1848, called *Hints Towards a More Comprehensive Theory of Life,* which is, in fact, an account of the creative or "imaginative" power of the "infinite I Am" functioning in the natural world.

There remains but one problem and I shall have finished. This is the problem of the source or sources of Poe's *Eureka.* He may have developed the theory explained in that essay from various studies in the astronomical speculation and discovery of Laplace and others. But his nebular hypothesis was much more far reaching than that of the astronomers, and had, moreover, a distinctly "transcendental" aspect. I shall here make no general investigation of the sources of *Eureka,* contenting myself with pointing out certain striking resemblances between its theories and those of Coleridge. As early as 1841 Poe shows special interest in the problem of cosmogony. The only irrefutable argument for the soul's immortality, he says at this time, —

or rather, the only conclusive proof of man's alternate dissolution and rejuvenescence *ad infinitum*—is to be found in analogies deduced from the modern established theory of the nebular cosmogony.[151]

---

[149] *Biographia Literaria,* I, 180–183.   [150] *Ibid.,* I, 188.
[151] Review of Macaulay's *Critical and Miscellaneous Essays, Graham's Magazine,* June 1841 (*Works,* X, 159–160).

The following passage from a letter to Lowell, July 2, 1844, further develops the idea suggested in the review:

Matter without atom or division is God, and its activity is the thought of God, and the individualizing of this activity forms intelligent creatures. It thus comes about that man is individualized by his material body; that when we die we merely undergo a change. The worm becomes the butterfly. The stars are the homes of such beings as death produces among us; and the unbodied individual, with power of motion, action, and knowledge, is visible to a sleepwaker.[152]

These ideas are set forth at length in "Mesmeric Revelation" (1844), which for a time he considered more important than "The Fall of the House of Usher."[153]

Eureka is Poe's attempt to explain the universe, material and spiritual. It is a queer mixture of mathematical calculation and transcendental speculation. He begins his treatise, as I have said, with the assertion that intuition is a surer road to truth than either induction or deduction. His theory may be briefly summarized as follows. There are two contending forces in the universe, attraction, or gravitation, and repulsion, or electricity. Gravitation is the physical principle, and electricity is the spiritual principle. Matter exists only by reason of the conflict of these two forces, and through matter spirit is individualized, reaching its highest development in the conscious intelligence of man. Originally God existed in spirit only and individually. Now He exists variously in the diffused matter and spirit of the universe. The diffusion originates in the Thought of God; but when diffusion is completed, God's Thought is withdrawn. Then commences the reaction, and the consequent conflict of the powers of attraction and repulsion.

The thought of God is to be understood as originating the Diffusion—as proceeding with it—as regulating it—and, finally, as being withdrawn from it upon its completion. *Then* commences Reaction, and through Reaction, "Principle," as we employ the word. It will be advisable, however, to limit the application of this word to the two *immediate* results of the discontinuance of the Divine Volition—that is, to the two agents, *Attraction* and *Repulsion*.[154]

---

[152] *Works*, XVII, 182–184.
[153] See Poe's letter to Griswold, Feb. 24, 1845 (*Works*, XVII, 201).
[154] *Eureka*, in *Works*, XVI, 238.

Eventually, by its tendency to draw to a single center, matter and spirit will be perfectly unified again.

The absolutely consolidated globe of globes would be *objectless*,—therefore not for a moment could it continue to exist. Matter, created for an end, would unquestionably, on fulfilment of that end, be matter no longer. Let us endeavor to understand that it would disappear, and that God would remain all in all.[155]

Conflict having ceased, with the consequent annihilation of matter as such, God, now existing variously as matter and spirit, will be again as He was at first, purely spiritual and individual—that is to say, Unity.

God—the material *and* spiritual God—*now* exists solely in the diffused Matter and Spirit of the Universe; and . . . the regathering of this diffused Matter and Spirit will be but the re-constitution of the *purely* Spiritual and Individual God.[156]

Eventually the "inconceivably numerous things which you designate as his creatures, but which are really but infinite individualizations of Himself,"[157] will become blended into one, and then will commence a new diffusion and a new cycle of life.

Think that the sense of individual identity will be gradually merged in the general consciousness—that Man, for example, ceasing imperceptibly to feel himself Man, will at length attain that awfully triumphant epoch when he shall recognize his existence as that of Jehovah. In the meantime bear in mind that all is Life—Life—Life within Life—the less within the greater, and all within the *Spirit* Divine.[158]

For purposes of comparison let me now summarize with like brevity the significant ideas of Coleridge's posthumous essay, *Hints Towards the Formation of a More Comprehensive Theory of Life*. To begin with, he objects to the division "of all that surrounds us into things with life, and things without life" as an "arbitrary assumption."[159] He himself defines life as "*the principle of individuation,* or the power which unites a given *all* into a *whole* that is presupposed by all its parts."[160] The mere act of growth, then, does not constitute the idea of life; in fact, he conceives of metals as having a low order of life, as evidenced by the irritability which they manifest to galvanism.[161] After

---

[155] *Ibid.,* p. 309.   [156] *Ibid.,* p. 313.   [157] *Ibid.,* p. 314.
[158] *Ibid.,* p. 315.   [159] *Theory of Life* (Philadelphia, 1848), p. 21.
[160] *Ibid.,* p. 42.   [161] *Ibid.,* p. 40.

establishing the tendency to individuation, he finds that the law or most general form under which this tendency acts is *"polarity,"* or the essential dualism of Nature, arising out of its productive unity, and still tending to reaffirm it, either as equilibrium, indifference, or identity.[162] He affirms that the "one great end of Nature, her ultimate object, is a tendency to the ultimate production of the highest and most comprehensive individuality."[163] Continuing, he says:

Life, then, we consider as the copula, or the unity of thesis and antithesis, position and counterposition,—Life itself being the positive of both; as, on the other hand, the two counterpoints are the necessary conditions of the *manifestations* of *Life*. These, by the same necessity, unite in a synthesis; which again, by the law of dualism, essential to all actual existence, expands, or *produces* itself, from the point into the *line*, in order to again converge, as the initiation of the same productive process in some intenser form of reality. Thus, in the identity of the two counterpowers, Life *sub*sists; in their strife, it *con*sists; and in their reconciliation it at once dies and is born again into a new form, either falling back into the life of the whole, or starting anew in the process of individuation.[164]

Here we find a suggestion of the cyclic process of creation and annihilation of matter and life which Poe likens to the rhythmic throb of the Heart Divine. In the following passage we have precisely Poe's idea of creation through the conflicting powers of attraction and repulsion:

If we pass to the construction of matter, we find it as the product, or *tertium aliud,* of antagonist powers of repulsion and attraction. Remove these powers, and the conception of matter vanishes into space—conceive repulsion only, and you have the same result. For infinite repulsion, uncounteracted and alone, is tantamount to infinite, dimensionless diffusion, and this again to infinite weakness; viz., to space. Conceive attraction alone, and as an infinite contraction, its product amounts to the absolute point, viz., to time.[165]

Coleridge objects to Milton's idea of a heterogeneous chaos, adding:

The requisite and only serviceable fiction, therefore, is the representation of Chaos as one vast homogeneous drop! In this sense it may be even justified, as an appropriate symbol of the great fundamental truth that all things spring from, and subsist in, the endless strife between indifference and difference.[166]

---

[162] *Ibid.*, pp. 50–51.   [163] *Ibid.*, p. 50.   [164] *Ibid.*, pp. 51–52.
[165] *Ibid.*, pp. 55–56.   [166] *Ibid.*, p. 68.

Here is a suggestion of Poe's definition of spirit or God in unity as unparticled matter.

Coleridge's work was published in 1848, but whether early or late, I do not know. His bibliographer says that "in some copies, evidently the latest issued, the recto of the final blank leaf carries the following *Postscript.*" This postscript bears the date October 17, 1848.[167] The postscript itself is unimportant here.

Eureka was published in March, 1848.[168] It is hardly possible, therefore, that Poe could have derived much benefit from the *Theory of Life,* supposing that he had an opportunity to read it. Yet he might have been influenced materially by Coleridge without having read his *Theory of Life,* for the germ from which this essay grew is to be found in the *Biographia Literaria.* I have already quoted the passage which defines intelligence as "an indestructible power with two opposite and counteracting forces."[169] In another place Coleridge says more specifically:

. . . grant me a nature having two contrary forces, the one of which tends to expand indefinitely, while the other strives to apprehend or find itself in this infinity, and I will cause the world of intelligences with the whole system of their representations to rise up before you.[170]

Further he says that

as something must be the result of these two forces, both alike infinite, and both alike indestructible; and as rest or neutralization cannot be this result; no other conception is possible, but that the product must be a *tertium aliquid,* or finite generation. Consequently this conception is necessary. Now this *tertium aliquid* can be no other than an inter-penetration of the counteracting powers, partaking of both.[171]

These passages alone, with their connotation, might have been sufficient to set Poe to work on a train of thinking that would produce such a theory as that of *Eureka.*[172]

It is hardly necessary to add a formal conclusion. I have tried to

---

[167] Thomas J. Wise: *A Bibliography of the Writings in Prose and Verse of Samuel Taylor Coleridge* (London, 1913), pp. 164–165.

[168] See Hervey Allen, *Israfel* (New York, 1926), II, 744.

[169] *Biographia Literaria,* I, 188.   [170] *Ibid.,* I, 196.   [171] *Ibid.,* I, 198.

[172] I am aware that Coleridge's ideas on this subject were probably borrowed. I am not now concerned with that problem. I submit, however, that since Poe, too, borrowed, it is highly improbable that he overlooked whatever of interest or value might be found in Coleridge. Both Coleridge and Poe usually absorbed what they borrowed and made something new of it.

collect and reduce to some order, not indeed all, but a representative body of reliable material on the basis of which each reader may judge the extent of Poe's debt to Coleridge. My object, as I have already intimated, was not to discredit Poe's intellectual achievement or to attack his reputation for originality; and if my labors help others as they have helped me to a better understanding of Poe and his work, I shall consider them well repaid. Perhaps, however, I ought to state my own opinion. It is that Poe was more deeply indebted to Coleridge in criticism and in speculative thought than has generally been supposed. In poetry the influence of Coleridge may easily be overestimated, and has been, perhaps, at times. On the whole, I agree with Woodberry's original opinion that Coleridge was "the guiding genius of Poe's entire intellectual life," and regret that he later substituted "early" for "entire."

VI. Poe as a Poet of Ideas

THE opinion is current that Poe was a clever melodist, an artist in words, but not a poet of ideas. This opinion, at best, is based on a half truth, which, if closely examined, proves to be no truth at all. It may be argued that his poems do not submit readily to analysis; yet ideas are there, nevertheless, for those who will take the trouble to seek them. His manner of presenting them may be made a subject of debate, but their presence in the poems is an indisputable fact.

But those who hold that Poe excluded ideas from his poetry will cite his own theory as evidence. In his critical essays we read, it is true, that "Beauty is the sole legitimate province of the poem,"[1] and that it is impossible to "reconcile the obstinate oils and waters of Poetry and Truth."[2] These generalizations are sometimes, unfortunately, detached from their contexts and interpreted as affording affirmation of the doctrine of art for art's sake. Nothing was further from Poe's intention. Other passages may be cited which apparently contradict these; for example, in his earliest critical essay, the "Letter to B——," he described poetry as music combined with an idea,[3] and in one of his latest, *Eureka,* he declared that "Poetry and Truth are one."[4] The fact is that he used these words, particularly the word "Truth," rather loosely, and one cannot hope to understand his meaning without taking into consideration the whole body of his criticism. If that is done, I think it will be found that when he opposes poetry to truth he uses the word "truth" as a synonym of "knowledge" or "science." He was led to make such ambiguous generalizations by his desire to check the didactic tendencies among his contemporaries. If we take *Eureka* seriously we must acknowledge that, with the transcendentalists, he held intuitive truth to be the highest and surest of all, and the most suitable for poetic treatment. In short, what Poe really believed was that poetry,

[1] *Complete Works of Edgar Allan Poe,* ed. James A. Harrison (New York, 1902), XIV, 197.
[2] *Ibid.,* XIV, 272; XI, 70.   [3] *Ibid.,* VII, xliii.   [4] *Ibid.,* XVI, 302.

like all the other arts, may depict or suggest truth, but may not preach or reason of it.[5] With this belief his practice is everywhere consistent.

Similarly, his definition of poetry as "the Rhythmical Creation of Beauty" is misleading if taken alone, because it attempts to generalize an entire theory in a single phrase. Poe conceived of beauty and truth as complementary aspects of harmony, the one being form and the other principle, the one concrete and the other abstract; hence in creating beauty the poet necessarily reveals truth. For the poet, therefore, beauty is the primary object, truth a secondary, whereas for the philosopher the reverse is true. The poet discards science or mere knowledge as prosaic because it leads to no perception of harmony.

There is in Poe's theory also the important idea that poetry and passion are discordant, that passion degrades whereas poetry elevates the soul. The higher love, however, the Uranian as distinguished from the Dionaean, is an excitement of the soul rather than of the heart, and hence is of all themes the most poetic.[6]

All of these ideas, besides many more, appear in his poetry, but in accordance with his theory of the indefinite he usually veils them in symbols, illusive images, and shadowy adumbrations. The idea of beauty predominates, as it does in his critical essays. I propose in this brief essay only to trace this idea of beauty through the body of Poe's poetry and to show how through it he reaches out to draw in such other ideas as may be made to harmonize with it.

The origin of Poe's idea that poetry and passion are discordant is to be found, I believe, in his early struggle for emotional tranquillity. He was a man of passionate temperament, but in his art as well as in his personal conduct he attempted to impose on the liberty of impulse the restraint of law. Out of this struggle grew his theory. "Tamerlane" is a veiled account of his effort to adjust himself to a new set of circumstances following the disruption of his love affair with Sarah Elmira Royster and his foster father's termination of his career at the University of Virginia. The hero of the poem, his pride broken, finds himself possessed by another passion—despair.

Poe, too, felt for a while the weight of despair, and attempted to save himself in the mood of reverie, as we may see in the two poems "Dreams" and "A Dream within a Dream." That failing, he sought relief by imagining a region of darkness, solitude, and terrifying mystery, where the person who has wronged him is reduced to humil-

[5] *Ibid.*, XI, 71; XIV, 275.   [6] *Ibid.*, XIV, 290.

ity and remorse. This mood produced "Spirits of the Dead" and inspired another poem, "Bridal Ballad," conceived at this period but not published until ten years later. But neither of these moods satisfied his need. Eventually he found in the contemplation and artistic creation of beauty the solace for which he yearned. The germ of this idea of beauty is to be found in "Stanzas," one of the poems of 1827. In a mood of spiritual exaltation he becomes conscious of a sudden but momentary illumination in which familiar objects assume a beauty and a meaning hitherto unsuspected. This experience, he asserts, is

> giv'n
> In beauty by our God, to those alone
> Who otherwise would fall from life and Heav'n,
> Drawn by their heart's passion.

Poe evidently means that poets are endowed with a sensitiveness and a power of insight not vouchsafed to ordinary men; for them beauty is an open sesame to truth and a protection divinely ordained against those passions which would otherwise destroy them.

As he explains in "Al Aaraaf," there are two kinds of beauty, the terrible and the fair,[7] symbolic of the power and the love of God as they are manifested in nature. Of the fair we can only catch glimpses in "Evening Star," "To Helen," and a few other poems, but the terrible is vividly revealed in many. We see in "The Lake" (1827) how through loneliness, mystery, and terror we are led from the idea of beauty to the idea of death, the ultimate solace for pain. This association of death and beauty accounts for nearly all that is most characteristic in Poe's poetry. In several of the poems of 1831 life's melancholy is represented as revived in death for those who are no longer mourned by their survivors on earth. The idea is most clearly stated in "Irene," the 1831 version of "The Sleeper," but is strongly suggested also in "The City in the Sea" and in "The Valley of Unrest." "The City in the Sea" is Poe's most perfect example of the poetry of somber beauty.

"Al Aaraaf" deals more fully than any other poem with the various aspects of the idea of beauty. It describes a starry realm ruled by an angelic spirit, Nesace, the special messenger of God and the personification of beauty, whose subjects, the spirits of those who in life were

---

[7] "Al Aaraaf," pt. I, l. 84. The text of all poems cited is that of the Killis Campbell edition of *The Poems of Edgar Allan Poe* (Boston, 1917); this work is cited as *Poems*.

lovers of beauty, aid her in transmitting by means of fantasy and imagination the wisdom of Heaven to all parts of the universe. These spirits represent artists, who, like Plato's inspired poet, reveal the divine truth in forms of beauty without themselves being conscious of its full significance. Thus they are pictured as existing on Al Aaraaf in a state of perpetual dream. In "Fairy-Land" poets are symbolized in the butterflies that, seeking heaven, catch on their wings fragments of those dissolving moons which, settling over earth at night, transform its daylight reality to a fairyland of beauty.

In "The City in the Sea" the poet finds a melancholy pleasure in scenes of death and decay, the somber beauty of which seems to spring from the romantic impulse in his genius. The fair and whole-some beauty of "To Helen" (1831), however, has its source, appar-ently, in an impulse to classicism. This little poem well illustrates the power of beauty to unify and control the diverse faculties of the poet. In "Israfel" the two impulses are fused. In the angel Israfel is typified the poet's ideal, but at the same time the poem explains why he can never hope to attain this ideal. Where Israfel dwells, beauty is perfect and universal, but on earth it is imperfect and evanescent. In Heaven, moreover, deep thoughts are a duty, and Love is a grown-up God. Truth and beauty, love and passion, are there perfectly harmonized; hence Israfel is not wrong in despising an unimpassioned song. The poet of earth, however, struggling with half-truths and degrading passions, finds no security but in beauty, which does not deceive.

I have already intimated that Poe's tendency in his later criticism was to expand the limits of the province of poetry so that it might include within the general idea of beauty such other ideas as truth and love. The same tendency is to be noted in the poems. This change is best illustrated in "Lenore." In its original form as "A Paean,"[8] written in 1831, the emphasis is placed on the beauty of the dead lady, whereas in the version of 1843, the first with the title "Lenore," the emphasis is on her innocence. Here is an obvious change in motif from the aesthetic to the ethical. In keeping with this change there is a corresponding alteration in the tone of the poem from the pagan to the Christian. "The Conqueror Worm," also composed in 1843, is a frankly philosophical allegory that can by no effort of the imagination be confined within the province of beauty. In "Dream-Land," which

[8] Campbell, in *Poems*, p. 68.

revives the romantic terror of "The City in the Sea," he confines himself to picture and symbol again, not of death this time, but of the chaotic realm of the opium dream.

"The Raven" is in perfect accord with Poe's theory. It surpasses "Lenore," an earlier study of the same mood, in the uniformity of its tone of sadness, in the subordination of the ethical motif, and in the greater intensity of its effect. "The Raven" is obviously the picture of a bereaved lover who finds a melancholy satisfaction in torturing his grief-stricken heart with thoughts of his deceased mistress. But the tragedy lies deeper than that. Aesthetically it lies in the knowledge of the irrevocable decay of beauty, and philosophically it lies in the growing certainty as the poem progresses that there is no life after death. The transience of beauty and the eternity of separation make the thought of death insupportable. In "Ulalume" the situation is essentially the same, but the lover's point of view is different. Here the picture is that of a lover bound unalterably to his beloved in spirit, but hopelessly deprived by her death of the companionship he needs. He hopes to find solace in a new love; but the very desire defeats itself, for the more eagerly he seeks the new, the more poignantly he remembers the old. His future is therefore as barren of hope as that of the lover in "The Raven." In "Annabel Lee" the situation is again the same, but the tone of the poem is not sorrowful because the lover's passion is here sublimated and so becomes a spiritual bond that is unaffected by death.

Even "The Bells" is not without its idea. The immediate aim of the poem is to reproduce the music of the four types of bells and to suggest the respective moods which they induce in the listener. Each stanza is longer, more complex, and more intense than the one preceding, giving the poem an effect of climax and tragedy. Its secondary object is to symbolize the four main stages in the emotional life of man: childhood, marriage, maturity, and old age ending in death; to this extent it is a philosophical poem. Another philosophical poem, "Sonnet—Silence," written earlier, encourages us to face the death of the body without fear, but warns us to beware of its shadow, which we may take to mean the death simultaneously of the spirit. Here, as in "The Raven," the poet shrinks from the idea that death is the end of all. "Eldorado" is a very wise commentary on idealism. From it we learn both the futility of pursuing the ideal and the impossibility of happiness without pursuing it. It is beauty, delusive, tantalizing, forever escaping yet forever leading on its pursuer in the path which eventually he must follow, either guided by its light or else blindly and alone.

Throughout most of his poetical career Poe had sought in beauty a solace for passionate strife and disappointment. But as time passed it seemed less satisfying than at first. "For Annie" is his confession that, after all, there is no perfect solace except death; no tranquillity but that passionless, half-sensuous but quiescent existence that he sometimes imagined would succeed the life on earth. One wonders whether "Eldorado" is his last word, or whether that is to be found in "For Annie." Their conclusions are different, but not really contradictory. "Eldorado" states his philosophy, a philosophy of cheerful resignation based on the reasoned decision of his intellect. "For Annie," on the other hand, is the wail of the vanquished, the cry of a weary heart, long buffeted by storms within and without, for that perfect rest of both mind and body which he is now willing to believe can be found only in death. However that may be, after reading all of Poe's poems in the light of our knowledge of his life and his philosophy, we are left with the melancholy thought that, as it was for him, so, perhaps, for all seekers of Eldorado there is no alternative but to ride, boldly ride, or else accept the cure of that cold hand whose touch alone allays the fever of life and soothes the spirit to dreams of perfect love and beauty.

VII. The Conscious Art of
Edgar Poe

ALTHOUGH Poe was not the social outcast Baudelaire conceived him to be, he was, and still is, perhaps the most thoroughly misunderstood of all American writers. His first biographer spread falsehoods about his life and character that a century of truth-telling has failed to dispel. Hence a distorted image of the man has become legendary and perhaps ineradicable in the popular mind. Like other interpreters of Poe, I have learned to live with this distorted image and almost ceased to agonize over it.

Of more immediate concern is the growth during recent decades of an equally distorted image of Poe the artist. I have no quarrel with those who dislike Poe's work so long as they understand it. Woodberry did not like it, yet he wrote a fair account of it and of its author. W. C. Brownell did not like it, but he included Poe among the six masters of prose writing in America. I am persuaded that much of the criticism of Poe in this century, whether favorable or unfavorable, has been done by people who have not taken the trouble to understand his work.

Most of Poe's critics fall into one of six categories.

1. Those who simply like to read Poe's poems, tales, and essays. If it is true, as T. S. Eliot said,[1] that Poe had "the intellect of a highly gifted young person before puberty," perhaps these readers, including myself, have intellects similarly retarded. However, persons of some literary reputation have confessed to a liking for Poe's work. In America, Paul Elmer More said, "In three of his essays he has developed his critical theory elaborately and consistently, in 'The Poetic Principle,' 'The Rationale of Verse,' and 'The Philosophy of Composition,' which together form one of the few aesthetic treatises in English of real value";[2] and, in England, Edith Sitwell said that Poe, "now derided by stupid persons," was the only American poet before Whitman whose work was not "bad and imitative of English poetry."[3]

[1] *From Poe to Valéry* (New York, 1948), p. 19.
[2] *The Demon of the Absolute* (Princeton, N.J., 1928), p. 79.
[3] Preface to *The American Genius* (London, 1951), p. xiii.

2. Those who are content to analyze and interpret individual works without evaluating Poe's worth as a writer. These are mostly the academic critics, old style, to whose work the nonacademic critics, so called, pay little attention.

3. Those who dislike Poe's writings so thoroughly that they simply cannot see what other intelligent readers appear to see plainly. I have already mentioned Brownell, who nevertheless did praise Poe's prose style. But the critic who qualifies most perfectly in this category is Yvor Winters, who became alarmed more than twenty years ago when, according to his own report, he awakened to the fact that some of his fellow-professors had almost established Poe as a great writer while he slept![4] Mr. Winters found many errors in Poe's theory, the most flagrant being his alleged failure to distinguish "between matter (truth) and manner (beauty)" and his alleged belief that truth should "be eliminated from poetry, in the interests of a purer poetry."[5]

4. Those who use psychoanalysis as a technique of criticism. D. H. Lawrence's essay in *Studies in Classic American Literature* (1923) was the first influential criticism of this kind. It was soon followed by Joseph Wood Krutch's *Edgar Allan Poe: A Study in Genius* (1926) and by Marie Bonaparte's *Life and Works of Edgar Allan Poe: A Psycho-Analytic Interpretation,* the original French version of which was published in 1933, the English translation in 1949. Other studies, long and short, French and American, have used psychoanalysis to some extent in the search for Poe's hidden secrets. These are not literary critiques at all, but clinical studies of a supposed psychopathic personality. I agree with Allen Tate's apt comment on the psychoanalytic critics in general: "To these ingenious persons, Poe's works have almost no intrinsic meaning; taken together they make up a *dossier* for the analyst to peruse before Mr. Poe steps into his office for an analysis."[6]

5. Those who like Poe but feel they should not. Perhaps the most notable critic in this category is Tate himself, who thinks of Poe as a "dejected cousin,"[7] and "the transitional figure in modern literature because he discovered our great subject, the disintegration of personality."[8]

[4] *In Defense of Reason* (New York, 1947), p. 234.   [5] *Ibid.,* pp. 240–241.
[6] "The Angelic Imagination: Poe as God," *Collected Essays* (Denver, 1959), p. 435.
[7] "Our Cousin, Mr. Poe," *ibid.,* p. 458.
[8] "The Angelic Imagination: Poe as God," *ibid.,* p. 439.

6. Those who do not like Poe but feel as if they ought to because certain French writers and critics whom they admire have praised him. T. S. Eliot stands authoritatively at the head of these critics. Though Eliot called Poe's intellect "immature" and Paul Valéry's "mature," he traced to Poe two notions which he says were brought to culmination by Valéry: (1) that a poem should have nothing in view but itself, and (2) that the composition of a poem should be as conscious and deliberate as possible.[9]

There are, of course, other ways of looking at Poe's work including my own, for which I claim no originality; indeed, I hope that it is the way of many intelligent readers who have no critical ax to grind. Although a large part of Poe's writing—perhaps more than the two fifths that Lowell called fudge—is trivial, artistically crude, and often in bad taste, the rest is of literary importance and merits detailed study without reference to its possible autobiographical significance. Some of his poems and tales are difficult, but they can be understood without the help of twentieth-century psychology, or any greater learning than what can be found in the literature and the reference works to which he had access. I believe the critic should look within the poem or tale for its meaning, and that he should not, in any case, suspect the betrayal of the author's unconscious self until he has understood all that his conscious self has contributed. To affirm that a work of imagination is only a report of the unconscious is to degrade the creative artist to the level of an amanuensis.

I am convinced that all of Poe's poems were composed with conscious art. How else can we account for his frequent and meticulous revision? Most if not all of them had their origin in thought and express or suggest clearly formed ideas. "Al Aaraaf" was written with the conscious purpose of suggesting Poe's aesthetic theory: that beauty is the province of art, that the artist reveals truth through beauty, and that he must keep his art free of passion. "To Helen" tells how an artist who has been lost on the turbulent seas of passion is restored to his artistic home through the beauty of woman. "Israfel" reminds us that in this imperfect world the poet can approach truth only through the veil of beautiful forms. "The Sleeper" and "The City in the Sea" present a series of images all developed from the trivial idea, or superstition, that those who die rest comfortably in their graves only so long as their surviving friends remember them and

[9] P. 28.

mourn. "Dream-Land" is just what the title promises: a description of the topsy-turvy world of dreams. "The Raven" describes the inconsolable grief of a bereaved lover unable to believe in life after death.

Poe did not tell us how he wrote "The Sleeper" and "The City in the Sea," but the several surviving versions of the poems record the process of their development. In the earliest version the initial idea was clearly stated, but the passage in which it appeared was later deleted, and so the idea remains only in the images that grew out of it. Certainly all the details were not preformed in his mind before he composed the first draft, but the overall pattern of the poem might well have been. I think it quite possible that "The Raven" was planned in advance of composition very much as Poe says it was in "The Philosophy of Composition." The difference between the early and late poems is chiefly in the technique of composition. The former are predominantly the lyric expression of moods in the style of the English romantic poets, particularly Coleridge; the latter are more dramatic in form, and characterized in style by novelties of rhyme, repetition, meter, and stanza structure, with elements of the fantastic not common before 1840. These novelties of style give the later poems the effect of seeming contrived; and indeed they may have been more completely the work of the deliberate craftsman than the earlier ones.

Analysis of the tales will yield similar results. "Ligeia" relates how the narrator, a student of German transcendentalism, becomes obsessed with the idea that he can, by the power of the will, incorporate his ideal of beauty in the person of a real woman. His first step is to convince himself that such a woman was once his wife; his second step is to impute to her a conscious spirit and the will to live by possessing the body of Rowena, a real woman, whom he has married. Actually the narrator kills Rowena, but attributes her death to the struggle with Ligeia's spirit. Of course the entire action is the hallucination of insanity. Presumably the narrator has recovered some degree of sanity when the story is written down. "The Fall of the House of Usher" describes how discrete objects, by long and close association, may develop a common identity. (Wordsworth suggests the same idea in the story of Margaret in Book I of *The Excursion*.) Roderick Usher is so sure of his identity with his twin sister that he will not believe that she can be dead while he himself still lives. The story ends with the strange invented episode of Ethelred and the dragon, which induces in both Roderick and the narrator (who has been affected also by his friend's theory of identity) the hallucination of Madeline's escape from the tomb and appearance before them. The destruction of the house by a storm at the time of Roderick's death seems to validate the theory. "William Wilson" is the story of a wilful and imaginative boy who becomes obsessed with the idea that a schoolmate by the same name, whose good conduct is a reproof to his own selfish egotism, is an embodiment of his own conscience. Wilson leaves school and never sees the other boy again, but the obsession grows upon him so that at intervals afterward he imagines his namesake intervenes to prevent some dishonorable action. Eventually William Wilson imagines he kills his personified conscience and thereafter acts without restraint. He, too, is apparently insane but recovers sufficiently to write the story of his life.

The origin of these and other imaginative tales was intellectual, but they differ from the tales of ratiocination in presenting their ideas less directly and in achieving their final effect through action rather than through logical analysis. Dupin solves the mystery of "The Murders in the Rue Morgue" because he brings the poetic imagination to the aid of the mathematician's logical reasoning. In "The Purloined Letter" Poe's hero almost meets his match in the Minister D__ who is, like Dupin, a poet as well as a mathematician.

Poe's criticism is less difficult than his tales and poems. His theory of the short story is stated, in essence, in the well-known paragraph of his review of Hawthorne's *Twice-Told Tales,* where he says the writer first deliberately conceives the single effect to be wrought, and then invents such incidents, arranges them in such order, and presents them in such a tone as will produce on the reader the preconceived effect. He adds that for fullest satisfaction, the story must be read with an art akin to that of its creator.

Poe's theory of poetry is similar, although less simply stated. According to this theory, every person is endowed by nature with the Poetic Sentiment, or Sentiment of Beauty, an insatiable desire to experience that Supernal Beauty which Poe conceived in Platonic terms as beyond the power of finite man wholly to possess. In this sense, Beauty is an effect, not an attribute. Sensuous beauty, the beauty of natural objects and artistic creations, though it is not an effect but only an attribute, is yet capable of evoking the Sentiment of Beauty, which is an effect, and thus furthering the soul's progress toward Supernal Beauty. Those who have found fault with Poe's definition of Beauty as an effect, not a quality, have failed to weigh sufficiently the sentence in "The Poetic Principle" in which Poe describes man's sense of the beautiful in language reminiscent of Plato as the "struggle, by multiform combinations among the things and thoughts of Time, to attain a portion of that Loveliness whose very elements, perhaps, appertain to eternity alone."

Though Poe denies the poet the use of the didactic method of inculcating the truths of the intellect and the moral sense, he insists that the true poet can and must suggest Truth through Beauty. He believes, with Emerson, that the Good, the True, and the Beautiful are aspects of one divine Unity; that though they are approached by different means, they are identical under the aspect of eternity. As he says in *Eureka,* a work of art is necessarily true, and an intellectual structure, because of the harmony of its elements, is necessarily beautiful. Indeed, as stated above, the imaginative and analytic faculties work best when they work together. The scientist uses intuitive reasoning, and the poet requires constructive skill. In *Eureka* he calls Kepler a greater man than Newton because Kepler imagined, or "guessed," the physical laws which Newton later demonstrated rationally to be true. This is not to say that Newton had no imagination, but only that Kepler had more.

If modern skeptics would read *Eureka* carefully and without prejudice, as Paul Valéry did, they might not be so ready to scoff at Poe's account of writing "The Raven" in "The Philosophy of Composition." Poe means that the poem began in the Poetic Sentiment, was shaped by the imagination, and then constructed according to the imagined pattern with deliberate and methodical skill in the manner best calculated to evoke in the reader the mood from which it grew in the mind of the poet. "The Raven," and with certain necessary individual differences, every other poem Poe wrote, was the product of conscious effort by a healthy and alert intelligence.

VIII. Mood, Meaning, and Form
in Poe's Poetry

I

My CONCERN in this essay is with Poe's poems, but since his theory and practice of poetry are so closely related that neither can be fully understood without reference to the other, the reader should be familiar with the basic ideas of his theory. In the preceding essays of this volume, and particularly in "Poe's Debt to Coleridge," I have discussed most of these ideas; therefore I shall content myself here with a brief summary of them and of his ideas on versification as finally detailed in "The Rationale of Verse."

The primary object of poetry, Poe believed, is pleasure, not truth. This pleasure is derived from the contemplation of the beautiful, and it is not sensuous merely but an excitement and elevation of the soul, which he calls the Poetic Sentiment, or Sentiment of Poesy. The poetic sentiment is innate, and is active in some degree in all people. It is stimulated by all forms of beauty, natural or artistic, physical or spiritual, in which, or through which, a responsive person may some-times catch glimpses of supernal beauty. Such glimpses are most likely to come through forms of beauty which have the quality of strange-ness, for then their effects are indefinitive and suggestive of the sublime. Although latent in all men, the poetic sentiment is most active in the artist, and especially the poet, who through his creative imagination and constructive skill as an artist in words has, to an unusual degree, the power to evoke it in others. Since the pleasure to be derived from music is the most indefinitive, it is the most entranc-ing of poetic moods. Hence Poe's earliest definition, formulated in 1831 in the "Letter to B——," was: "Music, when combined with a pleasurable idea is poetry; music without the idea is simply music; the idea without the music is prose from its very definitiveness." His latest definition, first formulated, I believe, in 1842 in the review of Longfel-low's *Ballads and Other Poems*, but best known through his last and most famous essay "The Poetic Principle," was: "I would define, in brief, the Poetry of words as *The Rhythmical Creation of Beauty*."

The poet's aim in creating beauty is to satisfy, insofar as that is humanly possible, the soul's thirst for supernal beauty—beauty that exists in no collocation of earth's forms. The poet cannot create supernal beauty, but he can suggest it through the original and novel combination of existing forms which the imagination so blends as to produce an integral whole and a single effect. Poe's statement that beauty is an effect, not a quality, which is explicit in "The Philosophy of Composition" and implicit in "The Poetic Principle," has been objected to as giving the word a meaning which it does not properly have. If the statement is read in its context, however, it will be seen that Poe does by no means deny that beauty may be a quality in all that appeals to the senses, but asserts that it may also be an effect, a sense, an intuition that transcends the power of the physical senses to perceive or the mind to understand. Cause and effect become one, and particular beauties are lost in the idea of beauty. For this sense of the term Poe could claim the authority of Plato, not to mention Coleridge, Emerson, and other contemporaries.

Since the excitement and elevation of the soul cannot be long sustained, the poem must be relatively brief. It must not be too brief, however, because more than a few lines are required to produce the excitement. Most of Poe's own poems range from twenty-five to approximately one hundred lines. The longer poems usually contain a limited narrative, whereas the shorter ones are predominantly lyrical. His famous comment in "The Poetic Principle" on the difficulty of reconciling "the obstinate oils and waters of Poetry and Truth" has been misunderstood because it is usually quoted out of context. The paragraph which ends with this begins: "With as deep a reverence for the True as ever inspired the bosom of man, I would, nevertheless, limit, in some measure, its modes of inculcation. I would limit to enforce them." Prose is the best medium for expressing perceptive truth because it appeals to the pure intellect. Poetry is the proper medium for representing truth because it appeals to the taste. As he states more specifically in *Eureka,* which was written about the same time as "The Poetic Principle," symmetry of form—that is to say formal beauty—is truth, and it is also poetical; therefore "Poetry and Truth are one." Rightly understood, then, the statement about the "oils and waters of poetry and truth" means only that the didactic, or rational, mode of inculcating truth and the poetic, or imaginative, mode are mutually exclusive. As the poet must not be didactic, so too he must avoid passion because it is discordant with the poetic mood, which is that mild sadness or melancholy growing out of the aspiration for a beauty not attainable in this world. It may be that Poe owed something to Wordsworth's statement in the Preface to the *Lyrical Ballads* that though poetry takes its rise in emotion, that emotion must be recollected in tranquillity before it is a suitable mood for poetic composition. In fact, it is only physical passion that is discordant; spiritual passion, what Poe called impassioned feeling, is not only acceptable but indispensable for the loftiest poetic effect. His goddess of love was not Venus, but Urania.

Essentially this is Poe's theory of poetry, or, rather, his theory of what he called "pure poetry." It is thoroughly romantic and even transcendental in spite of his occasional sharp criticism of transcendentalism, particularly that which emanated from New England. What he objected to was not transcendental idealism in itself, but the folly, as he believed, of trying to make it a criterion for judging the practical affairs of life. In such matters he was a realist. He might properly be called a transcendentalist only in the realm of aesthetics, although in his conception of married love he was certainly an idealist. He expressed admiration for a number of poems which did not fulfill all the conditions required of pure poetry. Some of them, like Thomas Moore's *Alciphron* and R. H. Horne's *Orion*, were long and largely narrative poems. Of the former Poe says that it "recounts a poetical story in a *prosaic* way."[1] Of the latter he said, "It is not to be regarded as a Poem, but as a Work . . ."[2] Though passion and poetry are discordant, he said, "we are willing to permit Tennyson to bring, to the intense *passion* which prompted his 'Locksley Hall,' the aid of that terseness and pungency which are derivable from rhythm and from rhyme. The effect he produces, however, is a purely passionate, and not, unless in detached passages of this magnificent philippic, a properly poetic effect." Tennyson's "Oenone," on the other hand, he thinks, "exalts the soul not into passion, but into a conception of pure *beauty*, which in its elevation—its calm and intense rapture—has in it a foreshadowing of the future and spiritual life . . ."[3] We are not to assume from these statements that Poe considered "Oenone" a more important literary composition than "Locksley Hall," but only a more nearly perfect example of pure poetry. He admired Longfellow's

---

[1] "Alciphron: A Poem. By Thomas Moore," *Burton's Gentleman's Magazine* (Jan. 1840). Reference is here made to *The Complete Works of Edgar Allan Poe*, ed. James A. Harrison (New York, 1902) (hereafter referred to as *Works*), X, 68.

[2] "Orion: an Epic Poem in Three Books. By R. H. Horne," *Graham's Magazine*, March 1844 (*Works*, XI, 251).

[3] *Ibid.*, 255.

genius and skill as an artist and acknowledged his high "Ideality," but complained that "his conception of the *aims* of poesy *is all wrong*."[4] The right conception is that the pure poem has its origin in the poetic sentiment, becomes a creation of beauty for its own sake, and has no other aim except to evoke and excite the poetic sentiment in the reader.

Nevertheless, the poem which arises spontaneously from the poetic sentiment requires craftsmanship for its construction; there must be process as well as theory, and the process should exemplify the theory. In all cases, he wrote in "Marginalia," "if the practice fail, it is because the theory is imperfect."[5] Failure to take account of this duality, theory and process, is partly responsible for the rejection by many readers of "The Philosophy of Composition" as a believable explanation of the composition of "The Raven." No poem, not even "The Raven," the critics protest, could have been composed so deliberately, so mechanically, in apparent contradiction even of the poet's own theory.[6] There really is no contradiction, although it must be admitted that Poe has repressed theory in order to emphasize process. A careful reading of "The Philosophy of Composition" will reveal also that he began with the idea of telling how a prose story is written, and then (because "The Raven" was so popular at the time) shifted to the poem. He explains that a poem is not composed in "a species of fine frenzy—an ecstatic intuition"—but with "vacillating crudities of thought" and "painful erasures and interpolations." The ecstatic intuition is not ruled out, but it comes first. Its work is done before the process of construction is begun. The poem has its inception in a mood, the poetic sentiment, and emerges into consciousness first as an idea on which the imagination sets to work. Only when that work is done or well advanced does the process begin. In this process the faculty of analysis is more active than the imagination. An analogy may be found in Poe's statement in *Eureka* that "Kepler *guessed*—that is to say, he *imagined*"—the laws of gravitation which Newton later demonstrated by logical processes.[7] The artist must be both Kepler

[4] "Ballads and Other Poems. By Henry Wadsworth Longfellow," *Graham's Magazine*, March 1842 (*Works*, XI, 67).

[5] "Marginalia III," *Godey's Lady's Book*, Aug. 1845 (*Works*, XVI, 69).

[6] In "The Poetic Principle" (*Works*, XIV, 272) Poe contrasts the method of truth and that of poetry. To inculcate truth, he says, "We must be cool, calm, unimpassioned. In a word, we must be in that mood which, as nearly as possible, is the exact converse of the poetical."

[7] *Works*, XVI, 197, 279, and *passim*.

and Newton. The Keplerian theory, so to speak, pre-existed in the poet's mind: that beauty is the sole province of the poem, sadness the tone of its highest manifestation, and the death of a beautiful woman the saddest of human experiences. Afterward the Newtonian process began. Poe does not tell us this precisely in "The Philosophy of Composition," but he does say: "Let us dismiss, as irrelevant to the poem, *per se*, the circumstance—or say the necessity—which, in the first place, gave rise to the intention of composing a poem that should suit at once the popular and the critical taste."[8] The circumstance could have been his need of the trifling sum he expected to receive as the price of publication, but the poem *per se* originated in a mood of sadness associated in his experience, or perhaps only in his imagination, with the death of a beautiful woman. The intention is another matter. He obviously intended to compose a poem that would appeal to the popular taste and at the same time satisfy the critics, including himself. From then on the poet's problem was one of analysis and construction: the choice of images and word patterns—meter, refrain, and stanza—best calculated, in his opinion, to produce the effect in both reader and critic most nearly akin to the mood that in him was a cause.

The reader who feels the effect intended in the poem has, in some measure, the genius of the poet. Such people, Poe declares, "are more abundant than is supposed." The poet differs from the responsive reader perhaps in the degree of his genius, but primarily in his constructive ability, which the reader, unless himself an artist, does not have. Constructive ability depends in part on the faculty of analysis, but also largely on the poet's exercise of the moral qualities of patience, purposefulness, and industry.[9] The poet also has more imagination than the reader. The imagination is the creative power, as distinguished from constructive skill, which enables the poet to translate the formless materials of experience into images of beauty in the mind. It is the architect; the analytic faculty is the builder. It chooses its materials usually from things already beautiful, but it sometimes chooses things in themselves ugly; for "even out of deformities it fabricates that *Beauty* which is at once its sole object and its inevitable test."[10] In "The Raven" there are elements of the grotesque in both

---

[8] *Works*, XIV, 195–196.

[9] "Marginalia III," *Godey's Lady's Book*, Aug. 1845 (*Works*, XVI, 66–67).

[10] *Works*, XII, 38–39. This excerpt is from a passage quoted at length in "Poe's Debt to Coleridge," p. 158.

the material and the style—"an air of the fantastic," as he puts it in
"The Philosophy of Composition," approaching the ludicrous—which
he says he introduces for contrast, "with a view of deepening the
ultimate impression."

Poe was always careful of the metrical patterns in his verse, but as
he grew older he became more and more meticulous. Some attention
must be given, therefore, to his formulation of what he termed the
"simple natural laws" on which poetic rhythms are founded. His
fullest treatment of the subject was the long essay "The Rationale of
Verse," published in the *Southern Literary Messenger* in 1848. This
was an expanded and less restricted version of an earlier essay entitled
"Notes on English Verse," which he contributed in 1843 to Lowell's
magazine *The Pioneer*. The added portions consist chiefly of a long
theoretical account of the origin and development of the art of verse
and, toward the end of the essay, an extended and rather ill-tempered
attack on classical prosodists and poets who have attempted to write
English verse on classical models.[11] "The Rationale of Verse" is too
long to be discussed in detail; it will be necessary here to point out
only its more salient features.

As we might expect, Poe finds the technique of verse very similar to
that of music, especially of the simple melody, but we have reason to
be surprised when he defines verse as "an inferior or less capable
Music." I suppose he means only that music, as he says in "The Poetic
Principle," is "the most entrancing of the Poetic moods." The principle
of music he identifies as "the perception of pleasure in the equality of
sounds." Likewise, verse "originates in the human enjoyment of
equality," which he explains as embracing the ideas of "similarity,

---

[11] "The Rationale of Verse" appears in *Works*, XIV, 209–265. Most of the
material retained by Poe from the early essay appears on pp. 211–216, 242–253,
262–265. A long paragraph on the subject appeared in "Marginalia VII," *Graham's
Magazine*, Nov. 1846 (*Works*, XVI, 111–112), and a somewhat longer discussion
was included in an anonymous review of Griswold's *Poets and Poetry of America*,
in the *Philadelphia Saturday Museum* (Jan. 28, 1843). The review is credited to
Poe by Harrison (*Works*, XI, 220–243), but some authorities, including Killis
Campbell (*The Mind of Poe*, Cambridge, Mass., 1933, pp. 226–227), question
Poe's authorship. Campbell thinks it was written by Poe's friend H. B. Hirst; if so,
Poe was probably a collaborator. The review contains one interesting variant of
Poe's definition of poetry (pp. 225–226): "Poetry, in its most confined sense, is *the
result of versification*, but may be more properly defined as *the rhythmical
personification of existing or real beauty*. One defines it as the 'rhythmical *creation*
of beauty'; but though it certainly is a 'creation of beauty' in itself, it is more
properly a personification, for the poet only personifies the image previously
created by his mind."

proportion, identity, repetition, and adaptation or fitness." He supposes the rudiment of primitive verse to have been the spondee—"the very germ of thought seeking satisfaction in equality of sound." As the art of verse developed, the spondee was found too monotonous and gave way to rhythmic units with alternating syllables of unequal accent, from which came the iambus and the trochee, and eventually the anapest and the dactyl. Finally, to achieve even greater variety, the foot of one long or accented syllable came into use, for which Poe appropriates the name "caesura" from classical prosody. For convenience he adopts the classical terms "long" and "short." Syllables are long if they are hard to enunciate; that is to say, if they are encumbered with consonants. An accented syllable, however, is always long, whether encumbered with consonants or not. Every long syllable must occupy naturally, or be made to occupy, "precisely the time demanded for two short ones" and every foot in the line must occupy precisely the time in enunciation of every other foot, though they do not have to be of the same type. When an anapest or dactyl is inserted in an iambic or trochaic line, the two unaccented syllables together occupy the same time as the one unaccented syllable of the iambus or trochee. When so used, he says, the anapest is a "bastard" iambus and the dactyl a "bastard" trochee. If a poet introduces a foot with three unaccented syllables in a dissyllabic rhythm, he will have made a mistake, but if the foot is properly pronounced in the line these three syllables must occupy also no more than the time of the one unaccented syllable of the iambus or trochee. If what seems to be an iambus or trochee is introduced into an anapestic or dactyllic rhythm, it must be pronounced as a spondee in order to fill the time equivalent of an anapest or dactyl. The caesura is always long, and though it consists of only one syllable it has the value and requires the same time as any other foot in the line in which it occurs. He explains, however, that the time is not all consumed in the mere enunciation of the syllable, but includes a pause preceding or following the syllable. The time of the accented syllable and the pause together must equal the time of the dominant foot of the line. The caesura frequently occurs at the end of a line, but may be also at the beginning, and may even be introduced into the middle of the line with good effect.

When Poe says a syllable is "accented," he does not mean it is to be enunciated with more force than a short syllable but that it is to be dwelt on longer. However, the reason for dwelling on one syllable more than another lies not in the structure but in some combination of the sound and meaning of the word in which it occurs. Poe may not have been aware of it, but he was in some difficulty here. He agrees that English is an accented language. The French language, he boldly declares, "is without accentuation and consequently without verse." He betrays considerable ignorance in saying that "Coleridge thought proper to invent his nonsensical *system* of what he calls 'scanning by accents'—as if 'scanning by accents' were anything more than a phrase." Here he gives himself away, for in the context he clearly means that there is no essential difference between scanning by accents and scanning by length of syllables, that is by what he calls the "true *laws*" of verse. He obviously admires "Christabel," and though he darkly hints at rough lines in it, he mentions none. He also hints that he is the one clever reader out of a hundred who can "both comprehend and admire it at first sight." But for the fact that Poe's whole system is based on equivalent intervals of time, one might suspect that he differs here from Coleridge to satisfy some inner egotistic compulsion, as he does in taking issue with him on the distinction between the fancy and the imagination.[12]

The one great weakness in Poe's theory—a weakness that is almost incomprehensible in the light of his practice—is that it tries to force poetry into a Procrustean frame of time limitations borrowed from music.[13] The only significant contribution he makes in this essay to the understanding of poetry, including his own early verse, is his new interpretation of the caesura as a monosyllabic foot, but even that is impaired by the overemphasis on time. The early essay "Notes on English Verse" avoids some of the errors of the later one. Among the passages in this essay that are omitted in "The Rationale of Verse" is the following: "Our usual prosodies maintain that a long syllable is equal, in its time, to two short; this, however, is but an approach to the truth. It should be here observed that the quantity of an English syllable has no dependence upon the sound of its vowel or diphthong, but chiefly upon *accentuation*. Monosyllables are exceedingly varia-

[12] See "Poe's Debt to Coleridge," p. 161.

[13] Although he admits that when we read a poem in which the poet has placed a naturally unaccented syllable, such as "and" or "the," in a position where the dominant rhythm requires an accent, we must "give up the sound for the sense," he adds that "the *perfection* of verse, as regards melody, consists in its *never* demanding any such sacrifice as is here demanded" (*Works*, XIV, 245). He would have done well, at this point, to recognize, as Robert Frost was later to do, the importance of "the sound of sense" in poetry and the fact that musical melody is inappropriate in the reading of poems that are not intentionally lyrical.

ble, and, for the most part, may be either long or short, to suit the demand of the rhythm. . . . Emphasis will render any short syllable long." [14] Among the passages introduced for the first time in "The Rationale of Verse" are several which I have not discussed dealing with the structure of the stanza, with the refrain, and with internal rhyme. These seem to have been by-products of his work on "The Raven" and "The Philosophy of Composition." They have little to do with the earlier poems, in which the mechanics of the craftsman are usually well concealed.

Let us turn now to the examination of the poems themselves, keeping in mind these theories of the nature, function, and technique of poetry. For convenience the poems may be arranged in three groups determined partly by chronology and partly by Poe's own treatment of them in his revisions. The poems originally published in the 1827 and 1829 editions constitute my first group; they received only minor revisions after 1829.[15] My second group consists of the poems first published in the 1831 edition, all of which were so drastically revised as to be the work as much of his middle years as of his youth, and all other poems published before 1845. The third group includes "The Raven" and all later poems. These were revised, but not materially altered, after their original publication. Although the poems of each group have certain characteristics in common that distinguish them from poems of the other groups, their primary importance is as separate and individual compositions. The poems Poe never collected are treated with the first group of poems.

II

Poe's most memorable short poems, of whatever period, are lyrical in form. They have their origin not in emotion, as that word is generally understood, but in moods which, though transient, are deeply felt. When the poet undertakes to transmit his mood to another person by means of words, which are symbols of ideas, and by images, which are

[14] *The Pioneer,* I (March 1843), 105.

[15] Some changes were made in reprinting these poems in the 1831 edition, but these changes were later abandoned and the 1829 text restored. In his 1845 edition, published with the title *The Raven and Other Poems,* Poe placed these poems at the end of the volume in a separate section he called "Poems Written in Youth." For some reason not easy to understand, he also placed the 1831 poem "To Helen" in this section.

visual impressions of ideas, the mood becomes meaningful; then the sound and movement of the words, in accord with their meaning, awaken in the responsive reader a mood akin to that felt by the poet. Much depends on the way the words are arranged; that is to say, on poetic form. In the two longer poems that Poe wrote and in a few of the shorter ones, it is possible that the idea preceded the mood in the process of composition, but if so the idea was soon dissolved, as it were, in the mood, and the final effect is essentially the same.

As it was first published in the 1827 edition, "Tamerlane" is a predominantly narrative poem that has as its theme the conflict of love and ambition. Its hero is represented as the medieval conqueror Timour, or Tamerlane, although the events narrated have no basis in historical fact. The story tells how Alexis, a Tartar youth, under the influence of the wild grandeur of his native mountains, aspires to power and fame, secretly leaves his village home and Ada, the girl he loves, succeeds in conquering half the world, and returns to bestow on her a queenly crown, only to learn that she is dead. Many years later, disillusioned and remorseful, he tells his story to a friar, not in the hope of forgiveness for his sinful pride, but like the Ancient Mariner from a resistless inner compulsion. The poem is without stanzas, but is divided in this version into seventeen numbered sections. The verse form is iambic tetrameter, rhyming, with a few exceptions, in couplets.[16]

As revised for the 1829 edition, "Tamerlane" contains only 243 lines. Of these only 87 are retained from the original text of 406 lines without revision; 88 are retained with revisions, and 68 are entirely new. More than two thirds of the lines omitted contain details of the narrative; they were cut out in order to reduce the narrative element to a minimum and to provide space for new lines that stress Tamerlane's state of mind. Other lines seem to have been omitted because they describe specific places not essential to the theme, because they are moralistic in tone, or because they represent the young lovers as too passionate. A number of lines scattered throughout the poem were doubtless omitted because they were faulty or trite, and some good lines were omitted because they were too obviously borrowed from well-known English poems.[17] In lines that are retained after revision

[16] Some pertinent comments on "Tamerlane" and the volume in which it was first published may be found in "Poet in Search of a Career," pp. 24–26.

[17] Line 365, "My heart sunk with the sun's ray," is an irregular but effective line; it may have been omitted because the idea expressed was too close to that of

improvements are made in various ways: to secure greater precision of meaning (the substitution of "withering" for "hatred" in line 25 and "searing" for "worldly" in line 26), an improved rhythm (as in line 66), unity of theme (changes in lines 144–150 that make ambition instead of love the aggressor), and originality in both diction and rhythm (as in the substitution of the monosyllable "white" for "silvery" in line 376). The imagery of the revised version is much more vivid; for example, in lines 174–176 the "astonished people" (not the "astonished earth") saw Timour "striding o'er empires" (not, as in 1827, outdoing Zenghis "with victory on victory"). Moreover, in this revision he reduced six weak lines to four strong ones. In general, the emphasis is transferred from events to character, from the man as hero to the hero as man, from the hollowness of fame to the waste of human love. The changed emphasis is felt everywhere in the new lines added in 1829, but especially in lines 21–26 (beginning "O craving heart"), in lines 177–190 (beginning "O, human love!" and ending with the fine metaphor "Hope, the eagle" turning homeward with pinions "bent droopingly"), and in the concluding lines on the betrayal of love by ambition.

In the 1829 version, although it is much shorter, the number of sections is increased from seventeen to twenty-three. The reason lies in the more accurate paragraphing of the later version, where each paragraph is a numbered section. The earlier version has twenty-four paragraphs. The gain in logic is apparent. When he reprinted the poem in 1845 he removed the numerals but retained the paragraph divisions of the 1829 text.

In the 1831 edition the poem contained 252 lines in twenty-four numbered sections which correspond to the sections of the 1829 text with two exceptions: section 13 (lines 128–138) is omitted, and two new sections are introduced as sections 8 and 24. The new section 8 is a revised version of "The Lake," which had appeared in both the 1827 and 1829 editions, and section 24 is a much altered version of a poem later titled "A Dream within a Dream," which had appeared in still different forms in both the 1827 and the 1829 editions but was omitted

---

Wordsworth's "Strange Fits of Passion Have I Known," in which the lover seeing the moon sink over Lucy's cottage fears that she may be dead. Other lines are omitted for similar reasons: lines 94–101 perhaps because they too closely resemble some lines from "Intimations of Immortality," and line 339 obviously because it is almost identical with Byron's line, "There was a sound of revelry by night" in *Childe Harold*.

in the 1845 edition. The omission of section 13, one of the weakest in the 1829 text, was an improvement, but most of the additions and changes (except in punctuation, which is nearer modern practice) were wisely discarded when he chose the text for the 1845 edition.[18]

Poe's longest poem, "Al Aaraaf," which contains 422 lines, was first published in 1829 and never thereafter materially altered, though it was very likely conceived as a longer and somewhat different kind of poem.[19] If, like "Tamerlane," it was planned as a little epic, the author changed his mind before publication. In Part I, out of 158 lines, only about ten are narrative in form, and these have to do with the function of the star Al Aaraaf rather than any character. In Part II, consisting of 264 lines, about sixty are narrative in form, telling how Angelo died, apparently in the Aegean island of Lemnos, was transported in spirit to Al Aaraaf, and "fell" therefrom because of his love for another spirit, Ianthe, which tempted him to fail in his duty to Nesace, the presiding spirit on Al Aaraaf.[20] Most of the lines in Part II, as in Part I, are descriptive of Al Aaraaf, its function as a messenger star of God, and the dedication of its resident spirits to the service of beauty. Since Al Aaraaf is the home of spiritual beauty and both Angelo and Ianthe are spirits, not flesh-and-blood mortals, we should not expect them to love with physical passion, and there is no evidence in what they say in the poem that they do; they are sitting quietly conversing about the earth, which is now at a great distance from Al Aaraaf, and about Angelo's experience in coming thence to the star which has been the instrument of his own death and of the earth's destruction. Yet they fail in their duty because they are so absorbed in each other that they do not hear Nesace's command, and there is a suggestion of passion in the last couplet: "They fell: for Heaven to them no hope imparts / Who hear not for the beating of their hearts." There is an obvious parallel in their fall from Al Aaraaf with the expulsion of Adam and Eve from Paradise; passion in Al Aaraaf was as illogical as evil in Paradise. If Poe really planned a little epic, he rejected most of

[18] The variant texts and collations appear in *The Poems of Edgar Allan Poe,* ed. Floyd Stovall (Charlottesville, Va., 1965).

[19] See "Poet in Search of a Career," pp. 28–32.

[20] Poe's geography and his chronology are vague, not to say confusing. Although Angelo dies on Lemnos, he tells Ianthe that the "last spot of Earth's orbit [he] trod upon" was the Parthenon, which is more than 150 miles away. He originally intended Angelo to be Michelangelo, it seems, and his footnote to the line about the Parthenon, "It was entire in 1687—the most elevated spot in Athens," may have been intended to inform us that he could have seen its beauty intact before his death in 1564. But he died in Italy, and the earth was not hurled into chaos as described in the poem. This catastrophe was prophecy, of course, not history.

the narrative part before publication, possibly even before composition was completed. Certainly the expulsion of Angelo and Ianthe from their aesthetic paradise, though integral to the theme of the poem as published, appears to be vestigial so far as the plot is concerned.

The beauty of the lyrics, particularly the second, which is usually the only part of the poem that finds its way into anthologies, has contributed to the neglect of the rest of it. Their beauty has not been exaggerated. It is easy to see why the second, a lilting song addressed by Nesace to Ligeia, the spirit of melody, is more popular than the first, which is more solemn and weighty because it is addressed to God and is Nesace's acknowledgment of God's will and her promise, as His messenger, to fulfill it. Their difference in rhythm and meter corresponds to their difference in mood and meaning. The best known lines of the song to Ligeia are probably the following, which illustrate the meter and the dominant rhythm:

> Ligeia! Ligeia! / My beautiful one!
> Whose harshest idea / Will to melody run,
> O! is it thy will / On the breezes to toss?
> Or, capriciously still, / Like the lone Albatross,
> Incumbent on night / (As she on the air)
> To keep watch with delight / On the harmony there?

I have arranged each pair of lines as one in order to illustrate their rhythmical continuity and to make scansion easier. The number of syllables in each pair of lines run from ten to twelve, but most have eleven. Of 43 pairs in the entire poem, two have ten syllables and eleven have twelve. Although there are no feminine rhymes in the lines quoted, there are fourteen in the poem, in one of which "maiden" is made to rhyme with "shade, and" and in another with "glade, and." In still another "you, Love!" is made to rhyme with "true love." There are two stresses in each line, or four in each pair of lines. The most common foot is the anapest. In a pair of lines of which the first has a feminine ending, and therefore an excess unstressed syllable, the first foot of the second is invariably iambic, though Poe would prefer to say that an anapest is made up of the excess syllable of the first line combined with the first two syllables of the second. The first four lines of the poem will illustrate this pattern:

> 'Neath blue-bell or streamer— / Or tufted wild spray
> That keeps, from the dreamer, / The moonbeam away—.

In each of the two pairs of lines with only ten syllables, there are two iambic and two anapestic feet. In each of the eleven pairs of lines with twelve syllables there are invariably four anapests, but if the first line of the pair ends with an excess unstressed syllable, that syllable combines with the first syllable (unstressed) and the second (stressed) of the second line to form one of the anapests. Poe could have cited this poem instead of Byron's "Bride of Abydos" to illustrate most of the comments he made in connection with that poem in "The Rationale of Verse," but if he had tried to force his own verses into the time system he applied to Byron's poem (each foot in a dactyllic or anapestic line having exactly the time requirement of four "short" syllables) he would have encountered the same difficulty he found in Byron. Out of the sixteen lines quoted from "The Bride of Abydos" there are two "caesuras" (so called because each consists of a "long" syllable at the end of the line when it is followed by a "long" syllable at the beginning of the next line), and three feet that are really trochees though Poe calls them spondees in order to give them the time interval of dactyls. He finds fault with Byron for distorting the natural stress, although he is the one who does so in an effort to convert the trochees into spondees. However, he admits that "not one person in ten thousand could, by ear, detect the inaccuracy." This statement renders the entire argument absurd. In the first sixteen lines of Poe's own lyric there are five iambic feet among the anapests which, by his system, are no less inaccurate than Byron's trochees. If he had accepted natural stress as the principle of English verse he would have found no inaccuracy in either Byron's poem or his own.[21]

The first lyric of "Al Aaraaf" is very irregular and is less melodious than the second, but it has rhythmic beauty if it is read with attention to the sense of the words. Conventionally scanned, the dominant rhythm is iambic and the prevailing line pattern is trimeter; yet there are lines in which there seem to be four feet ("From their príde, and

[21] For Poe's discussion of the lines from "The Bride of Abydos," see *Works*, XIV, 242–247. An explanation of my own system of scansion may be needed here. I accept accent as the basis of rhythm in English poetry, and I assume therefore that each foot, as a rhythmic unit, has one accented syllable and only one. Since stress is relative the reader of dissyllabic verse will naturally stress one syllable more than the other, depending upon the basic pattern of the line. The pyrrhic and spondee are both illogical and unnecessary for scansion. The monosyllabic foot is a useful term by which to designate a foot in which the normal unaccented syllable or syllables are omitted but compensated for by a rhetorical pause or by some juxtaposition of consonants that makes enunciation more deliberate than usual.

from their throne") and lines in which there seem to be only two ("In
the deép ský"). One line ("Thó' the beíngs whóm thy Nésacé") might
even be scanned with five stresses. The sensitive ear may find fault
with the concluding line ("In the environs of Heaven"). If we stress
the second syllable of "environs," we produce a shrill sound out of
keeping with the tone of the context, but if we choose the alternate
pronunciation, stressing the first and last syllables, we make the line
very weak.

The beauty of "Al Aaraaf" is by no means confined to these two
lyrics. Indeed, the fifteen introductory lines of Part I, though they do
not sing, have a pronounced lyrical quality. The rhythm is predominantly iambic, and each line has four feet except the last, which seems
to have only two. They fall consecutively into three groups of four, six,
and five lines. The first line ("O! nothing earthly save the ray") is
repeated to begin the second group except that "thrill" is substituted
for "ray," and the third group begins with a similar line ("Oh, nothing
of the dross of ours"). The basic statement of all three groups is that
the only earthly things on Al Aaraaf are Beauty and Love expressed
through music and flowers. The change from the "O!" of the first and
fifth lines to the "Oh," of the eleventh suggests that the poet is
consciously reducing the intensity of the earlier mood before mentioning the "dross" of our world in contrast to the quiet beauties that
"Adorn yon world afar, afar— / The wandering star." The repetition
of "afar" and the shortening of the last line suggest, to me at least, the
subsiding motion and abrupt termination of a flight from Al Aaraaf to
earth. I believe the poet felt something like this effect himself, even if
he did not consciously design the lines with the intention of reproduc-
ing it in the reader.

The main body of the poem, consisting of the remaining 283 lines, is
written in pentameter verse, predominantly iambic, and the lines are
arranged, with five or six exceptions, in rhymed couplets. The most
frequent metrical variation is the substitution of a trochee for an
iambus at the beginning of the line, but there are many less conventional variations, such as the wrenching of the normal stress to describe an irregular movement (Part I, line 150: "Lest the stárs tótter in
the guílt of mán"), or the reduction of the normal five stresses to four,
with weak syllables between, to hurry the movement (Part II, lines
52–53: "From the wíld enérgy of wánton haste / Her cheeks were
flúshing, and her líps apárt"). Sometimes a line with six stresses will

be followed by a line with only four by way of compensation, as in Part II, lines 243–244: "Dréad stár! that came, amid a níght of mírth, / A red Daedálion on the tímid Eárth." This is the way in which the lines would be normally read, though of course they can be readily forced into the regular pattern by lifting some of the stress from "Dread" and adding some to "on." At other times a thought or a mood is emphasized by a line in which seven or eight syllables (often separate words) must be given almost equal stress, as in Part II, line 177, where we are told that Heaven imparts no grace "To those who hear not for their beating hearts." Here the reader will naturally be inclined to give more stress to the alternate syllables, but the line is more effective if the difference is minimized.

Many other examples could easily be produced to illustrate the skilled craftsmanship of this poem. There are a few logical inconsist-encies, as in Nesace's song to Ligeia, where she says in one place (II, 90–91) that the spirits were lulled to rest by "kisses of true love," but elsewhere in the same lyric (II, 146–147) that their slumber was produced by music. These are trivial flaws. More weighty is the alleged vagueness of the poem, although that has often been exagger-ated. There are some weaknesses in structure that I have pointed out in "An Interpretation of 'Al Aaraaf,'" but I may have exaggerated these. I am more than ever convinced that it is a better poem than most critics have acknowledged. Its worth is not recognized because critics do not read it for the purpose of understanding it. Poe is himself partly to blame for its neglect, for he sometimes referred to it disparagingly as a juvenile poem. He did so at first, I suspect, to disarm the critics; but later he may have been misled by some faulty criteria of his own, especially such as he laid down in "The Rationale of Verse." Justice requires that it be allowed a central position among all of Poe's poems published before 1845.

Of the nine short poems in the 1827 volume, four were not reprinted by Poe even in the 1829 edition. These were "Dreams," "Evening Star," and two poems then without titles but by later editors given the titles "Stanzas" and "The Happiest Day—the Happiest Hour." The poorest of these, both in style and in structure, is "Stanzas," a vaguely mystical meditation that might have been meant for an imitation of Wordsworth. "Dreams" is a little better, but it is a juvenile imitation of Byron revealing such things as would-be unhappy boys are made of. "The Happiest Day—the Happiest Hour" could have been written only by a boy in comfortable circumstances imagining, in a Byronic mood, that he had lost happiness and now had nothing to do but nurse his "sear'd and blighted heart." "Evening Star" is a simple lyric with some good lines, but it lacks consistency of form and logical development. It is probably a very early poem, one written perhaps before Poe had read Byron. "Imitation" is presumably an imitation of Byron. Though not as bad as some of the others, it was almost completely rewritten for the 1829 volume. Of the original twenty lines he retained, with revisions, only about half a dozen. Most of the forty lines in the revised poem are inferior to the 1827 version, but about a dozen pleased John Neal, and he printed them in his magazine *The Yankee* in December 1829. In deference perhaps to Neal, Poe appended these lines to "Tamerlane" in his 1831 *Poems,* but he omitted them from his 1845 edition. With further revisions and additions, these lines were published by Poe in *The Flag of Our Union* in 1849 as "A Dream within a Dream." In its final form the work is much improved, though hardly recognizable as the same poem he started with. Like the later "Lenore" it well illustrates Poe's hoarding of early ideas and images and his habit of frequent republication and revision.

The best of the 1827 poems were a ballad beginning "I saw thee on thy bridal day" (in 1829 "To ___ ___," and later "Song"), "Visit of the Dead" (in 1829 and later "Spirits of the Dead"), an untitled ballad-like poem (in 1829 and later "A Dream"), and "The Lake" (in 1829 and later "The Lake— To _____"). The first two betray a note of irony not often heard in Poe's verse. This has contributed to the opinion that they express a feeling of resentment and wishful thinking on the part of the poet: the former because the girl he loved has married another, the latter because his foster father, John Allan, has exercised his parental authority wilfully and oppressively. The poems may have had their origin in this mood of resentment, for there is a degree of comfort after injuries received, real or supposed, in imagining that the person responsible for them will some day suffer comparable injuries from others, or will be made unhappy by regret or remorse.[22] "A Dream" lost its initial stanza in the 1829 version, but otherwise remained much the same. Judged merely on its merits, the deleted stanza appears to be as good as the rest of the poem, but it smacks of personal narrative, whereas the basic images develop the contrasting moods of present sorrow and remembered joy. "The Lake" was an

[22] This mood of wishful thinking is often felt by children and adolescents and sometimes it finds expression in poems such as Tennyson's "Locksley Hall."

excellent poem even in the 1827 version and the revisions in 1829 and later made it surely one of Poe's best short poems. Three of these four poems were included in the 1845 edition, but for reasons which are not obvious to me, "Spirits of the Dead" was excluded.

The text of the 1827 edition is full of printer's errors that Poe would undoubtedly have corrected if he had seen proof copies. By contrast, there are relatively few errors in the 1829 text. All of the five poems reprinted were improved by revision, and only one, "A Dream within a Dream," was materially altered thereafter. Poe's taste, though obviously romantic, was already sure in 1829, and his artistic maturity was far beyond his age. This is evident in all but one of the six new poems first published in 1829. The exception is "To M___," which Poe never reprinted, although Griswold, in his 1850 edition, printed eight lines of it (the first two stanzas) from a signed manuscript in Poe's handwriting, a clean copy with no revisions. These lines contain five verbal changes from the text of 1829: in the first line "O!" is omitted and "heed" is substituted for "care"; the fourth line has "hatred" for "fever," the fifth, "mourn" for "heed," and the seventh, "sorrow" for "meddle." All of these are improvements; and so is the omission of the last three stanzas, which are not only morbid but out of harmony with the mood of the first two. The other five poems are the untitled sonnet prefixed to "Al Aaraaf" (later called "Sonnet—To Science"), the poem called "Preface" prefixed to the section of "Miscellaneous Poems" (later called "Romance"), "Fairyland" (later "Fairy-Land"), "To ___ ___," and "To the River ___." The last two were omitted from the 1831 volume though Poe published them in the *Broadway Journal* in 1845 and included them in the 1845 edition. Neither has distinction of thought or diction. In 1831 "To Science" was again placed, without title and without verbal changes, before "Al Aaraaf" as a prologue. The original twenty-one lines of "Romance" were reprinted in 1831 with only two or three verbal changes, but twenty-four new lines were inserted after the tenth line and twenty-one more at the end. These forty-five lines were all dropped in subsequent publications of the poem. Since the enlarged version was the first poem of the 1831 volume and was called "Introduction," Poe must have intended it as an autobiographical "apology" for his verses. Of course, the autobiography was mostly fanciful, but even so its inclusion was, like some other aspects of this volume, inconsistent with his theory. Only half of the forty-six lines of the 1829 "Fairyland" are kept in the 1831 version, but forty new lines are introduced at the beginning to make a story. Most of these lines are so obviously inferior that Poe must have written them hastily before sending the manuscript to the printer in the hope that they would lighten the tone of his book. They were dropped in subsequent printings.

Certain characteristic aspects of mood, meaning, and form in these early poems require particular attention. I have said elsewhere that "the predominant moods of the 1827 volume as a whole are those of wounded pride and resentment for the wrongs, real or imagined, that he had suffered," and that the dominant tone of the 1829 volume "is one of disillusionment with the world and escape into some more congenial realm of dream or of the imagination."[23] These are generalizations and may perhaps oversimplify the facts. They will best be understood, and perhaps modified, when examined in the light of an analysis of the poems Poe thought worth revising and reprinting. It should also be remembered that Poe was temperamentally averse to revealing the facts of his personal life. This aversion sometimes induced him to make up stories about himself which his early biographers uncritically accepted as literal fact.

For this reason if for no other we should be on our guard against reading the poems as autobiography. The bride in "Song" who blushed on her bridal day when she saw her rejected suitor may have been associated in the poet's mind with Elmira Royster, but there is nothing in the poem itself to support such a conjecture. We cannot be sure that the poem was written after Elmira's marriage to A. B. Shelton, or even after her engagement to him.[24] The situation of the resentful rejected suitor is fairly common in both literature and life. Our knowledge that romantic poets have sometimes made their own woes the subject of a song leads us to assume too readily that Poe has done so in this case. The conjecture that "Spirits of the Dead" was suggested by Poe's resentment against the restrictive authority of John Allan is still less justified by the evidence of the poem itself. Actually, the mood of this poem is not one of resentment so much as weary hopelessness under the domination of the thought of death. The spirits of the dead mentioned in the second stanza are the personified memories of the person described, and the "red orbs" of the third are symbols of his own depressing thoughts. The "mist upon the hill" in

[23] Quoted from the introduction to Stovall, p. xx, *The Poems of Edgar Allan Poe*, 1965.

[24] Apparently Poe was not in Richmond at the time of Elmira's marriage. See Hervey Allen's *Israfel* (New York, 1926), I, 234; II, 877.

the last stanza is a symbol of the impenetrable veil which enshrouds the soul in such a mood. If we did not know from other sources of Poe's troubles with his foster-father we should not think of associating the poem with him. In this poem the poet addresses himself, or any one in such a mood, not John Allan specifically. The images—the beamless stars, the mysterious mist, and the overshadowing will of surrounding spirits—constitute an objective correlative by which the mood is realized. The things and places described need have no existence except as they are used by the poet. Several of Poe's poems, both early and late, can be understood only through this device.

"The Lake— To _____" is the most perfect illustration of the device among the early poems. Here the mood is loneliness, a loneliness which can be both lovely and terrible.[25] The lake, surrounded by black rock and tall pines, is lovely by day, but under the "pall" of night, with the "mystic" wind murmuring in the pines, the beauty awakens terror—terror that is not ordinary fright, but a feeling delightful though indefinable. In "The Lake" (1827 version) Poe says this feeling is "undefined, / Springing from a darken'd mind." This was changed in 1829 to "A feeling not the jewell'd mine / Should ever bribe me to define— / Nor Love—altho' the Love be thine." The reason for rejecting "darken'd mind" is clear. It is inconsistent with the mood of loneliness because "darken'd" connotes something bad, whereas the loneliness of the lake is delightful. Having eliminated "mind," he cannot find a way to keep "undefin'd" as a rhyme, and rewrites and extends the passage. Presumably he introduced "jewell'd mine" to rhyme with "define," but then found the lines a bit obscure and so added the line about Love. Having done that (with "thine" as a rhyme word), it seemed desirable, for the sake of consistency, to change the title so that the poem would seem to have been addressed to some one who might love. If I am right, these changes, once "darken'd" is got rid of, are purely technical and do not affect the meaning. The last stanza has led some interpreters to believe that Poe, as a boy, contemplated suicide by drowning himself in a lake. Such an interpretation is a misreading of the lines and is not supported by the final version. In the 1827 version he wrote "a fitting grave / For him who thence could solace bring / To his dark imagining." In 1829 "dark" was changed to "lone." It is possible that Poe meant that the lake would be a place in which, because of its loneliness and its beauty, a lonely lover of

[25] Cf. "Al Aaraaf," I, 83–85: "In the deep sky, / The terrible and fair, / In beauty vie!"

beauty might fittingly seek death. The idea is not unlike that of Keats's "Ode to a Nightingale," in which the poet, enchanted by the beauty of the bird's song, is "half in love with easeful Death."

The mood of the poems of 1829 is one of disillusionment and escape from the world of material realities, but this mood needs further defining. As I have tried to demonstrate in the essay on "Al Aaraaf," an "escape" from earth to Al Aaraaf, as in Angelo's death, is symbolic of the artist's renunciation of all aims for his art except the creation of beauty. The artist who makes such a renunciation does not die, of course, and may live in the world as other men so long as his art remains uncorrupted by worldly aims. In "Sonnet—To Science" Poe condemns science only in so far as he is an artist; as a rational and social being, he approved the knowledge man has achieved through science. Like time, science changes all things; it destroys our illusions, especially our nature myths, and replaces them with the realities of everyday experience. Yet we do not lose illusion entirely; we only come to recognize it for what it is and distinguish it from reality. The Hamadryad is not destroyed, but driven from the wood to another and more congenial world of the imagination. This world we can know only through what Coleridge described as "that willing suspension of disbelief for the moment, which constitutes poetic faith."[26]

"Romance" is not only a good poem but an interesting one for what it reveals of Poe's theory of poetry and his development as a poet. In the first four lines of the original and shorter version, he defines "romance" as a bird in green leaves which are visible only as they are reflected in "the bosom of some shadowy lake." This definition is in keeping with Poe's theory that the effect of poetry should be indefinitive and that it presents to the reader not truth itself but truth reflected in forms of beauty. The remaining six lines of the first stanza tell us that for him, as a boy, romance was imitative, a paroquet, and a painted one besides, which suggests that the sentiments expressed in the earliest poems were insincere. The eleven lines of the second stanza, in so far as they are autobiographical, state that "of late," that is, during the years 1827–29, his life has been so full of real trouble that he has had no time (and presumably no taste) for the trivial cares that inspired his first verse. When he has known calmer hours in which he could write at all, he has felt that it would be wrong to express any mood except that of complete sincerity. If we may inter-

[26] *Biographia Literaria*, ed. J. Shawcross (2 vols.; London, 1907), II, 6.

pret this stanza as a definition of romance as it appeared to him in his more mature years (1828–29), and should appear to every serious romantic poet, it is a real bird, not a painted one, and it is not a paroquet but a bird that sings its own individual song and through it expresses its genuine nature and feelings. In the expanded version of 1831 the poem represents three periods of development, seeming to separate in time the years of tumult and the calmer hours. Poe's reason for dropping the new lines, in addition to the desire to be less openly autobiographical, was the recognition that the calmer hours did not come all at once at the end of a period of trouble, but came, in his own life as in that of others, as intervals between periods of trouble.

"Fairy-Land" is also closely related to "Al Aaraaf" and suggestive of his poetic theory. The place described is an unreal one, where the reflected light of the moon, or moons, prevails over the starlight, which would be direct, like the light of the sun. Moonlight clearly suggests the world of the imagination, not the real world. When the "easy drapery" of moonlight buries the real world in the deep "passion" of sleep, we have a condition similar to that on Al Aaraaf. When the hovering moon rises into the sky the next day, it dissolves in a shower of atoms, which are brought back to earth on the wings of "those butterflies" that "seek the skies." That the butterfly is a symbol of the poet is evident enough in the original version of 1829 and is merely blurred in 1831 by the introduction of an enfolding story. The story was very properly dropped after 1831.

The craftsmanship of these short poems of 1829 is equal to that of "Al Aaraaf." Poe was never fond of the sonnet form, and "Sonnet—To Science" may have been written as a prologue for "Al Aaraaf" for no better reason than that Byron had prefixed a sonnet to his "Prisoner of Chillon." Nevertheless, this sonnet, though irregular in its rhyme sequence, is a good example of the Shakespearean type. The rhythm is pleasingly varied, the stresses are those of natural speech, and the progression of the thought is in harmony with the structural development of the sonnet. "Romance" is more lyrical, of course, being arranged in tetrameter couplets, but a sing-song pattern is avoided by an occasional displacement of stress, as in the line "Among the green leaves as they shake." "Fairy-Land" has a fluid movement that is appropriate to both the mood and the meaning. This is secured by the skillful arrangement of vowels and consonants in iambic trimeter, with variations in both rhyme and rhythm to avoid monotony. On the evidence of these poems I think it may be said without exaggeration that by the winter of 1829–30 Poe had arrived at aesthetic maturity and had very nearly mastered his craft.

Little need be said about the half dozen early poems that Poe never collected: "Alone," "Elizabeth," "An Acrostic," "Serenade," "Latin Hymn," and "Song of Triumph." The first three were written in albums, and it is quite possible that Poe did not keep a copy of any of them. Even if he did he would probably not have thought them good enough to be published in editions issued subsequent to their composition. "Alone" is perhaps the best of the three, but it is undistinguished even among the early poems in either meaning or form. "Elizabeth" is better metrically, but it was presumably written after the 1831 volume was published and excluded from the 1845 edition because of the higher standards by which Poe selected the poems for that collection. Originally the other two poems were a part of the story "Epimanes" and by themselves are insignificant. Of the poems attributed to Poe, "O, Tempora! O, Mores!" is a not very clever satire on the manners of the time and in particular on a certain "beau" and "counter-hopper" by the name of Pitts, who is assumed to have been an acquaintance of Poe's in Richmond in the 1820's. "A West Point Lampoon" is better, but it is only a fragment. "To __" ("Sleep on, sleep on," etc.) is a lyric of considerable beauty; "Fanny" is not so good, partly because the meter falters in the second line and in one or two others. "Ballad" is somewhat in the mood of the 1827 "Song" ("I saw thee on thy bridal day"), but it is inferior both in meter and in structure.[27] "The Musiad," which Poe may have written or helped to write, is a witty satire, much superior to "O, Tempora! O, Mores!" Why he did not preserve and acknowledge it, if indeed it was his work, I do not know unless it was because, if included in any of his collections, it would have appeared incongruous among the poems evolved from moods rather than from ideas.[28]

III

Besides "Scenes from *Politian*," Poe published seventeen new poems before 1845, six of them in the edition of 1831. Some of his finest lines may be found in the original versions of these six poems. Yet if the 1831 texts are compared with the best of the earlier poems—"The

[27] For an account of the discovery and publication of these poems, see Stovall, pp. 290–298.

[28] See "Poe and 'The Musiad.'"

Lake," "Romance," "Fairy-Land," and "Al Aaraaf"—it must be admitted, I believe, that they are not remarkably superior. Only after much revision over the ensuing twelve to fourteen years did they come to be the masterpieces that we rank among Poe's best. In their final form, therefore, they are the products not alone of his youth but equally of his middle years. Looking at them in the light of his poetic theory, we recognize in them the richer poetic moods of his early period presented with the technical mastery of his second period. Fortunately, he applied his acute critical judgment chiefly to improvements in diction and imagery and rarely tampered with the original moods or rhythms. In the final version of "Lenore" there is some evidence of the application of the metrical theories of "The Rationale of Verse," but even there the changes in metrical pattern from "A Paean" of 1831, through the *Pioneer* version of 1843, are more apparent than real. They consist in changes in the length of the lines, hardly at all in the rhythm, rhyme, or total effect. In other poems changes of title or the omission of lines cause some alteration in meaning, but this again is more apparent than real. My interpretations are based on the final versions of the poems except where reference to earlier ones is necessary to clarify meanings.

The first thing to be said about "To Helen" is that far too much effort has been expended trying to prove its sources and not enough trying to understand it. The poem may have been inspired by Mrs. Jane Stith Stanard, as Poe wrote Mrs. Helen Whitman in 1848,[29] but if so the fact is merely incidental. The much discussed "Nicéan barks" and "perfumed sea" may have been derived from Milton, or Homer, or elsewhere,[30] but their source has little or no importance in determining the meaning of the poem, although the words and the images contribute to its beauty. "To Helen" consists of three stanzas of five lines each, rhyming *ababb, ababa, abbab*. It is irregular in form. The dominant rhythm is iambic but it is varied by trochees and anapests both at the beginning of the line and within the line. Lines 5, 9, and 10 do not fit comfortably into this pattern, and line 15 not at all, since it can have only two feet. If "way-worn" is pronounced naturally, as it should be, line 4 really has five stresses, and the necessary pause between "own" and "native" (because of the two *n's* coming together)

[29] *The Letters of Edgar Allan Poe*, ed. J. W. Ostrom (Cambridge, Mass., 1948), p. 385.

[30] For a good summary of many theories see Edward Snyder, "Poe's Nicéan Barks," *Classical Journal*, XLVIII (Feb. 1953), 159–169.

compensates for the missing unstressed syllable in line 5. Lines 9 and 10 are pedestrian if given four stresses; they are more effective if read with three or even two, the natural lingering of the voice on "glory" and "grandeur" again compensating for the lost stress, and the extra unstressed syllables absorbing the expected time interval. The shortening of the last line adds to the resonance of "Holy-Land!"

The first two stanzas are not difficult to understand. The simile in the first compares Helen's beauty to a boat that returns the weary wanderer to his native land. In the second this beauty is made specific in the terms "hyacinth hair," "classic face," and "Naiad airs," and the "home" to which this beauty has returned him, as by a boat, is the home of beauty, the same which he had symbolized in the star Al Aaraaf. These lines were first printed in their final form in 1843; earlier versions had "beauty of fair Greece" and "grandeur of old Rome." The change from "beauty" to "glory" suggests the quality of beauty, and the change from "of fair" to "that was" makes glory not merely a characteristic of Greece but the synonym of it. The last stanza develops the idea, first explored in "Al Aaraaf," that beauty is related to truth and dwells with the soul in a region which, for the poet, is holy. In 1843 the "folded scroll" of the original version was changed to "agate lamp." The lamp is a better symbol of transcendental truth than the scroll, and in making the lamp base agate, which has many colors suggesting the colors of the spectrum, Poe symbolizes beauty supporting truth. This is best understood in the equation: beauty is to truth as the colors of the spectrum are to the single ray of sunlight. Both beauty and truth, in the image of the lamp, are upheld by Psyche, the soul, which can perceive beauty as truth. The Holy Land of the last line is not Palestine, but Al Aaraaf, the home of beauty and the true native land of the artist, the lover of beauty.

"Israfel" is, like "To Helen," a thematic poem, but it is more specific about the nature and limitations of the earthly poet. It was much revised and improved in phrasing and structure after 1831, but its essential meaning remained the same. Israfel is wise and sings an impassioned song because he dwells in Heaven, where deep thoughts are a duty and where Love is a "grown-up" God—that is to say, where love is spiritual, not sensual. The poet of earth, however, is limited by the imperfections of mortality and, it is implied, must avoid in his singing both truth except as imaged in forms of beauty and passion unless it is spiritualized. Nevertheless this poem comes nearer than any other new poem of 1831 to what Poe later called the "heresy of the didactic." The most striking change after 1831 is in the structure of the stanzas. In the early versions the first, third, and fifth had the same rhyme sequence; all three were altered by the addition of one or two lines or the fusion of an original line in two or three new ones. The gain is not only in greater variety of structure, but in the lyrical effect of the stanzas. Some of these changes were made in 1841, but the final form was not attained until 1843. The original first line of the last stanza was broken into two, probably because it was the only one that had internal rhyme. In some of these changes it is possible to see the operation of the metrical theories of "The Rationale of Verse." By substituting "grown-up God" for "grown God" in the fourth stanza he may gain something in precision of meaning, but in regularizing the meter he sacrifices the beauty of the rhythm.

"The City in the Sea," "The Sleeper," and "The Valley of Unrest" constitute a distinct group because they are all similar in form and closely related in theme. Their mood is that of melancholy at the thought of death and its consequences, one being a dim consciousness on the part of the dead person that his friends are forgetting him and that he will inevitably sink into oblivion. The first two have the same metrical pattern, iambic tetrameter varied by the frequent substitution of trochaic or anapestic feet and the displacement in the line of one or two stresses. "The Valley of Unrest" begins as trochaic tetrameter "catalectic" (to use a pedantic term) and that seems to be the domi-nant pattern, although at least ten lines, including the last five, begin with an iambic foot and are hence iambic all the way, and two of the couplets have feminine rhymes. These variations break up the tripping movement of the first lines and avoid the intrusion of a lightness out of keeping with the serious mood of the poem.

The basic image of a city that sinks into the sea may have been borrowed from antiquity, but Poe's city, where Death reigns, is not a real city and never existed except in his imagination. It is, in fact, more like a cemetery, and it is the symbol of the soul's temporary quiet after death before it begins to sink into oblivion, which is symbolized by the sea. The poem has been frequently misunderstood because of attempts at literal interpretation. Poe's early titles for it contributed to the misunderstanding. The original title was "The Doomed City," which, in itself, is not inconsistent with my interpreta-tion, for all people are "doomed" to die and be eventually forgotten. When Poe reprinted it in the Southern Literary Messenger in 1836, however, he gave it the title "The City of Sin," and this has led some

readers to think the sinking of the city into Hell represents a punishment for its sins. But the fourth line, which is in all texts, clearly states
that both good and bad have found "eternal rest," or will find it, in
this city. In the *American Review* for April 1845 Poe called it "The
City in the Sea. A Prophecy." In a sense it is a prophecy, since it is a
foreshadowing of a common fate. Later in the same year the poem
was published in the *Broadway Journal.* There, "A Prophecy" was
dropped from the title. The concluding lines have bothered some
readers: "Hell, rising from a thousand thrones, / Shall do it reverence." But this "Hell" is not the place which Christians have been
taught to believe unredeemed sinners will be condemned to inhabit
after death. It is simply the place to which all the dead go, something
like the Greek idea of Hades. In fact, in the 1836 text Poe substituted
"All Hades, from" for "Hell, rising." I think he restored the word
"Hell" because it gives rhythmic strength to the line, whereas the
dissyllable "Hades" weakens it.

The original title of "The Sleeper" was "Irene" (pronounced as
three syllables), the name of the lady in the poem who sleeps the
sleep of death. She lies on a bed with a canopy which the wind,
coming through an open window, waves so that the moonlight causes
it to cast moving shadows on the floor and on the wall. In the 1831
version the questions asked in lines 18 to 36 are said to be "hummed"
by the moon—possibly reflecting the same fantasy that produced a
moon ray with a "tune" in the 1831 version of "Fairy-Land." Fortunately he removed the fantasy in both poems. Yet the moon does exert
its influence. In "The Sleeper" it exhales a vapor which "steals drow-
sily and musically / Into the universal valley." The valley is said to be
universal because, like the city in the sea, it is no particular place but
the symbol of a mood, or a condition of the mind. This mood is developed by the images of the rosemary that nods on the wave (sym-
bolizing forgetfulness), the lily that lolls on the wave, and the lake
that looks like Lethe. In conjunction with these images I should like
to draw attention to lines 41 to 59 of the original poem. There we are
told that the soul of one who has died sleeps peacefully as long as it is
remembered and mourned, but when "light laughter chokes the sigh,"
it leaves the tomb and goes to "some remember'd lake," and there

> Pores for a moment, ere it go,
> On the clear waters there that flow,
> Then sinks within (weigh'd down by wo)
> Th' uncertain, shadowy heaven below.

These nineteen lines were omitted in all versions published after 1831, possibly because Poe thought them too specific a statement of the ideas he had already suggested by the images of the rosemary, the lily, and the lethean lake, and possibly also because they were so obviously connected with "The City in the Sea." The wish expressed in lines 38–48, that Irene's sleep will be deep, is in effect a wish that her surviving friends will not cease to remember her and mourn her death.

The third poem of this group, "The Valley of Unrest," was originally called "The Valley Nis," and was reprinted with that title in the *Southern Literary Messenger* in 1836. These versions also contained sixteen introductory lines omitted when the poem was published in 1845 with its present title. These lines contribute little or nothing to the meaning of the poem, but they have some interest with respect to the origin of the early title. The valley "Nis" is said to be far away in the "golden east," and is also said to be the subject of a "Syriac tale" that is all about "unhappy things." The last two of the lines omitted are: "But 'the valley Nis' at best / Means 'the valley of unrest'!" The remaining lines were much revised, but their meaning was not significantly changed. Instead of "each visiter" in the ninth line, the early version had "the unhappy"; a person named "Helen" is addressed at this point in the early version, and later the sky is described as "terror-stricken." These phrases were dropped, I suspect, because they were too specific. In the final version the poem conveys the intended mood and meaning entirely through symbolic images.[31]

The valley had not always been a place of unrest. Once it had been "silent," which, in the context, means without sound or movement. The people who had inhabited the valley did not "dwell" there any more because they had gone to the wars and had presumably been killed. The word "dwell" means, I believe, to exist as a living human being. Presumably the people were buried there, but the valley was still "silent" because, though dead, the people were not forgotten.

[31] The original title may have used "Nis" as an inverted spelling of "Sin," as Campbell suggested. "Sin" was a moon-god worshipped some four or five thousand years ago, according to the *Encyclopaedia Britannica*, by wandering tribes in the valley of the Euphrates. Rees's *New Cyclopaedia* (1810) does not mention this, but says that Ptolemy identifies by that name a country in India near the Ganges. Rees also identifies Sin, or Zin, as a city of Arabia Petraea, from which the area was called the "wilderness of Sin." Perhaps the "Syriac" tale was invented by Poe in connection with one or another of these places. The source of the title, however, is of little importance. In so far as it is meaningful for this poem, it may also explain the 1836 title of "The City in the Sea," which was "The City of Sin," although that was in the west, not in the east.

Now any visitor to the valley will notice that nothing there is motionless aloft, although the air near the ground is still and brooding. The clouds are driven and "rustle" through the heavens, and yet there is no wind. The lilies "wave" though the air is motionless, and the grave over which they wave is nameless. The person buried there, the poem seems to say, has now been forgotten. The valley's supernatural restlessness is the symbolic consequence of the buried person's sinking into oblivion. Of course the word "dwell" may be taken literally. In that case we must assume that the person buried is forgotten because the people who might have remembered him have gone away and been killed in the wars. Either interpretation proves the poem to be closely related in theme to "The City in the Sea" and "The Sleeper."

"Lenore" is different both in theme and in form. As published with the title "A Paean" in 1831 it consisted of eleven ballad-like stanzas which vary in metrical pattern for no reason. The first and eighth have the regular four-foot line alternating with a three-foot line, but the second, fifth, and ninth stanzas vary slightly from this pattern, and the rest of them definitely have three feet in each of their four lines. Poe seemed to recognize the inferiority of "A Paean," for he revised it many times, the last only a few weeks before his death. The first drastic revision was made for the *Pioneer* in 1843. There the poem was titled "Lenore" and arranged in irregular lines with end rhymes except the third, which had internal rhyme but no end rhyme: "Let the bell toll!—A saintly soul." I suspect this was an editor's change or a printer's error, for when the poem was soon afterward published in the Philadelphia *Saturday Museum* this line was broken into two in conformity with other lines. In 1831 the story is told by the lover, and the statements of the family of the girl (whose name Helen is mentioned there but later dropped) are given in the third person. The *Pioneer* version presents for the first time a dialogue between the lover and the family. The final form of the poem combines two or three of the *Pioneer* lines into one of seven feet; most of these long lines therefore have internal rhyme as well as end rhyme. If the two versions are read aloud to a person who has not seen the printed poems, his ear will hardly detect a difference except where verbal changes have been made. The long lines were first used in 1845, doubtless under the influence of "The Raven." One change that may be significant is that in the early version the girl's beauty is stressed, whereas in 1845 the stress is on her innocence. Otherwise the theme remains the same, expressed by the lover's singing a paean instead of a dirge because in dying the girl escapes from her wicked family to the happiness of heaven.

After 1831 Poe was so busy editing magazines, reviewing books, and writing tales for periodicals that he found little time for serious poetry. His longest composition in verse was written probably during the year 1833 or 1834. This was the poetic drama *Politian—A Tragedy,* which was never completed, and of which only five scenes were published. These appeared in the *Southern Literary Messenger* in the issues of December 1835 and January 1836. The poem has little or no value as a drama, although it was probably conceived and begun in the desperate hope that it might be staged and earn the money required for his support. Before it was finished he had found a career in journalism. The play is written in blank verse, some of it very good, but Poe's genius was for lyric, not dramatic, poetry. The chief character, Politian, never comes to life, and the style is derived from models long out of fashion. The plot is melodramatic, based, it is generally believed, on newspaper accounts of a murder and court trial that occurred a few years before in Kentucky, but the scenes and characters are transported to Rome in what appears to be the sixteenth century. Politian, who is English, is sensitive to beauty, and his moods are reminiscent of some of Poe's earlier verses. He is the same person in conception as the Visionary in the tale of that name (later "The Assignation") and has affinities with several characters in the prose fiction.

The short blank verse poem "The Coliseum" was incorporated in the manuscript of *Politian,* but it may have been written independently since it was submitted in the *Saturday Visiter* literary competition during the summer of 1833. When the scene in which it appears in the manuscript was published, "The Coliseum" was omitted. Its style is similar to the lines spoken by Politian elsewhere in the play, and its tone of sonorous melancholy is but a deepening of the one we have heard in earlier verse. Poe here displays such command of blank verse that one wonders whether, after all, his genius was exclusively lyrical.

Though its setting is very different, "To One in Paradise" expresses a mood not unlike that of "The Coliseum," but it is even closer to the mood of some of the earlier poems, "A Dream," for example, or "A Dream Within a Dream," or even "Romance." The last stanza of "To One in Paradise" has been much admired, and justly so, for its melody in iambic trimeter is perfect. Yet the first three stanzas, in which the rhythm is less regular, are equally charming. In the first stanza the rhythm flows smoothly through the first two lines, but in the third line is sharply broken by the displacement of expected stresses: "A green isle in the sea, love." The excessive stress of the line eases in the next line, "A fountain and a shrine," where there are only two natural stresses instead of the expected three. Again in the last line of the second stanza ("Mute, motionless, aghast!") we have two stressed syllables to begin with and then three unstressed ones before we arrive at the strong third one in "aghast!" Both the lyrical form and the theme are characteristic of Poe's early period. In its finished form, the poem is much improved over the first version, which was incorporated in "The Visionary," a tale published in *Godey's Lady's Book* for January 1834. It was probably composed at about the same time as "The Coliseum."

Three other poems of this period are the lines incorporated without title in "Morella," afterwards called "Catholic Hymn" and finally "Hymn"; the lines first published in 1835 with the title "To Mary" and years later reprinted as a compliment to Mrs. Osgood with the title "To F——"; and the poem first published as "Lines Written in an Album," eventually also used to compliment Mrs. Osgood and given the title "To F——s S. O——d." These poems have no personal significance, of course, in Poe's relationship with Mrs. Osgood, except as polite compliments, and they probably had no greater significance for any other relationship; hence there was no impropriety in his sending to one woman a poem that may have been previously addressed to another.

"Bridal Ballad" is much better and shows an advance in technique. First published in January 1837, it is reminiscent of "Song" and may have been inspired by the same incident. But the existence of two such poems composed ten years apart minimizes the likelihood that either has any autobiographical significance. These two illustrate the growth of Poe as a poet. The earlier poem is equal to the later one in the simpler forms of poetic art, but the poem of 1837 is much more sophisticated. Every line has but three stresses, yet the number of syllables to the line varies from six to eight. The dominant rhythm is iambic, and yet fourteen of the thirty-three lines begin with an anapest, three with a dactyl. Thirteen of the lines have feminine endings, and lines in each stanza that have the same rhyme range in number from two to five. The second and final line of each stanza rhyme, but in the fourth stanza a third rhyme is introduced. In this poem, for the first time, Poe made effective use of repetition, not only in the last line of each stanza, which is a varied refrain, but within the stanza, as in the fourth: "And, though my faith be broken, / And, though my heart be broken."

Poe is known to have written only five sonnets. Two of these, "Sonnet—to Zante" and "Sonnet—Silence," belong to this period, the former to 1837 and the latter to 1840. "To Zante" is a rather conventional sonnet of the Shakespearean type in which the fair isle of Zante becomes accursed ground because there he once knew a happiness that is now departed. "Silence" is unconventional and irregular in several ways: it has fifteen lines, its rhyme sequence is *abab cdcd c efef gg*, thus breaking the Shakespearean pattern with an excess *c*-rhyme, and the development of the thought does not follow the usual four-part structure indicated by the rhymes. However, if the reader is unaware as he reads that a sonnet is intended, he will find the development of the thought entirely satisfactory. Poe was not a conventional writer, a fact which this poem, as well as many others, makes perfectly clear. Unlike Poe's earlier work, this poem appeals to the intellect more than to the feelings. The two silences are the corporate, produced by the death of the body, and the incorporate, produced, one must suppose, by the death of the soul, though the idea is not directly stated. Probably Poe does not try or wish to elucidate this idea, since it obviously lies beyond man's understanding, if not beyond his experience. To meet this nameless shadow, the last lines seem to suggest, is to face the thought of final annihilation—the prospect of becoming nothing, or if not nothing, something unimaginable. The mood is related in a vague way to some of the tales of this period, particularly to "The Fall of the House of Usher," "William Wilson," and "The Man of the Crowd."[32]

Poe's two best known poems from the years around 1840 are even more closely associated with his prose fiction. "The Haunted Palace," though first published separately, in April 1839, was a few months later incorporated in the first printing of "The Fall of the House of Usher." Whether it was written specifically for that story I cannot say, but that seems a reasonable conjecture. If Poe had analyzed this poem critically he would have been obliged to call it a work of the fancy, not of the imagination, and therefore not of the highest order. The idea of the head as the palace of the monarch Thought suits well enough at

---

[32] Other stories suggest the mind's rejection of the thought of the soul's annihilation; for examples, "The Conversation of Eiros and Charmion" and "The Colloquy of Monos and Una."

first, but when the metaphor is carried into detail—the hair as banners on the roof, the eyes as windows, and the mouth as the door—it becomes a bit ridiculous. The images of rational thought as spirits moving musically and of irrational thought as vast forms moving to a discordant melody are effective, and the total impact of the poem, especially on first reading, is considerable. The appeal is chiefly to the intellect, however; the poetic sentiment is not deeply felt. There are six stanzas, each with eight lines rhyming *ababcdcd*. The dominant line pattern is trochaic tetrameter, alternating acatalectic and catalectic; variations occur in the sixth line of each stanza, which has but two feet, and in lines 2 and 4 of the fourth stanza and line 8 of the fifth and sixth stanzas, which have three.

"The Conqueror Worm" was first published separately in 1843, but in 1845 it was incorporated, for the first time, into the tale "Ligeia," where it is somewhat intrusive because it violates the theme. The five stanzas of the poem correspond roughly to the five acts of a play. The universe is the theater, the human world the stage, and the celestial worlds the orchestra, which plays the "music of the spheres." The play is really a puppet show in which the actors are human beings, described as "mimes in the form of God," blindly chasing in circles an illusive phantom. Vast formless things, presumably such powers as Fate, Time, and Circumstance, control the scenery and the puppets. The audience is made up of angels, veiled perhaps so that they cannot be recognized or because they cannot bear to witness the madness and horror unveiled. The hero is Death, the "Conqueror Worm." One might say that the play is the tragedy "Man," as the poem states, except that it presents human life as futile and meaningless. The mood is not one of melancholy but rather of cynicism, and the manner is ironic. Each stanza has eight lines rhyming *ababcbcb*. The fourth stanza illustrates the basic metrical pattern, iambic tetrameter alternating with iambic trimeter. But there are numerous variations in both rhythm and meter. Five lines, all in the first two stanzas, begin with trochees, and approximately twenty-five anapests are scattered through the forty lines. The first line of the first stanza is "Lo! 'tis a gala night," which has only six syllables. According to the basic stanza pattern it should have four stresses, and perhaps Poe meant it so; but in that case we must read the first syllable as a monosyllabic foot, the second and third feet as trochees, and the fourth, "night" as an incomplete trochee or another monosyllabic foot. Moreover, the second line, which normally would have three stresses, obviously has four. In the second stanza the third line, which would normally have four, has only three stresses, and the sixth, which would normally have three, has four, while the last line, "Invisible Wo!" can be made to bear more than two stresses only by distorting the pronunciation. I mention these variations not because they are defects. On the contrary, they contribute unmistakably to the effect of the poem and were probably designed. It must be acknowledged, however, that both "The Haunted Palace" and "The Conqueror Worm" are idea poems and please rather by their display of technical skill than by any evocation of the poetic sentiment.

"Dream-Land," on the other hand, though the latest published of the poems in this section, is a mood poem closely related in theme to some of Poe's early verse. Some of the phrases and images closely resemble passages in "Fairy-Land" and "Spirits of the Dead," but it is nevertheless an original creation superior in nearly every way to the early poems as they were first published. It is not an exaggeration to claim for it the best of both periods, the somber tone and obscure symbolic imagery of 1829–31 and the technical mastery of the 1840's. The obscurity of the images has led to some misinterpretations. The title states specifically that the place described is the land of dreams. The Eidolon who reigns there is not Death but Night, as the third line plainly states. The dim Thule is the land of dreams, and it is out of time and space because what the dreamer does and sees is free of these normal limitations of sense experience during waking hours. "These lands" are simply the actual world as the dreamer finds it after waking; hence, as we are informed in the last stanza, he has "wandered home" from the land of dreams, which is to say he has awakened and is describing his dream in complete consciousness of what he is doing. The intervening four stanzas, constituting the main body of the poem, describe what he seemed to see and what he felt during the dream experience as he remembers it. The landscape of the second stanza has no feature that does not exist in some real landscape, but in their relationship to one another these features are distorted. They can be distorted because they are not controlled by laws of time and space. The vales seem bottomless and the floods boundless because their forms and limits are obscured by the foglike dimness—the "tears that drip all over." The mountains seem to be toppling into shoreless seas and yet they never really topple because their movements are free of the limits of time. The "Ghouls" of the third stanza are the "Memories" described farther on; they are sheeted because they are ghostlike, and they are ghostlike because they are forms dredged up from that part of the mind which is usually submerged in waking hours; they are shrouded because they appear to be the forms of persons now dead. The fourth stanza has led some readers to conclude that the dream described is one induced by opiates, but there is nothing in the poem that requires such an interpretation. The dreamer whose waking life is unhappy finds the dream soothing, despite its melancholy aspect, because it does not affect him as reality; he drifts passively through it without obligation and without passion, in a state not unlike that of the inhabitants of Al Aaraaf. He cannot understand what he sees, but he feels no desire to understand. In the first stanza, as also in the last, we are told that this Thule is haunted by "ill angels" only. This does not mean that the forms the dreamer meets are wicked or that they are images evoked by remorse. We learn in the third stanza that some places in Thule are "unholy." I take this to mean only that they are unhallowed. This must be so because the experience is amoral; if there is no joy in it, neither is there grief or pain. It is sublime because it is out of space and time, beyond understanding.

The line pattern is trochaic tetrameter almost equally divided between catalectic and acatalectic. The rhymes are by couplets, some of them imperfect, such as "floods—woods," "discover—over," and "river—ever." Occasionally a line begins with an iambus or anapest, and there are a few displaced stresses; on the whole, however, both the rhythm and the meter are exceptionally regular for Poe. The effect is somewhat monotonous in keeping with the mood. This effect is enhanced by internal rhyme and various types of repetition and parallelism. Lines 18–19 will serve to illustrate these devices: "Their lone waters—lone and dead,— / Their still waters—still and chilly." These lines are repeated with variations in the next stanza. The last stanza of six lines is identical with the first six lines of the first stanza except that "reached these lands" in the first stanza becomes "wandered home" in the last, and "an ultimate" becomes "this ultimate." These two stanzas constitute a kind of envelope for the other stanzas. In no earlier poem, unless possibly in "The City in the Sea," had Poe achieved such a high degree of unity in mood, meaning, and form.

IV

Poe published thirteen poems during the last five years of his life, whereas during the preceding ten years he had published only six.

Eleven of the thirteen made their first appearance in print during his last four years, after he had given up editorial work and had almost ceased to write prose fiction.[33] There was, then, a revival of interest in the composition of poetry in Poe's third and last literary period, although it did not equal the enthusiasm of 1827–1829 that in three years had produced two long poems and fifteen short ones. His mind was weary from uncongenial work, and the routine of reviewing had, perhaps, dulled his imagination. Part of the time, in 1846 and 1847, he was ill, especially just before and after the death of Virginia on January 30, 1847. He continued to write book reviews, though few important ones, and he composed *Eureka* during this period as well as several of his most important critical essays. But he was emotionally disturbed much of the time and consequently unable to compose poetry, even though he could still concentrate sufficiently to write good critical prose.

"The Raven" made him famous, and it remains, in the popular mind, his greatest achievement in poetry. Probably it was composed during the latter half of 1844, after he had left Philadelphia and before he joined the staff of the *Mirror*. He was living in the country at the time, a few miles outside the city.[34] He may also have been working out the theories of "The Rationale of Verse," of which "The Raven" seems to be a conscious exemplification. It is hard to tell, of course, whether Poe's poems are based on his theories or his theories on his poems, or whether, as is most likely, they grew to consciousness together. Many of the theories formulated in "The Rationale of Verse" were exemplified in his early as well as in his late poems, but the elaborate patterns of parallelism, repetition, refrain, and internal rhyme, together with the shift from the principle of stress to the principle of time equivalence in the determination of rhythm, are characteristic exclusively of the late poems. The first conspicuous use of parallelism, repetition, and refrain was in "Bridal Ballad," dating from 1837, and the next and only other poem in which they were used before 1845 was "Dream-Land." Poe's tendency toward greater and greater elaboration of metrical patterns between 1843 and 1849 parallels, in a general way, the

[33] The *Broadway Journal* expired with the issue of January 3, 1846. Although Poe continued to hope for a more elite journal of his own, he did no more regular editorial work. Only seven tales and sketches were published after January 1846, and of these only "The Cask of Amontillado" (November 1846) is of the first rank.

[34] See A. H. Quinn, *Edgar Allan Poe, A Critical Biography* (New York, 1941), pp. 430–433; also *Letters*, pp. 259–262.

development of his theories between the publication of his "Notes on English Verse" in 1843 and the publication of "The Rationale of Verse" in the fall of 1848.[35]

This preoccupation with the mechanics of verse contributed, no doubt, to the composition of two acrostics, like those which he sometimes inscribed in ladies' albums when he was a young man but did not himself preserve or collect for publication.[36] The earlier and the better of the two was written in 1846 as a compliment to Frances Sargent Osgood and read at a Valentine party that year. Poe revised it later because in his first manuscript he had misspelled Mrs. Osgood's middle name. The first version was published February 21, 1846, in the *Evening Mirror,* but whether by Poe's permission I do not know, since all the poems read at the party were published in the same issue. The revised poem was published with Poe's permission in *The Flag of Our Union,* March 3, 1849, and apparently without his permission in the March number of *Sartain's Union Magazine.* The second acrostic, which Griswold called "An Enigma," was also published in the March number of *Sartain's,* with no title except "Sonnet." Although it was written as a compliment to Sarah Anna Lewis, it is really less a compliment than a squib on the trivialities of contemporary sonnet writing. Had Poe issued a collected edition of his poems after the publication of these two poems I suspect he would have omitted them as he had omitted the early acrostics from all collected editions.

Poe wrote four other complimentary poems that may be briefly considered. Two were written to Mrs. Marie Louise Shew, who had shown great kindness to him and had nursed Virginia in her last illness. One was addressed to Mrs. Sarah Helen Whitman in 1848 at the time he was paying court to her. The other is a sonnet expressing affection for Virginia's mother, Mrs. Maria Clemm. The first of the poems to Mrs. Shew, entitled "To M. L. S——," was apparently written as a valentine in February 1847, shortly after Virginia's death. It was published in the *Home Journal* about a month later. The second, published in the *Columbian Magazine* for March 1848, with the title "To ___ ___ ___," but entitled "To Marie Louise" in a manuscript, is somewhat better, and more finished than most of Poe's personal poems. Obviously both are expressions of deep gratitude. The poem to Mrs. Whitman was published in *Sartain's* in November 1848, with the title "To ___ ___ ___," but given the title "To Helen," by Griswold in his edition of 1850, prob-

---

[35] See above, p. 194.   [36] See above, p. 36.

ably on the authority of a manuscript. It consists of 66 lines of blank verse, some of which are effective, though none achieve the sonorous beauty of the blank verse of "The Coliseum." The sonnet "To My Mother" is one of the best, as it is the most sincere, of the personal poems.

Three other poems of the late period that need only brief discussion, although they are superior to the personal poems, are "Eulalie—A Song," "Eldorado," and "Annabel Lee." The first is a melodious and rather gay lyric, in mood like the 1829 "To the River ___," and in metrical pattern somewhat like "Lenore," especially in its 1843 arrangement. In the first stanza, lines 1 and 2, which rhyme, have only two feet each. Line 3 has three feet and rhymes not with the first two but with lines 4 and 5. The rhyme words of lines 4 and 5 are identical, but that of line 3 is not. The first three lines taken together, therefore, constitute the equivalent of a line of seven feet. Lines 4 and 5 differ from this first composite line not only in their having identical rhyme, but also in their initial repetition, their parallelism of statement, and their lack of a caesura after the fourth foot. The second and third stanzas have eight lines each instead of five. This is because in each stanza the pattern, though not the language, of lines 1–3 is repeated in lines 4–6. Each of these groups of three lines makes a composite line of seven feet. Lines 7 and 8 of the second stanza have identical end rhymes, and the end words of lines 3 and 6 rhyme with them but are not identical. This rhyme pattern is repeated in the third stanza. It is an interesting stanza and musically effective as well as pleasing to the eye. The rhythm of "Eulalie" is similar to that of Shelley's "The Cloud," but the language is not noticeably similar unless possibly in lines 4–6 of the second stanza:

> And never a flake
> That the vapor can make
> With the moon-tints of purple and pearl.

Poe had no need to borrow metrical patterns, for he was a master in the invention of them; and any echo of Shelley that we detect here in Poe's language is probably accidental.

The stanza structure of "Eldorado" is essentially the same as the group pattern formed by the first six lines of the third and fourth stanzas of "Eulalie," but the effect is different because of the absence of trisyllabic feet in the dissyllabic pattern, and also because of the variation produced by the introduction of dialogue. The fact that nearly half the lines begin with a trochee instead of an iambus lends to the rhythm a vigor suggestive of a galloping horse. The images are carefully counterpoised to emphasize the irony of the theme, which is developed through a progressive change in the meaning of the word "shadow." The word is repeated in each stanza as a rhyme to "Eldorado." In the first "Shadow" is simply a shade, in the second it is a synonym of doubt, in the third it is a Platonic equivalent of unreality, and in the fourth a symbol of death. The poem is perfectly unified in mood, meaning, and form, and is perhaps the most impressive of the short poems of Poe's last period.

"Annabel Lee" has been the most popular of the late short poems, but critics often dismiss it as meaningless or damn it with faint praise for its alleged "simple" melody. Analysis reveals some degree of sophistication. In theme it is akin to Poe's tale "Eleonora": the love of two young people that transcends death and survives in a spiritual union. The rhythm is predominantly anapestic varied with frequent iambic feet and one initial trochee. The line and stanza patterns are simple at first but become more complex as the poem progresses. Parallelism appears inconspicuously in the second stanza and internal rhyme in the fourth. The first, second, and fourth stanzas have six lines, but the third has eight, the fifth seven, and the sixth eight again. The seventh stanza has parallelism in lines, repetition of phrases, and identical rhyme, and also a kind of syzygy in the unit "ever dissever." The last stanza is the most complicated of the six. The end rhyme sequence is *ab cb dd bb,* and all of these rhymes are identical except "side" and "bride" in lines 5 and 6. Although lines 1 and 3 have no end rhyme, each has an internal rhyme, as does also line 5. The last two lines are parallel in thought and syntax, and also have initial and terminal repetition. Thirty-one lines have end rhyme, and nineteen of these end with the words "sea," "Lee," or "me," in different sequences, and two others end with "we." The name "Annabel Lee" occurs seven times and the phrase "kingdom by the sea," five. The word "love" is used four times and "loved" twice. Only 118 different words are used in the entire poem out of a total of 303. The last stanza, with 68 words, has only nineteen that have not appeared in the preceding stanzas. The hypnotic effect of the repetition of harmonized sound and sense through the poem, building up to a climax in the last stanza, should be pleasing to most readers, whether naive or sophisticated. The value of the poem subsists more in its form than in its meaning.

I have reserved for final consideration the four longest poems of this period: "The Raven," "Ulalume," "The Bells," and "For Annie." Like "Annabel Lee," "The Raven" is more important for its form than for its meaning. The raven, as Poe states at the end of "The Philosophy of Composition," is the symbol of "mournful and never-ending remembrance." The mood is sadness, or melancholy, and the action shows how this mood, as felt by the bereaved lover, shifts from a cherished hope that he will be reunited with his beloved Lenore in some future life to the conviction that he will not. Since there is no evidence that the lover feels remorse, the intellectual meaning of the poem is that he does not believe in the survival of identity after death and never really did. His questions addressed to the raven, which begin in a spirit of amusement, become more serious under the influence of his mood and the somber aspect of the bird, and are finally an expression of superstitious terror and despair. Knowing the raven's answer must be "nevermore," he asks precisely those questions which, when so answered, will torture him most. This self-torture finally leads to a temporary madness in which he believes the raven is both demonic and prophetic. The poem is not difficult, and its meaning should be evident to any careful reader. If it is not, he has only to turn to Poe's own explanation in "The Philosophy of Composition."[37] Some people have thought this explanation a hoax, perhaps because they have never tried writing poetry themselves and suppose, as Poe remarks in his essay, that poets compose "by a species of fine frenzy—an ecstatic intuition." Poe believed in intuition, but he thought it a factor only in the inception of the poem. It produces what he calls "the poem, *per se*," but the gathering of suitable materials and the skilled labor of construction must be left to the analytic faculty of the mind.[38] Early in the essay Poe repeats the two basic ideas that Beauty is the province of the poem and sadness the highest tone of its manifestation. He does this in an effort to clarify his theory, which he says some of his friends "have evinced a disposition to misrepresent."[39]

Poe explains his use of the refrain, his choice of the key word to be repeated, and the means of its invariable repetition, but he does not tell us much about the structure of "The Raven." He explains the rhythm as trochaic and the meter as "octameter acatalectic, alternat-

---

[37] *Works*, XIV, 193–208. "The Philosophy of Composition" has been frequently reprinted and discussed.

[38] I have commented on this point above, p. 190.

[39] This disposition to misrepresent Poe's meaning has been evinced not only by his contemporaries but by some later critics.

ing with heptameter catalectic repeated in the *refrain* of the fifth verse, and terminating with tetrameter catalectic." One hesitates to disagree with a poet about the meter of his own verse, yet surely Poe has made a mistake in calling the alternate verses "heptameter catalectic," for they are obviously octameter catalectic.[40] He claims originality for nothing except the structure of his stanza, but he does not analyze the stanza to show how it is original. This I shall undertake to do.

The rhythm is monotonously regular. Of a total of 792 feet in the poem, 776 are trochees, and 16, or about 2 per cent, are dactyls; but most of these dactyls are such as "many a" and "fiery," which can be and often are pronounced as trochees. Poe's earlier poems have many more irregularities of rhythm. Comparing two earlier poems largely trochaic in rhythm, we find that "Dream-Land" (1844) has irregularities in 12 per cent of the feet and "The Valley of Unrest" (1829) in at least 15 per cent.

The end rhymes have the same sequence, *abcbbb*, in all stanzas of "The Raven," the *a* and *c* rhymes are always feminine, and the *b* rhyme of line 5 is always identical with that of line 4. In lines 1 and 3 also the fourth trochee always rhymes with the eighth. One other invariable pattern is that the fourth trochee of line 4 always rhymes with the fourth and eighth trochees of line 3. Other internal rhymes are irregularly placed in a variety of patterns. Line 2 has internal rhyme in only two stanzas: in the second stanza the fourth trochee of line 2 rhymes with the eighth of line 1, and in the third the first trochee of line 2 rhymes with the second trochee, thus producing syzygy. In line 4 of stanzas one, two, and four, the fourth and fifth trochees are composed of the same word repeated and rhyme with the fourth and eighth trochees of line 3. In all other stanzas, only the fourth trochee of line 4 rhymes with the fourth and eighth trochees of line 3. The internal rhyme of line 5 varies somewhat. In stanza one only, the fifth trochee rhymes with all the rhyme words of lines 3 and 4 and is identical with the eighth trochee of line 3. In stanzas three, thirteen, fourteen, and sixteen, the fourth trochee rhymes with all the rhyme words of lines 3 and 4 and is identical with the fourth trochee

[40] Perhaps Poe's mistake was inadvertent. I have tried to account for his statement by reference to "The Rationale of Verse" and his theory of "bastard" iambics and trochees. For example one may make seven feet of the second line by the following scansion: "Ŏver|mány ă|quaínt and|cúriŏŭs|vólŭme ŏf fŏr|gótten| lóre." This, however, requires that the three unstressed syllables in the fifth foot shall be pronounced in the same time as the second syllable of "gotten" in the sixth foot. This is unnatural and perhaps impossible.

of line 4. In all the remaining stanzas line 5 is without internal rhyme unless the rhyme word occurs in a phrase repeated from line 4 in a pattern common to all the stanzas. Usually these repeated phrases occur at the end of the line, but in a few cases, as in stanzas three, seven, and sixteen, they occur at the beginning.

The poet secured further variety in rhythmic effects by placing the caesural pause at different and unexpected points in the line. Several lines seem to have no caesural pause (line 2, stanza one, line 4, stanza three, line 2, stanza eight). If they have one it is only because of the reader's tendency to pause at the end of the fourth foot, especially if it is a rhymed word (for example, line 2, stanza two, or line 1, stanza eleven). The reader naturally expects a caesura after the fourth foot of an octameter line; therefore the poet must arrange words carefully if he wishes to avoid it or to push it forward or back. It is made to fall after the first trochee in line 2 of stanzas three and five, after the second in line 5 of stanza five and in line 1 of stanza twelve, and after the seventh in line 4 of stanza five. There is no clear case of the caesura falling after the second syllable of the fifth and sixth trochees, but it falls after the first (the stressed) syllable of the fifth trochee in line 3 of stanza eight and after the stressed syllable of the sixth trochee in line 2 of stanza twelve. In several lines there are two caesuras; for examples, line 3 of stanza three, line 2 of stanza four, and line 5 of stanza five. In two or three lines there are perhaps three caesuras; for examples, in line 3 of stanza fourteen and line 1 of stanza seventeen.

The manipulation of these devices, together with others more common, such as refrain, alliteration, and assonance, enabled the poet to adapt the sound and movement of his verse to the shifting mood and developing theme of the poem. Its composition was the performance of a virtuoso; its appeal is therefore more to the intellect than to the feelings. The reader is not moved deeply because the poetic sentiment is less in evidence than craftsmanship; but if he has not already lost interest in the poem through familiarity, he may find its verbal architecture a challenge and a delight.

The mood and theme of "Ulalume" are similar to those of "The Raven," but the metrical pattern is quite different though almost as complex. It was first published in December 1847, nearly a year after Virginia's death. Taken literally, it represents a bereaved lover walking alone in the woods late at night, presumably in the hope of finding solace for his grief after the death of his beloved Ulalume. As he proceeds, his rational mind, the "I" of the poem, converses with his soul or intuitional mind, the "Psyche" of the poem, about the appearance at the end of the path they are following of the planet Venus in the form of a crescent, or, more probably, the crescent moon which the rational mind tries to convince Psyche is Venus. Just before the dialogue begins, the poem states that the crescent is Astarte, the ancient goddess of fertility who in Greek times was sometimes associated with Diana as well as with Venus. The rational mind identifies the star with Venus because it wishes to believe that it is beneficent, an augury of hope, perhaps signifying the dawn of a new love; it says, "She is warmer than Dian" and that she shines on them "With Love in her luminous eyes." She "has come past the stars of the Lion," indeed in spite of them. These would be the stars of the constellation Leo. In the zodiacal calendar the sun enters the sign of Leo on July 21. In astrological symbolism, therefore, Leo is fire and so might be considered antithetical to the softer light of love. But since Astarte has come past Leo, the lover must suppose the zodiacal sign to be not Leo but Virgo, representing Venus, and so favorable to love. The sun enters the sign of Virgo on August 22 and leaves it about a month later. On September 23 it enters the sign of Libra, and on October 24 enters Scorpio. The reader already knows, although the lover does not yet, that the actual time is October, possibly late in the month since the leaves are sere. Symbolically, Libra, the balance, is neutral and Scorpio malign. Both were less favorable than Virgo.

Psyche, of course, has no knowledge of the zodiacal calendar, but she mistrusts the star, citing its unnatural pallor in contrast to the brightness of Venus. She knows intuitively that they should not go on and advises that they hasten away. But the rational mind persuades her and they do proceed, only to come at length upon the tomb of Ulalume. The lover then remembers that it was exactly a year before, in October, that he had brought here the corpse of his beloved Ulalume and placed it in this tomb. He also recognizes now the region of Weir into which he has wandered, near the dank tarn of Auber. With this memory and the reawakening of his grief, the rational mind and the intuitional mind are reconciled, and the strange dreamlike experience is ended. The only explanation they offer for the apparition is that the ghouls who dwell in this region had taken pity on the lover and tried to prevent his discovery of the tomb of Ulalume by drawing up the "spectre of a planet" from limbo. The merciful ghouls would have been successful had the lover followed his intuition instead of his rationalizing mind. Those who like to read poetry as autobiography may interpret "Ulalume" as the symbolic revelation of an actual debate in Poe's mind, after Virginia's death, over whether he should seek the love of another woman and marry a second time. According to this interpretation, Poe made the effort, but discovered that in pursuing a new path of love he inevitably revived his memory of Virginia and renewed his grief for her death. The fact that Poe did pay court to several women during his last two or three years makes such an interpretation tempting. But I am skeptical of the wisdom of reading any poem as autobiography, especially if the statements and images in it are treated as documentary evidence. One may reasonably conjecture that the circumstances of Poe's life after Virginia's death suggested the mood and the imagery of the poem, but to identify it more closely with the poet's own experience would unjustifiably restrict its meaning as a work of art.

"Ulalume" has ten stanzas varying in length from nine to thirteen lines. The rhythm is predominantly anapestic, although 47 of its 104 lines begin with an iambus. Lines 8 and 9 of stanza seven begin with a monosyllabic foot ("Wings | till they trailed | in the dust," and "Plumes | till they trailed | in the dust"), which in "The Rationale of Verse" he called a "caesura." Thirteen feet in the poem are what he called in that essay "bastard anapests." They consist of three "short" or unstressed syllables and one "long" or stressed syllable.[41] Each stanza has four lines with feminine endings except the fifth stanza, which has five, and the eighth, which has only three. Repetition and parallelism combined with the swinging trimeter movement give the poem a music that has been, not inaptly, compared to a funeral march. No line is repeated entire, but often the line as repeated has but a word or two not in the first one. This form of incremental repetition may occur in only two lines of a stanza, as in stanza one ("The leaves they were crispéd and sere— / The leaves they were withering and sere"), or it may run through as many as seven lines, as in stanza five. The peculiar tone of "Ulalume" is created by the frequent recurrence of long vowels in stressed syllables; o, e, and i, the most common, give the sound to nearly half of all the stressed syllables of the poem. The short vowel sounds of e and i also occur frequently, producing the dominant

---

[41] These are in line 3 of stanza one, lines 1, 7, and 9 of stanza three, line 8 of stanza four, line 3 of stanza five, line 10 of stanza six, line 6 of stanza seven, line 11 of stanza seven (two examples), line 3 of stanza nine, and lines 3 and 10 of stanza ten.

sound of more than a fourth of all the stressed syllables, but they usually occur in words whose meaning is more significant than the sound of their vowels; such words, for examples, as "restlessly," "memories," and "nebulous," or "withering," "dim," and "limbo." The long *o* sound is by far the most common, and it occurs with greatest frequency in the first four and the last two stanzas. It has been suggested that the name "Ulalume" was selected for the poem because of the mournful sound of its first and last syllables, and one might expect that sound to be the most frequent. It does occur 20 times, but the long *o* sound occurs 51 times, the long *e* sounds 42, and the long *i* sound 40. It is, however, the stressed sound in the end rhyme of seven out of ten lines in stanza eight. The trimeter line of this poem does not lend itself to internal rhyme. Even if it did, internal rhyme would be superfluous in verse containing so much repetition.

Poe's skill in creating unusual rhythmic patterns and sound effects led, one might almost say inevitably, to the composition of "The Bells," which was begun in the summer of 1848 but not finished until the autumn of 1849. This poem is in the form of a quaternion representing the four ages of man's life: childhood, youth, middle age, and old age terminating in death. The silver bell is appropriate for childhood, and its tinkling suggests a merry mood. The golden bell is the right one for youth, and its mellow sound is suited to the church wedding. The brazen bell, used for fire alarms, represents by its harsh and discordant note the turbulence and danger of middle age. The iron bell is suited to old age because of its heaviness and melancholy tone, and also because it is associated with the funeral knell. The mood of each of the four stanzas is developed through rhythmic movements that synchronize with the tempo of the age represented.

The rhythm is predominantly trochaic, but irregular. The chief stress falls usually at the end or near the middle of the line. The lines vary in length from one to eight feet and from one to fifteen syllables. The stanzas increase in length in proportion, apparently, to the intensity of the mood. The first stanza has 14 lines, the second 21, the third 34, and the fourth 44. There are four end rhymes in the first stanza, four in the second, eleven in the third, and nine in the fourth. The reason for the large number of rhymes in the third stanza in proportion to the total number of lines is that there are more separate ideas, or statements, in that stanza than in any other, even the longer fourth. There are several dimeter lines rhyming in couplets which might as well have been combined into one line with internal rhyme. There is only one line with internal rhyme as printed; that is in the second stanza ("To the swinging, and the ringing"), and it might more consistently have been made into two dimeter lines. Line 91, in the fourth stanza, consists of the single word "Rolls," but this appeals to the eye more than the ear, which hears it as part of the rhythm of the following line. The lengthening of the successive stanzas is achieved mainly through repetition, especially in the fourth and climactic one. The word "bells" occurs 10 times in the first stanza, 13 in the second, 16 in the third, and 24 in the fourth. Other words frequently repeated for tonal effect are "time" and "toll" or "tolling."

The mood and tone of the several stanzas are produced by the denotation and connotation of the words themselves, but also, more than in most poems, by the sounds of the vowel and consonant combinations. Because of the frequent repetition of the words "bells," "time," and "toll," the vowel sound of short e and the consonant sound of t occur most frequently, but they do not much affect the mood or tone of the poem. The vowels and consonants that do this more than any others are the short and long i sounds in the first stanza, the o and u sounds in the second, the long i sound in the third, and the long o and i sounds in the fourth. Of course the effect of the vocalic sound is often altered by a change of the adjacent consonant. The liquids and nasals are the most numerous consonants, and they occur most frequently in the fourth stanza. In the mellow second, g and l are most common, and in the harsh third, combinations with ang endings, along with k, are prominent in stressed syllables. The k sound and the long e sound do not occur in any stressed syllable in the second stanza. I do not wish to overemphasize the importance of these mechanical devices, but they cannot be overlooked by any one who seriously engages himself to understand and appreciate Poe's verse. In "The Bells" the sounds of the syllables, taken by themselves and in their context, are doubtless more important than the denotative meanings of the words.

The last of Poe's poems to be discussed is "For Annie." This poem was inspired by Mrs. Nancy Richmond, of Lowell, Massachusetts, whom he always called "Annie." He first met her in July 1848, when he lectured in Lowell, but the poem was probably not written until early in 1849 for he sent her a copy of it in a letter dated March 23, 1849. It is not a love poem, unless of the Platonic kind, for it contains no suggestion of physical passion. The fact that it was intended for the public, not exclusively for Mrs. Richmond's private reading, is proved by his having already sent a copy for publication to *The Flag of Our Union,* where it was first published April 28, 1849. In the letter accompanying the manuscript sent to Mrs. Richmond he tells her he has sold the poem; he thinks it the best he has written, but asks for her honest opinion of its worth. It is not directly addressed to "Annie," who is referred to in the third person.

Like "The Raven" and "Ulalume," "For Annie" is about death, but the mood is quite different, for the death that has occurred is his own, and the mood is one of relief and even happiness. Death is welcome because it cures him of the fever called "Living." The poet has exchanged the agitations of life, symbolized by the myrtles and roses, for the final peace of death, symbolized by the rosemary odor commingled with pansies and rue. Consciousness remains, though dim; grief is softened to regret, and memory is purified and no longer painful.[42] The spiritual self survives; and whereas in life it was tantalized, it now reposes in a state not unlike that of a pleasant dream of life rather than life itself. There is no evidence in the poem that Poe longed for death at the time he wrote it. He was reasonably well physically, more successful than usual with his writing, and intellectually more active than he had been for the preceding two years. The mood is reminiscent of that of "Al Aaraaf," but there is a difference. In the earlier poem he imagined a world or a state of being apart from good and evil in which the aesthetic spirit could live for beauty alone, whereas in "For Annie" he imagined a state of being in which both truth and beauty, seen through the veil dropped by death, are dreamlike. In so far as the poem reveals Poe's state of mind in the late winter and spring of 1849, it suggests that he was relieved to be free of the uncertain and frenzied emotions with which he had courted and proposed marriage to Mrs. Whitman, and content in the more spiritual love of Mrs. Richmond. Since she had a husband and was loyal to him, the poet was not tantalized by the question of marriage. Annie was his "sweet *sister,*" the "wife" of his soul, a relation which remained the same in death or life.

Like "The Raven" and "Ulalume," "For Annie" was intended to appeal to the eye as well as the ear. Yet its metrical pattern is not intricate; it is arranged in lines of two feet, and the dominant rhythm

---

[42] In several of Poe's prose sketches and essays he represents sentience as continuing after breathing ceases and the heart stops beating. The nature of sense impressions after "death" is described in some detail in "The Colloquy of Monos and Una," *Works,* IV, 200–212.

is anapestic. Of the fifteen stanzas, ten have six lines each, four have eight lines, and one has ten lines. Only the even numbered lines have rhyme. In fact, the structure is most clearly seen if each pair of lines is thought of as one line having four feet. In that form each stanza would have three, four, or five lines, and all the lines of a given stanza would have end rhyme. In the stanzas with three such lines, the third rhyme word would always be identical with the second; in three of the four stanzas with four such lines, the rhyme word of the last three would be the same, but in one the rhyme word of the fourth line would be identical with that of the second; in the one stanza with five such lines, the first and third would be identical and the second, fourth, and fifth identical. These identical rhymes are the result of repetition, which occurs most frequently in lines having such rhymes. Variations in rhythm are few. Ten lines, out of a total of 102, have initial iambic feet, and five have initial trochaic feet. However, if we read the poem without regard to line divisions, keeping strictly to the rhythm, we find that (except for the first foot of the first line) the rhythm is trisyllabic and may be scanned thus (for each pause equal to an unstressed syllable I insert an asterisk):

Thank Heav|en! the cri|sis—The dan|ger is past,|And the lin|gering
ill|ness Is o|ver at last.|**Sad|ly, I know|I am shorn|of my strength,|And
no mus|cle I move|As I lie|at full length—|But no mat|ter!—I feel|I am
bet|ter at length.|And I rest|so compo|sedly, Now,|in my bed,|*That an|y
behold|er Might fan|cy me dead—|*Might start|at behold|ing me, Think|
ing me dead.

It will be seen that in the three stanzas (18 dimeter lines) quoted without regard to line and stanza divisions, the trisyllabic rhythm moves without break after the initial iambus to the end of the first stanza (after the word "last"). The second stanza begins with what most scanners would call a trochee followed by an iambus. If I understand Poe's "Rationale of Verse," he would call the first foot of the second stanza a "caesura," or monosyllabic foot, the pause following the preceding line being equivalent to two "short" syllables. Thus scanned, the anapests begin again with the second syllable of "Sadly" and continue until we arrive at line 15, where we seem to have an initial iambus, "That an | y." Poe would say that the pause after "bed" at the end of line 14 is equivalent to one "short" syllable. Such a regular trisyllabic rhythm is anapestic if the first syllable is not stressed, but if it is, the rhythm is dactyllic.[43] In spite of the morbid details of "For Annie," its swinging rhythm sustains the mood, which is essentially happy.

This concludes my analysis of Poe's poems, a process which the reader, if he has been patient enough to follow me to the end, must have found tedious at times in its details. He may also find fault with me for being more analyst than critic. I have no apology to make on that account, for my purpose has been not to evaluate Poe's poetry but to understand it, and to discover, if I could, how his poetic conceptions grew from mood, to meaning, to form; in other words, how the "Poetic Sentiment," which I suppose to be originally formless, is conveyed through form so that it is felt by the sensitive reader, or hearer, in something like the force that moved the creative imagination of the poet. In Poe's early poems mood dominated form, in the middle period meaning tended to assert itself, or perhaps I should say to impose itself on mood, and in the third period form dominated both mood and meaning. His most satisfactory poems, perhaps, are those which were originally composed between 1827 and 1831 but were improved by later revision after he had become a master craftsman. It would be difficult, however, to demonstrate their superiority, for the best poems of each period are excellent in their kind, and all are equally characteristic of Poe's genius.

[43] Poe illustrates such a rhythm in "The Rationale of Verse" by printing a number of lines from the beginning of Byron's "Bride of Abydos" without line divisions: *Works*, XIV, 244–245.

IX.   The Poetic Principle in Prose

POE defined the poetry of words as the rhythmical creation of beauty, and in "The Poetic Principle" he made the following explicit distinction between poetry and truth: "In enforcing a truth, we need severity rather than efflorescence of language. We must be simple, precise, terse. We must be cool, calm, unimpassioned. In a word, we must be in that mood which, as nearly as possible, is the exact converse of the poetical. He must be blind, indeed, who does not perceive the radical and chasmal differences between the truthful and the poetical modes of inculcation." Yet on the title page of *Eureka*, which is obviously an expository essay written in a style that could be described as "simple," "precise," and even "terse," he announced it as "A Prose Poem." Is this not inconsistent with his conception of poetry and particularly with the statement I have just quoted? His brief Preface to *Eureka* will help us to understand that it is not, and had best be quoted in full:

> To the few who love me and whom I love—to those who feel rather than to those who think—to the dreamers and those who put faith in dreams as in the only realities—I offer this Book of Truths, not in its character of Truth-Teller, but for the Beauty that abounds in its Truth; constituting it true. To these I present the composition as an Art-Product alone:—let us say as a Romance; or, if I be not urging too lofty a claim, as a Poem.
>
> *What I here propound is true:*—therefore it cannot die: or if by any means it be now trodden down so that it die, it will "rise again to the Life Everlasting."
>
> Nevertheless it is as a Poem only that I wish this work to be judged after I am dead.

These statements are very carefully phrased. The author anticipates two kinds of readers: those who feel and those who think. To the latter he boldly affirms that what he propounds is true and therefore cannot die even though it be rejected at first. To the former, whose dreams are intuitions of the reality behind appearance, he offers his book as a poem only, knowing that they will discover its truth through its beauty. The poetry of *Eureka,* in fact, is not the poetry of words but of ideas, or concepts, of which words are the symbols. Its beauty inheres in the consistency of these ideas and in the totality of effect they produce on the intuitive mind.

My purpose is not to analyze and evaluate Poe's theory of the cosmos but to discover, if possible, why he called his explanation of it a poem. This will require looking into his essay for clues. He begins by stating his "ruling idea" or "general proposition": "In the Original Unity of the First Thing lies the Secondary Cause of All Things, with the Germ of their Inevitable Annihilation."[1] By what he calls "an intuition altogether irresistible" Poe arrives at the conviction that God's original and sole creation was matter in its state of utmost simplicity, that is, without form or particles and indivisible except by himself. This primordial particle was not matter as we know it but spirit, like God himself, and his willing it into existence was not so much an act as a conception. It was spirit because it was unparticled matter; yet it was infinitely divisible, and by another exercise of volition God diffused it throughout a limited sphere in space to constitute the universe we know. As thus diffused, these particles of matter became subject to the law of gravitation, the effect of which will be that eventually all matter as atomic substance will be annihilated by returning to its original state as unparticled matter, or spirit. The unity now obscured by the diversity of forms will have been restored and become absolute again. Poe illustrates the paradox of unity in diversity by an example of how the eye may receive the impression of oneness in viewing a multiform scene. "He who from the top of Aetna casts his eyes leisurely around, is affected chiefly by the *extent* and *diversity* of the scene. Only by a rapid whirling on his heel could he hope to comprehend the panorama in the sublimity of its *oneness.*" (186) Emerson illustrates a similar idea in his essay "Experience" by reference to an elementary laboratory experiment once used to demonstrate the phenomena of light. He says, "The party-colored wheel must revolve very fast to appear white."[2] Emerson also believed that the apparent chaos of sensible nature can be known through intuition as a condition of unity in variety. Poe's conception of intuition in *Eureka* is described in terms suggestive of modern psychology. He explains it as "the conviction arising from those inductions or deductions of which the processes are so shadowy as to escape our

---

[1] *Works,* XVI, 185–186. Hereafter page references to *Eureka* will be inserted in the text by numbers in parentheses.

[2] *Complete Works* (Centenary Edition; Boston, 1904), III, 57.

consciousness, elude our reason, or defy our capacity of expression."
(206) This way of knowing may not be essentially different from what
Emerson called "reason" as distinguished from the "understanding."[3]

Once matter is diffused to the extent intended, the divine will which
had forced the diffusion is withheld. Then the law of gravitation acts
freely and would produce rapid coalescence of all atoms and the
collapse of the universe at once but for the fact that in each atom
there is a repulsive force that repels every other atom to prevent or
delay the process of coalescence. Poe identifies this force with electricity, although he does not pretend to understand it. For the sake of
clarity he discards the terms gravitation and electricity and prefers the
simpler but equivalent terms attraction and repulsion. "The former,"
he explains, "is the body; the latter the soul: the one is the material;
the other the spiritual, principle of the Universe. *All* phenomena are
referable to one, or to the other, or to both combined." In fact, he
concludes, "attraction and repulsion *are* matter." (214) Since without
the diffusive force of the divine will all things tend to return to their
original state of unity, the universe will eventually collapse into the
aboriginal particle. This particle contains all that had composed the
universe, but since there is no longer either attraction or repulsion,
there is no matter, only spirit, the divine purpose having been fulfilled.
Poe believes, however, that the same process will be repeated over
and over in the eternal pulsation of the divine heart. The physical
universe exists for the purpose of individualizing spirit; it is God made
the object of his own thought, or, in a phrase borrowed from literary
criticism, the objective correlative of God's meaning.

Whatever may be the strength or weakness of *Eureka* as science
and philosophy, it is, and probably was intended to be, chiefly significant as a demonstration of the essential identity of truth and beauty,
and of Coleridge's and his own proposition that the artist's imaginative creation is a manifestation on a limited scale of the same power
by which God created the universe. In his discussion of the laws of
attraction and repulsion Poe arrives at the conclusion that they demonstrate in the divine creation a perfect adaptation of part to part.
Then he points out that the perfect adaptation of part to part is also
the aim of the literary artist, although he cannot hope to attain it. "In

[3] Emerson speaks of intuition in many contexts. Perhaps the best known of these
is the essay "Self-Reliance," where he calls it "primary wisdom." "We lie," he
says, "in the lap of immense intelligence, which makes us receivers of its truth and
organs of its activity" (*Complete Works*, II, 64).

the construction of *plot*, for example, in fictitious literature, we should aim at so arranging the incidents that we shall not be able to determine, of any one of them, whether it depends from any one other or upholds it." Such perfect reciprocity is not possible in a human construction, but the plots of God are perfect. "The Universe is a plot of God." (292) In its form it is beautiful because it is symmetrical, and it is true because its governing laws are consistent. He has said in other contexts that the sentiment of poetry, or of beauty, is inherent in all men. Here he says also that "the sense of the symmetrical is an instinct which may be depended upon with an almost blindfold reliance. It is the poetical essence of the Universe—*of the Universe* which, in the supremeness of its symmetry, is but the most sublime of poems. Now symmetry and consistency are convertible terms:—thus Poetry and Truth are one." (302)

Poe is supported in these ideas by some of his more transcendental contemporaries. In his essay "The Poet" Emerson defined the good, the true, and the beautiful as three aspects of one reality;[4] and in "A Song of the Rolling Earth" Whitman described the earth as a poem. Furthermore, Poe's spiritual ether, which pervades space and is "ever in attendance upon matter" (305) is very much like Whitman's divine soul which fills and swells "the vastnesses of Space." Both identify themselves with God through this ether, or as Whitman calls it, "the float forever held in solution."[5] Like Whitman, Poe finds himself unable to believe "that anything exists *greater than his own soul*," (312) and he differs from him little, if at all, in saying that "God—the material *and* spiritual God—*now* exists solely in the diffused Matter and Spirit of the Universe." This view alone, he adds, makes evil either intelligible or endurable. (313) In this view what we call fate is simply the operation of the laws that control the universe and our own being, and sorrow is seen to be self-imposed. Poe would have agreed, I think, with Whitman's definition of Freedom as "the fusion and combination of the conscious will, or partial individual law, with those universal, eternal, unconscious ones, which run through all Time, pervade history, prove immortality, give moral purpose to the entire objective world, and the last dignity to human life."[6] It is man's

---

[4] *Complete Works*, III, 6–7.

[5] This idea is common in Whitman's poems, but see especially "Crossing Brooklyn Ferry," sections 2 and 5, and "Passage to India," section 8.

[6] *Prose Works 1892*, ed. Floyd Stovall (New York, 1964), II, 538. Many other passages throughout Poe's writings could be cited as evidence that he had much in

identity with God through participation in these universal laws that Poe has in mind when he speaks of his inherent sense of the beautiful and his intuition of truth through that sense.

A distinction must be made between the word "truth" as it is used in *Eureka* and the same word as it must be understood in "The Poetic Principle," especially in the context of passages in which he relegates truth to the intellect alone, by which he means the rationalizing faculty.[7] By the truthful mode of inculcation he clearly means didacticism; all he is saying is that poetry should not inculcate truth in an overt manner. It is equally clear that by the poetical mode of inculcation he means imagination, the presentation of truth through beauty. The "obstinate oils and waters of Poetry and Truth," therefore, symbolize not poetry and truth themselves, but the imaginative and didactic modes. Poetry exists for its own sake, is its own end; to believe that its purpose is moral instruction is "the heresy of *The Didactic.*" Prose is the proper medium for didactic writing. A composition in verse, judged by Poe's criteria, is not a poem if it exists for a purpose outside its own beauty. As I have mentioned before, he called the effect of Tennyson's "Locksley Hall" passionate, not poetical; and of the two long poems that he reviewed most favorably, Moore's *Alciphron* and Horne's *Orion,* he said the former "recounts a poetical story in a *prosaic* way," and that the latter is not to be regarded as a poem but as a "work."[8] *Eureka* might be designated a poem, like *Alciphron,* because it recounts the poetical story of the creation in a prosaic way.

There are, in addition to *Eureka,* several other examples in Poe's work of the incorporation of a poetic idea or story in prose. These are rational in method and expository in purpose, though they differ from *Eureka* in containing a story element with human characters. Some of them develop ideas and moods closely related to those of the early poems. The first of these to be published was "The Conversation of Eiros and Charmion."[9] The two characters are men of earth who have died and now dwell in spirit in a region Poe calls Aidenn. They retain their identities and memories, but for reasons not explained they have

---

common with the transcendentalists he sometimes ridiculed, especially in the areas of aesthetics and metaphysics.

[7] "The Poetic Principle," in *Works*, XIV, 266–292. I have not thought it necessary to give page references for quotations from Poe's shorter works.

[8] See the essay "Mood, Meaning, and Form in Poe's Poetry," p. 189.

[9] First published in *Burton's Gentleman's Magazine*, Dec. 1839 (*Works*, IV, 1–8).

received new names. Three-fourths of the piece is devoted to a description by Eiros, who has died recently in a conflagration that has destroyed all life on earth, of how he felt and what he saw in experiencing this catastrophe. The conflagration, he says, was produced by the passage of the earth through the gaseous substance of a comet. All the nitrogen gases were extracted from the air, leaving only the oxygen; the result was "a combustion irresistible, all-devouring, omni-prevalent, immediate," which he recognizes as a fulfillment of the prophecies of the Bible.[10] The soul of Eiros then joined that of Charmion, whose earthly body had died earlier.

In "The Colloquy of Monos and Una,"[11] whose names also must have been assumed after their death, we have a pair of lovers, presumably husband and wife, and the interest developed is in the experience of death itself. Though Monos died first, both have been dead for about a century, during which their "slumbering senses" have kept no account of time. The experience began, Monos tells Una, with "a breathless and motionless torpor; and this was termed *Death* by those who stood around me." Volition had not departed but was powerless, and though the senses were active they were eccentric, assuming each other's functions at random. All his perceptions were purely sensual; they conveyed nothing to the understanding, which was "deceased." Yet the following night, when Una came to him and kissed his brow there arose in his bosom "something akin to sentiment" that was responsive, but it quickly faded away "into a purely sensual pleasure as before." Then came a "sixth sense," a sense of time like pulsations in the brain, but independent of the succession of events. He knew when decay began because then he felt a "dull shock like that of electricity" and all senses became "merged in the sole consciousness of entity, and in the one abiding sentiment of duration." After a year in the grave, his "consciousness of *being*" was giving way to "that of mere locality," and "the idea of entity was becoming merged with that of *place*." When Una died, her body was buried with him in the same grave. Then, Monos recalls, "came *that* light which alone might have had power to startle—the light of enduring *Love*." But soon that light also was extinguished and "the autocrats *Place* and *Time*" reigned supreme until Monos and Una were "born again," as reported at the beginning of the story. Monos remembered that even during his life-

---

[10] I have pointed out in "An Interpretation of 'Al Aaraaf' " (p. 106) how Poe's description of this imagined event is related to that poem.

[11] First published in *Graham's Magazine*, Aug. 1841 (*Works*, IV, 200–212).

time the many evils growing from man's thirst for knowledge and his perversion of taste had become oppressive. After his death, they seem to have become unendurable, so that man and all earthly life with him were destroyed. This was a "purification" by fire, after which earth had become a new paradise and a fit dwelling place "for man the Death-purged—for man to whose now exalted intellect there should be poison in knowledge no more—for the redeemed, regenerated, blissful, and now immortal, but still for the *material* man."

"The Colloquy of Monos and Una" is related, in a somewhat similar way, to the poem "Al Aaraaf," written twelve years earlier, and to *Eureka*, written seven years later. In "Al Aaraaf" the world is destroyed because, it seems, men have conceived God in their own image and sought to understand his mysteries despite the fact that such knowledge is forbidden to them. In *Eureka*, at its conclusion, we are asked to think that in some future state "the sense of individual identity will be gradually merged in the general consciousness—that Man, for example, ceasing imperceptibly to feel himself Man, will at length attain that awfully triumphant epoch when he shall recognize his existence as that of Jehovah." It is unlikely that Poe, whose intellectual pride is well known, would consign the human race to ignorance by condemning knowledge itself as an evil. Monos makes the point that it was the combination of "intemperance of knowledge" with the perversion of taste that separated man from Beauty and Nature and hurried him to destruction. To save the artist from such a fate, Poe created the metaphor of Al Aaraaf, a place where man, so long as he remains there, knows only the beautiful and has no intellectual thirst for knowledge. Yet truth is available to him in that place through beauty. So in *Eureka* we learn that the highest truths of the universe are revealed to the intuitive philosopher, as they were to Kepler, through his sense of symmetry and consistency; that is, through the sentiment of the beautiful, which is at the heart of the poetic principle.[12]

Another conversation in Aidenn, this time evidently between two men—Agathos, who has been dead three hundred years, and Oinos, who is "a spirit new-fledged with immortality"—is reported in "The

---

[12] In the description by Monos of the survival of the senses after death the reader will recognize ideas that entered into the making of "The Sleeper" and to a lesser extent of "The City in the Sea" and "The Valley of Unrest," among Poe's early poems, and of "For Annie" among the later ones.

Power of Words."[13] The idea of knowledge and the idea of creation suggested here are at once more specific and more fanciful than in *Eureka*. Agathos tells Oinos that "Not even here is knowledge a thing of intuition." This is startling, for it seems to contradict several statements concerning intuition, later as well as earlier, in Poe's writing. The succeeding conversation makes it clear, however, that it is only perfect or complete knowledge that cannot be attained, even in Aidenn, by intuition. Only God could know all, and whether even he knows all or not may be the one thing unknown to him. For lesser beings, to know all would be a curse, for happiness exists not in knowledge but in its acquisition. For angels, as for men of earth, the power of intuition is limited. Agathos says also that God directly created only in the beginning; yet creation continues indirectly through the power of thought exercised by beings created and endowed with that power by God. In the last few paragraphs we learn that the earth has "lately perished" and that Agathos and Oinos have paused in their movement through stellar space and are hovering over a "fair star" where many beautiful flowers grow, but where also there are active volcanoes. Agathos, weeping, ends the story with this explanation: "It is now three centuries since with clasped hands, and with streaming eyes, at the feet of my beloved—I spoke it—with a few passionate sentences—into birth. Its brilliant flowers *are* the dearest of all unfulfilled dreams, and its raging volcanoes *are* the passions of the most turbulent and unhallowed of hearts." This rather sentimental conclusion is a bit incongruous; but it is obviously a myth illustrating the idea of mediate creation—creation by the power of human thought deriving from the original creative thought of the deity. It is not to be taken literally. And this star has no more real existence than the messenger star Al Aaraaf.

Poe wrote a number of stories involving the exercise of mesmeric power and its revelations, but only one contains ideas sufficiently like the metaphysics of *Eureka* to require comment here. This is "Mesmeric Revelation,"[14] which purports to record the answers made by a man in a state of hypnosis to questions concerning the nature of God, man, matter, spirit, and immortality. Vankirk, who was something of a philosophical thinker, had been under mesmeric treatment for "con-

---

[13] First published in the *Democratic Review*, June 1845 (*Works*, VI, 139–144).
[14] First published in the *Columbian Magazine*, Aug. 1844 (*Works*, V, 241–254).

firmed phthisis" for several months. Finally, believing himself about to die, he called in the mesmerist for the purpose of being questioned while in the mesmeric state about these matters and about certain "psychic impressions" which he had lately experienced. He had been accustomed to deny the existence of the soul, but admitted that there had always existed, in the very soul he denied, "a vague half-sentiment of its own existence." Recently this feeling had deepened and had come "so nearly to resemble the acquiescence of reason" that he could hardly distinguish the two. This new feeling he attributes to the mesmeric treatments he has received, on the hypothesis, he says, "that the mesmeric exaltation enables me to perceive a train of ratiocination which, in my abnormal existence, convinces, but which, in full accordance with the mesmeric phenomena, does not extend, except through its *effect,* into my normal condition. In sleep-waking, the reasoning and its conclusion—the cause and its effect—are present together." This hypothesis, which resembles Poe's definition of intuition in *Eureka,* he wishes to test by the mesmerist's direct questioning. It is necessary only to summarize briefly Vankirk's answers to the mesmerist's questions. There are, he reports, gradations of matter from metal to ether; the grosser impels the finer and the finer pervades the grosser. Ether, the finest, is unparticled matter; it permeates all things and "*is* all things within itself. This matter is God." All created things are the thoughts of God. Man can never be divested of his "corporate investiture," since then he would not be man but God. There are two bodies, the rudimental and the complete body. The latter is the ultimate one, which escapes the rudimental senses because it is unorganized and so can perceive all things except the nature of God's thought itself. The style of "Mesmeric Revelation" is matter of fact, and the story has nothing of the poetic except the idea of unity in all things, God and man, matter and spirit.[15]

Very different from these metaphysical tales, but equally illustrative of the poetic principle expressed in prose, are "The Domain of Arnheim" and two related pieces, "The Landscape Garden" and "Landor's Cottage." "The Landscape Garden," the first to be published,[16] is hardly a story at all, but it contains all the theory developed by Ellison on the art of landscaping that governed the creation described

[15] Another story, "Mellonta Tauta" (*Works,* VI, 197–215), which seems to have been written in 1848 shortly before *Eureka,* contains much the same thought as the first portion of that essay.

[16] In the *Lady's Companion,* Oct. 1842 (*Works,* IV, 259–271).

in "The Domain of Arnheim," and is repeated there. Ellison is represented in the latter[17] as quoting "from a writer on landscape-garden-
ing" a paragraph distinguishing between the "natural and the artificial" styles of landscape gardening. The natural style "seeks to recall
the original beauty of the country," changing only the order of nature
so as to remove defects of harmony. The artificial style adds to natural
beauty through "a mixture of pure art," as "an evidence of care and
human interest."[18] Ellison rejects the natural style as having merely
"negative merit." He agrees, in principle, with the definition of the
artificial style, but suggests that "there *may* be something beyond it."
A landscape gardener who is a poet, he says, might "so imbue his
designs at once with extent and novelty of beauty, as to convey the
sentiment of spiritual interference." Thus, he adds, "the sentiment of
interest is preserved, while the art intervolved is made to assume the
air of intermediate or secondary nature—a nature which is not God,
nor an emanation from God, but which still is nature in the sense of
the handiwork of the angels that hover between man and God."
Ellison has devoted his high poetic gifts and his stupendous wealth to
the achievement of these ideals in a garden whose beauty seems to
combine nature and art in a way that transcends mere craftsmanship.
The remainder of "The Domain of Arnheim" is devoted to Ellison's
search for a suitable situation, which he found in a secluded and
narrow valley with a stream running through it, and to a description
of the domain by the narrator as he approaches by canoe. Although
the handiwork of the artisan is nowhere visible, he feels himself
"enwrapt in an exquisite sense of the strange," and he notes everywhere a "weird symmetry, a thrilling uniformity, a wizard propriety"
in the valley, which nevertheless seems still natural. There is nowhere
a dead limb, a withered leaf, or a stray pebble, and the gorgeous

[17] "The Domain of Arnheim" was first published in the *Columbian Magazine*,
March 1847 (*Works*, VI, 176–196). Ellison's theory is discussed by Robert D.
Jacobs in "Poe's Earthly Paradise," *American Quarterly Review*, XII (1960),
404–413. He points out that "The Domain of Arnheim" develops Poe's general
concept of the purpose of art.

[18] Poe places this paragraph in quotation marks, as if he quoted it verbatim
from a published work. I have looked at a number of works on landscape
gardening, from Horace Walpole's essay "On Modern Gardening" (*Works*, London, 1898, II, 517–545) to A. J. Downing's *A Treatise on the Theory and Practice
of Landscape Gardening, Adapted to North America* (New York, 1841), including
a number of periodical reviews, but I have not found a passage which contains
any substantial portion of Poe's quotation, though the general ideas in it are
common enough.

flowers on the slopes of the hills are mirrored in the crystal-clear water. He is soothed by a melancholy music, a "divinest melody," which seems to have no origin unless in the ripples that break gently about the canoe. He comes to a "gigantic gate or rather door of burnished gold" which slowly opens and admits him into a vast amphitheater, in the midst of which rises the dwelling place of Ellison and his wife, "a mass of semi-Gothic, semi-Saracenic architecture, sustaining itself as if by a miracle in mid-air, glittering in the red sunlight with a hundred oriels, minarets, and pinnacles; and seeming the phantom handiwork, conjointly, of the Sylphs, of the Fairies, of the Genii, and of the Gnomes."

The poetic principle is most active in the conception of Arnheim and in the strange beauty with which it is surrounded, but it is overwhelmed by the flamboyant architecture of the central structure. I should like to think that Poe became dissatisfied with the magnificence of Arnheim and that he wrote "Landor's Cottage"[19] as a corrective. The cottage is in the midst of an artistically improved natural valley like that of "The Domain of Arnheim," but smaller, and all the structures are on a reduced scale. "Everywhere was variety in uniformity. It was a piece of 'composition,' in which the most fastidiously critical taste could scarcely have suggested an emendation." The cottage itself was very simple and not much larger than Poe's own cottage at Fordham, which may have suggested it. In its architecture it was strange, yet not *outré*. Its *"tout ensemble"* struck the narrator "with the keenest sense of combined novelty and propriety—in a word, of *poetry*." "Its marvellous *effect*," he adds, "lay altogether in its artistic arrangement *as a picture*." He records the exact dimensions of the cottage and describes the interior arrangements of the front rooms. He was admitted by a young woman about twenty-eight years old, Landor's wife, whose name proved to be Annie. His first impression of her was of "the perfection of natural, in contradistinction from artificial *grace*." His second and stronger impression was that of *enthusiasm*. "So intense an expression of *romance*, perhaps I should call it, or of unworldliness as that which gleamed from her deep-set eyes, had never so sunk into my heart of hearts before." He then explains what he means by romance here by equating it with womanliness, saying that "what man truly *loves* in woman, is, simply, her *womanhood*." Her hair was "light chestnut" and her eyes were "spiritual gray." This

[19] Published in *The Flag of Our Union*, June 9, 1849 (*Works*, VI, 255–271).

sketch was written about the same time as the poem "For Annie," and both were inspired by Mrs. "Annie" Richmond, of Lowell. The landscape of "Landor's Cottage," like its mistress, has more of natural than of artificial grace; and though in many ways it resembles that of Arnheim, it is a more appropriate setting for a cottage than for a Gothic castle or Saracenic palace. One must feel that Landor's cottage would have been a more suitable residence for Ellison the poet than the one he built, and that Annie would have been a suitable companion. Unfortunately there is no description of Ellison's wife except the statement that she "was the loveliest and most devoted of women."

"The Island of the Fay"[20] was originally published in *Graham's Magazine* for June, 1841, to accompany an engraving with the same title by John Sartain. The first half of "The Island of the Fay" is an essay on solitude developing the idea, also found in "The Domain of Arnheim," that man's greatest happiness is in the contemplation of natural scenery, alone and in a place of seclusion. The presence of any other person or of animal life in any form "is at war with the genius of the scene." The narrator imagines the earth, with its rocks, forests, and mountains, as a sentient whole, somewhat like a great animal, "whose life is eternity" and "whose thought is that of a God." In words which are almost identical with those with which he concludes *Eureka,* he asks: "As we find cycle within cycle without end—yet all revolving around one far distant centre which is the Godhead, may we not analogically suppose, in the same manner, life within life, the less within the greater, and all within the Spirit Divine?" In "To Think of Time" Whitman exclaimed, "I swear I think now that every thing without exception has an eternal soul!" In much the same spirit Poe decries man's erring pride in denying a soul to "the clod of the valley" for "no more profound reason than that he does not behold it in operation."

The second half of the sketch relates how once, "amid a far-distant region of mountain locked within mountain, and sad rivers and melancholy tarns writhing or sleeping within all," the narrator came upon a small and verdant island and sat down on the green turf to doze and contemplate it. The walls of the forest closed it in on all sides except the west, where the sinking sun caused the flowers and other vegetation to glow, as it seemed, "with a deep sense of life and joy." By contrast, a "sombre, yet beautiful and peaceful gloom" pervaded all

[20] *Works,* IV, 193–199.

things at the eastern end of the island. Small hillocks among the trees
there had the aspect of graves, but were not, although the grass had
the dark tint of cypress, and rue and rosemary clambered over and
about them. As the sun descended lower and lower, each tree shadow,
he fancied, "separated itself sullenly from the trunk that gave it birth"
and became absorbed in the general shadow in the depths of the
stream. He could see pieces of the white bark of the sycamore floating
around the island on the eddying currents. The place seemed enchanted. "This," he mused, "is the haunt of the few gentle fays who
remain from the wreck of the race."[21] Then it appeared to him that he
saw "one of those very Fays," standing erect in a tiny canoe that
floated out of the light into the shadow and presently reappeared after
completing the circuit of the island. Her attitude seemed joyful in the
light but sorrowful as she entered the shadow. He imagined that each
revolution about the island marked a year in the brief life of the Fay.
After a few more revolutions, her form becoming less distinct with
each one, she finally was lost in the heavy darkness on the water.

The narrator says, "My position enabled me to include in a single
view both the eastern and western extremities of the islet"; he was
therefore looking from a point along the side of the island, either
north or south. In the engraving, however, the artist's point of view is
near the east end, for the glow in the sky was directly before him, seen
over the trees. The Fay appears as a very small figure, standing in her
tiny boat, not far from the southeastern point of the island. Presumably Poe altered the point of view in order the better to contrast the
east and west sides and so bring out his symbolic values. The mood of
Poe's sketch, very much like that of his early poem "The Lake," is not
that of the picture, which includes some animal life, and it does not
suggest the cycle of life. The style of "The Island of the Fay," like the
mood, is closely related to the style of Poe's early poems.

"Eleonora" was probably written only a few months after "The
Island of the Fay," and it is even more poetic in mood and style.[22] Its
method is metaphorical, and in rhythm as well as in diction it resembles Poe's poetry. It is all narrative and descriptive except the first two

[21] This idea probably led Poe to reprint, at the head of this sketch, as it was
published in *Graham's Magazine*, his "Sonnet—To Science"; it was omitted in all
later publications of "The Island of the Fay."

[22] "Eleonora" was published for the first time in *The Gift*, an annual for 1842;
Works, IV, 236–244. Annuals were usually published in September or October of
the year preceding their printed date. Both "The Island of the Fay" and "Eleonora"
were reprinted in 1845 in the *Broadway Journal*.

paragraphs. In the first paragraph the narrator says men have called him mad, but he raises the question whether what is called madness is not the loftiest intelligence; whether "much that is glorious" and "all that is profound" does not come from "disease of thought"—that is, "from *moods* of mind exalted at the expense of the general intellect." I take it that by "disease of thought" he does not mean mental illness, but an exalted state in which the mind obtains "glimpses of eternity," in which the rational processes give way to intuition, as in the mesmeric trance. It is in that state of mind, as he says in the Preface to *Eureka,* in which waking dreams become the only realities. These intuitions closely resemble what Poe has elsewhere described as "psychal impressions" that arise in the soul "at those points of time where the confines of the waking world blend with those of the world of dreams," and afford it "a glimpse of the spirit's outer world."[23] In the second paragraph the narrator recognizes two distinct conditions of his mind: one of lucid reason in all that he relates of the first epoch of his life, and another of "shadow and doubt" in his recollection of the second epoch. He advises his reader to believe what he relates of the earlier period and to give the rest "such credit as may seem due," if he cannot doubt it altogether, and "play unto its riddle the Oedipus."

This story is probably well known to most readers; even so, if I am to play the Oedipus to its riddle I had best provide a brief summary. During the first fifteen years of Eleonora's life and the first twenty of the narrator's, they lived in the Valley of the Many-Colored Grass, through which the River of Silence ran in "mazy courses." Almost inaccessible to the outside world because of the surrounding mountains and the dense foliage of trees, this valley was covered with "soft green grass, thick, short, perfectly even, and vanilla-perfumed, but so besprinkled throughout with the yellow buttercup, the white daisy, the purple violet, and the ruby-red asphodel, that its exceeding beauty spoke to our hearts, in loud tones, of the love and of the glory of God." But one day, "locked in each other's embrace, beneath the serpent-like trees," they looked down at their images in the River of Silence and drew therefrom the god Eros. Then were kindled within them the passions and fancies of their forefathers which "breathed a delirious bliss" over the valley and brought a change in it. The tints of the green grass deepened and the white daisies withered, but the red asphodels multiplied tenfold. Animal life appeared for the first time,

---

[23] "Marginalia V," *Graham's Magazine,* March 1846 (*Works,* XVI, 88–89).

the flamingo, gay-colored birds, and golden and silver fish; and then a cloud floated in from the west, "all gorgeous in crimson and gold, and shut them, as if forever, in a prison-house of grandeur and glory." At length the knowledge of death came to Eleonora, and she perceived that she must die. Though innocent of guile, she grieved to think that, after her death, her companion would leave the valley and transfer his love to some maiden of the outer world. To comfort her he gave his promise never to love another and invoked upon himself a curse if he should forget it. So she died in peace, assuring him that she would watch over him in spirit, sighing upon him in the evening winds, and, if permitted, would return to him visibly in the watches of the night.

As he begins the second part of his story, the narrator says, "I feel that a shadow gathers over my brain, and I mistrust the sanity of the record." Yet he continued to dwell in the valley for several years, although a second change had come over it. The tints of the green grass faded, and the ruby-red asphodels withered, and "there sprang up, in place of them, ten by ten, dark eye-like violets that writhed uneasily and were ever encumbered with dew." All life left the valley —the flamingo, the gay birds, and the gold and silver fish went away, the stream became silent again, and finally the covering cloud drifted back into the west, taking away the glories of the valley. Yet he kept his promise. A "holy perfume" still floated about the valley, and at lone hours he could hear soft sighs in the winds. Once, but once only, he was awakened from slumber "by the pressing of spiritual lips" on his own. But at length the valley pained him through its memories of Eleonora, and he left it forever for the "vanities and turbulent triumphs of the world."

He found himself in a strange city, hoping that the pageantry of a stately court, the clangor of arms, and "the radiant loveliness of woman" would blot from recollection the sweet dreams he had dreamed so long in the Valley of the Many-Colored Grass. For a while he kept his vow and felt indications of the presence of Eleonora in the night. Suddenly these manifestations ceased and he "stood aghast" at the thoughts and temptations that beset him; for "there came from some far, far distant and unknown land" the beautiful Ermengarde, before whom at once he "bowed down without a struggle, in the most ardent, in the most abject worship of love," compared to which his "passion for the young girl of the valley" was as nothing. The curse was not visited upon him when he married Ermengarde, and once, in the night winds coming through his latticed window, he thought he heard soft sighs that "modelled themselves" into the familiar voice, saying: "Sleep in peace!—for the Spirit of Love reigneth and ruleth, and, in taking to thy passionate heart her who is Ermengarde, thou art absolved, for reasons which shall be made known to thee in Heaven, of thy vows unto Eleonora."

Some interpreters of "Eleonora" believe that it is an idealized account of the life of Poe and his cousin-wife Virginia. The early version lends some support to this interpretation, for in that version Eleonora's mother lived with them and continued to live with the narrator as long as he remained in the valley, as Virginia's mother lived with her and Edgar. It is supposed that about the time of the composition of the story, Virginia was so ill that Poe anticipated her early death, and that in this tale he was imagining what life would be like for him afterward. Ermengarde would represent the woman he imagined might take Virginia's place. In fact Virginia did become ill about the middle of January 1842, after bursting a blood vessel in her throat while singing, and for a while Poe despaired of her life. It seems probable, however, that the story was written before that happened.[24] The relationship of the two lovers in the first part of the story may have been suggested by his situation with Virginia and her mother, but its meaning is more general and more subtle than such an interpretation would permit; at least it came to be in the revised version. The most significant fact about the revisions is that they not only removed Eleonora's mother from the scene, but eliminated the specific description of the physical appearance of the girl. This would suggest that Eleonora, finally, is meant to be an ideal, not a real, person. As first conceived, Eleonora seemed to have "two separate souls," reflected in her alternate moods of melancholy and mirth. Also in the early version Ermengarde is apparently intended to be identical with Eleonora, perhaps a reincarnation. There was, the narrator records, "a wild delirium in the love I bore her when I started to see upon her countenance the identical transition from tears to smiles that I had wondered at in the long-lost Eleonora." This passage was deleted in

[24] Although prepared for the 1841 Christmas trade, *The Gift* was certainly published as early as September 1841, since "Eleonora" was reprinted in the Boston *Notion* on September 4, 1841, with a note saying it was from *The Gift* for 1842. The story was reprinted with a similar note in the New York *Weekly Tribune*, September 18 (see Quinn, p. 328 note). So far as has been established, Virginia had had no earlier illness that could have led to Poe's anticipating her death.

the revision.[25] This representation of Eleonora and Ermengarde as
identical and as each having two separate moods should be sufficient
to disprove the theory that Virginia seriously influenced Poe's conception of either of them. The desire to remove, in revision, all factual
particulars that might interfere with an ideal representation has been
noted in earlier essays of this volume as characteristic of his method in
trying to perfect the early poems.

The first question likely to occur to the reader is, What is the
significance of the names of the two girls? One of them, at least, is not
difficult. Eleonora, like Lenore, is one of several variants of Helen,
which originally meant Light, and through literature and tradition has
come to mean Beauty, or, as one writer on the subject of names says,
"the eternal woman, the unattainable ideal."[26] Poe's fondness for the
name Helen is well known. I have said that in the early poem "To
Helen" Beauty is personified in a woman, but in the tale under
discussion, I think Poe might also have intended Eleonora to mean
that which in woman is eternal, the unattainable ideal. Ermengarde, I
suppose, as the dictionaries of names all say, means literally, or almost
literally, "Her people's guard." If Poe selected the name because it has
a special significance in the story—and of course one cannot be sure
he did—this definition does not help much. Poe might have intended
Ermengarde to mean the guardian or protector of love, and a symbol of the reconciliation of spiritual and passionate love. In a sense she
is also the protector of the narrator from the temptations of the world.
He has lost his innocence and acquired experience in passing from the
paradise of the Valley of the Many-Colored Grass into the outer world
with its conflict between good and evil. Eleonora was an inseparable
part of that paradise, for although she was capable of passion, she
could not sustain it, and she was so unfitted for knowledge that she
died almost as soon as she learned of her own mortality. The seraphic
beauty which he had lost in Eleonora he recovers when he looks into
the "memorial eyes" of Ermengarde. Thus he is saved from the world-
liness of the great city and is absolved from his promise to Eleonora,
whose spirit seems to reassure him that because the "Spirit of Love
reigneth and ruleth" in the world as well as in paradise, the love that
began in innocence may survive in experience. Paradise is not forever
lost, and the ideal may be found in the real.

[25] These deleted passages appear in the notes to this tale in *Works*, IV, 312–316.
The revised text is that of the *Broadway Journal*.

[26] Evelyn Wells, *A Treasury of Names* (New York, 1946), p. 90.

The second question is, Why does the narrator mistrust the sanity of his record in the second part of the tale? This section appears to be much more realistic and probable than the first part. The answer may be found in what I have just said of the two women: we can believe beyond doubt that the ideal really exists in its proper sphere, apart from the world, but whether it exists also at the heart of reality as perceived through the senses may remain in doubt. If it does exist there, we can know it only through intuition so long as we remain subject to mortal limitations. This suggests a close relationship between "Eleonora" and most of the prose pieces we have been discussing. The description of the Valley of the Many-Colored Grass bears a striking resemblance to the description of the valleys by which we approach the domain of Arnheim and Landor's cottage. The "unworldliness" that gleamed from the "spiritual gray" eyes of Annie Landor may be the same that the narrator saw in the depths of Ermengarde's eyes. Perhaps Ellison saw it also in the eyes of his wife, who shared his happiness at Arnheim, "a woman, not unwomanly." The beauty of Ermengarde is not made specific, but one suspects that it possessed, more than did that of Eleonora, the quality of strangeness superadded to natural beauty, not by artificial means, but by her foreign origin and her culture. To put the case formally, the strange beauty of Ermengarde is to the natural beauty of Eleonora as the beauty of Arnheim is to that of the natural landscape before Ellison's poetic art perfected it. This strangeness of Ermengarde, like the strangeness of Ligeia in an earlier tale, seems to have been in her eyes, and perhaps accounted for the narrator's recognizing their memorial quality.

It is possible that the conception of "Eleonora" was derived from Poe's experience rather than strictly from his thinking, and to that extent it is autobiographical. It may be a kind of parable in which he tries to reassure himself that in turning from poetry to prose writing about 1832 he had not really been unfaithful to his genius. In this interpretation the years spent with Eleonora in the Valley of the Many-Colored Grass were the youthful years he devoted exclusively to poetry, and the later period, after leaving the valley, represents his turning from poetry to fiction and criticism. Eleonora would symbolize his poetic genius, her death would suggest his discouragement brought on by critical neglect, and his meeting Ermengarde would stand for his discovery that the poetic principle can become active in imaginative prose as well as in poetry—the poetic principle being that which he thought he lost in Eleonora but recovered in Ermengarde. In this sense prose (Ermengarde) becomes the protector or savior of his poetic genius (the spiritual love first awakened by Eleonora). I offer this interpretation merely for its suggestive value. To wrench specific meanings out of such tales as "Eleonora" does violence to their effect of beauty; like poems they exist, as Poe said, for themselves and not for any meaning that can be drawn from them and stated.

The early version of the tale in which the identity of Eleonora and Ermengarde seems to be physical as well as spiritual, is, in that respect, parallel with "Morella" and "Ligeia."[27] The heroine of each of these tales is a very learned woman with a Germanic background. Morella loved her husband but her love was not returned by him, although he admired her intellect. He even came to hate her and wish for her death. She did die while still young, and in dying gave birth to a daughter who proved to be strangely like her mother. Yet he gave the daughter all the fervent love which the mother had longed for but never received. The child grew physically with abnormal rapidity, and her mind seemed to be already mature even as a child. He did not give her a name until she was ten years old; then, standing by the baptismal font in the presence of the priest, perversely and as if compulsively, he pronounced the name "Morella." The daughter replied, "I am here," and died immediately. When he opened the family tomb, he found no traces of the body of the first Morella. We are expected to believe that the physical substance of Morella's corpse had, during the preceding ten years, passed into and formed the living body of her daughter. This, of course, is so incredible as to be ridiculous. It is the great flaw in the plot, for it destroys any possibility of verisimilitude. If Poe had been content to imagine an identity of spirit only, or of consciousness, between mother and daughter, or if he had prepared us to believe that the emptiness of the tomb was apparent to the narrator only, we could have assumed that he was suffering from some psychic disorder and so have found the story plausible.

The plot of "Ligeia" is handled more skillfully. Ligeia, like Morella, is a beautiful and learned woman of Germanic origin and education. Like Morella also she loves the narrator passionately, and for this reason chiefly she clings desperately to life. She is said to have been

[27] *Works*, II, 27–34; 248–268. "Morella" was first published in the *Southern Literary Messenger* (April 1835); "Ligeia," in the *American Museum* (Sept. 1838).

much affected by a passage represented as coming from the writings of Joseph Glanvill affirming the belief that man yields to death only through the weakness of his will. But she died, and afterward the narrator went to England, married the fair-haired Rowena, and retired with her into an ancient abbey in a remote part of the country. He fitted up his gloomy abode with fantastic and morbid taste; the bridal chamber in particular, with its ghastly and funereal decorations, was such a nightmare that Rowena became ill within a month after she was brought there. Even before his marriage the narrator, as he informs us specifically, had become a slave to opium and had recognized in himself an "incipient madness." He says he hated Rowena from the beginning "with a hatred belonging more to demon than to man." He thinks of Ligeia constantly, loves her far more passionately than he did while she was living, and dreams of restoring her to life. Finally Rowena dies amid the phantasmagoria of the bed chamber after a series of illnesses, each more devastating than the one before. Her death is hastened by drinking a goblet of wine which may have been poisoned by the narrator, though he says that as he handed the glass to her he saw four large drops of a ruby-colored fluid fall into it as if dropped from the air by ghostly hands. He admits, however, that he was wild with "an immoderate dose of opium." About midnight, after Rowena had been prepared for the tomb, he sat alone with her body, again strongly under the influence of opium. He heard a sob coming apparently from the corpse and soon after saw a tinge of color in her cheeks. He had been thinking of Ligeia, but as soon as he aroused himself sufficiently to think of doing something for Rowena, she relapsed into the pallor of death. At once he resumed his thinking of Ligeia, and again the corpse showed signs of life. This cycle occurred several times, the signs of life being stronger each time; yet each time, as soon as he began to think of Rowena instead of Ligeia, there followed at once a new and more positive relapse. This succession of events indicates that it was the narrator's thought of Ligeia that seemed to bring back life into Rowena's corpse, and that it was his interrupting his thought of Ligeia to give attention to Rowena that caused the relapse. But finally, in one of these cycles, life became so strong in the body of Rowena that she rose from her bed and stood as if alive before the narrator; but these movements loosened the cerements from about her face and head, and he recognized the dark eyes and raven tresses of Ligeia. He took a step toward her, but she shrank away from him. So ends the story.

"Ligeia" has intrigued many readers, and there have been a number of interpretations, several that come close to the heart of it without quite reaching it, or so it seems to me. Ligeia is obviously another personification of beauty, this time both strange and ideal. The strangeness is suggested in the mysteriousness of her origin and early life, but especially in the expression of her eyes. In her origin and perhaps also in her eyes she resembles Ermengarde. If we assume that she is a real woman, we must believe the narrator's statement that in dying she left him a large fortune, that subsequently he becomes in some degree insane, that his studies with her in the mystic and romantic philosophy of the Germans, especially Schelling's transcendental idealism, have inspired in him the insane belief that the soul of Ligeia could be drawn from the regions of the dead, transplanted, so to speak, and made to live again in the physical substance of the dying Rowena. To this end he marries Rowena and brings about her death, convincing himself, in his madness, that it was the spirit of Ligeia who, in her surviving desire for life, had poisoned the wine. This is a better plot than that of "Morella" because we can with reason believe that the apparent rebirth of Ligeia through the body of Rowena is a hallucination induced by madness and opium. There are many reasons why we may be sure that the rising of Ligeia from the deathbed of Rowena is a hallucination, but I need mention only two or three here. In the first place, if the soul of Ligeia has assumed the physical body of Rowena, it would seem that the narrator should have seen the features of Rowena, not those of Ligeia. In the second place, why did the apparition of Ligeia shrink from his touch if what he saw was real and not a hallucination? In the third place, if Ligeia was literally brought to life in the substance of Rowena, what became of her afterward, since obviously she is not alive when the narrator writes his story? As I have already intimated, it was the narrator's will and not Ligeia's that undertook to restore her to life. The story involves the idea of identity, but the identity is not between Ligeia and Rowena but between Ligeia and the narrator. The passionate love which in life she felt for him, he now feels for her, or for the image of her that lives on in his mind. Her belief in the power of the will to overcome death becomes his belief and leads to the demonic purpose of his marriage and the fantastic events that follow.

I am inclined to go further and say that the identity is not between the narrator and a real Ligeia either in life or in death, but with the idea only of Ligeia. If she had existed, there must have been some

record of their marriage, of her death, and of the legal process by
which he acquired her wealth. He cannot remember anything that
would identify her, yet he remembers her person and describes her
features in minute detail. The strange expression of her eyes is not that
of a real person. He cannot understand this expression although he
has found in nature a "circle of analogies" to it; and he has also felt it
in the sound of stringed instruments and in passages from books,
especially the passage on the power of the will that becomes the motto
of his story. This strange expression in Ligeia's eyes must be the means
by which he becomes identified with her, just as the narrator in
"Eleonora" recognizes the identity of Ermengarde with Eleonora
through her eyes. The Ligeia of the story is the creation of a poetic
but abnormal imagination. Her creator has endowed her with all the
beauty that is natural to woman, then enhanced that, as Ellison
enhanced the beauty of nature, with a spiritual, almost a supernatural,
quality that lifts it out of nature into the realm of the ideal. She not
only has all the beauty that can be imagined of woman, but she has
also all the intellectual power that can be imagined of the most
learned man. Her creation is the work of intellectual idealism di-
vorced from nature and even from rationality. The idealist, the narrator in this case, conceives of the physical, mental, and spiritual characteristics of the ideal woman and then sets about creating, not by art
but merely by the power of his will, a real person corresponding to the
ideal. The attempt is a madman's interpretation of what he supposes
to be the transcendental idealism of Friedrich Schelling. In "Eleonora"
we saw how the ideal can be found in the real through love; in
"Ligeia" we are shown the folly of trying to preserve the ideal in
contempt of the real by sheer human will power.[28]

Poe's most successful use of the theory of identity is in "The Fall of
the House of Usher,"[29] where it is associated with another speculative
notion, that of the sentience of vegetable and even inorganic matter.
This story is too well known to require a summary. There have been a
number of excellent interpretations of it. I cannot add much that is

[28] Many parallels may be found in literature. I will mention only two, both from
American writers who were Poe's contemporaries. In "The Birthmark" Aylmer
tries by his "science" to remove a birthmark, the sign of human imperfection, from
the cheek of Georgiana and kills her in the process. In *Moby-Dick* Ahab insanely
ignores common sense and humanity in his attempt to impose his conception of
the ideal on real people and events, with disastrous consequences.

[29] First published in *Burton's Gentleman's Magazine* (Sept. 1839), just a year
after "Ligeia" appeared (*Works*, III, 273–297).

new, but I will mention two or three ideas which have not, I think, been specifically proposed before. The mood of the story is that of gloom, and the dominant effect intended and produced is terror. These are suggested in the first paragraph and emphasized throughout. The narrator feels the gloom and a sense of terror when he first sees the house and attributes them to certain combinations or arrangements of particulars in the house and its surroundings. Thinking a different point of view might relieve his feeling of terror, he looks at the reflection of the house in the adjacent tarn, but in this view the effect is intensified. He suspects that there is a peculiar atmosphere, a pestilent vapor, that has "reeked up" from the tarn and the decayed trees to envelop the house and the entire domain. Roderick, we learn later in the story, in connection with his ideas on the sentience of vegetable and inorganic matter, has also observed, in fact has long been aware of, this peculiar atmosphere, which he attributes not only to the tarn and the decayed trees, but to the arrangement of the stones in the house and, above all, to the "long undisturbed endurance of this arrangement" and to "its reduplication in the still waters of the tarn." This long undisturbed endurance extends to the family as well as to the house. There were no collateral branches, but the family descended through many generations directly from father to son in a direct line until the present generation, which consists of a brother and a sister. They have a certain degree of identity, however, because they are twins. Roderick has a strange illness which has left him physically weak, though his senses have become abnormally acute, and mentally depressed. He thinks this illness is parallel to and caused by the deterioration of the stones and the decay of vegetation all about the house. The recent serious illness of his sister Madeline has contributed to his depression. Their relationship was close but quite normal; there is no evidence whatever that it was, as some critics have alleged, of an incestuous nature. Roderick seems to believe, however, that there has come to be an extraordinary degree of identity between himself and his sister and the house they live in. This belief was no doubt a principal source of the fear that consumes him. Early in the story Roderick tells the narrator that he will die of this fear; and indeed it is fear, an overwhelming terror, that in the end is the immediate cause of his death.

Madeline dies soon after the arrival of the narrator, and the two men deposit her in her coffin, with its lid tightly screwed down, and place it temporarily in a copper-lined room lying at a great depth directly under the narrator's chamber. There they leave her, fastening securely behind them the heavy iron door to the vault-like room. These facts are clearly stated by Poe, I think, so that the reader will know that, even if Madeline had been placed living in her coffin, as Roderick presently comes to believe, she could not possibly have escaped and climbed the many flights of steps to appear, still living, at the door of the narrator's room. Yet many readers have believed that, despite the weakness consequent upon a long illness, Madeline really did exert the preternatural strength necessary to burst out of the coffin, open the heavy iron door, and climb the many stairs. Nothing like this really happened. For several days after Madeline's death there was no observable change in Roderick's manner, but then he grew daily more nervous and distracted, and seemed always to be listening as if he were trying to hear some sound from far away. His strange manner was the result of a growing fear, knowing as he did that Madeline's illness had shown symptoms of catalepsis, that he had placed her in her tomb alive. He believed that because of his acute senses he could hear her movements in the coffin. Roderick's fear was genuine, and infected the narrator. "I felt creeping upon me," he said, "by slow yet certain degrees, the wild influences of his own fantastic yet impressive superstitions." One night during an electric storm, presumably engendered by the miasma of the tarn, Roderick, in great trepidation, joined the narrator in his room. To try to amuse him and distract his attention from the storm, the narrator picked up a book that happened to be on a table in his room and began to read a fantastic story of a medieval knight's fight with a dragon. As the reading progressed, with its report of clanging shield and shrieking dragon mingled with the sounds of the storm, both Roderick and the narrator imagined they heard the sounds of the coffin being ripped open and the iron door creaking upon its rusty hinges. At the climax of the knight's battle with the dragon, the door of the narrator's room swung open and Madeline stood there a moment, then advanced and fell against the person of Roderick, dying there and bearing him to the floor also a corpse. The story clearly indicates that the narrator shares Roderick's terror and his hallucination, for their close association for weeks under conditions both strange and exciting had brought his mind into a state of sympathy and temporary subjection to that of Roderick Usher. But with Roderick's death he is suddenly released and rushes from the house just in time to escape its collapse into the tarn.

"William Wilson"[30] is another prose tale in which Poe employs insanity and hallucinations to account for incredible events. Since there is not much of the poetic in this story, it requires no more discussion than a brief comment on the crucial questions of Wilson's relationship with another boy named Wilson and of his hallucinations. One must believe, on the basis of the first part of the story, that during his school days at Dr. Bransby's academy William Wilson, the narrator, had a schoolmate by the same name whose superior moral character and kindly efforts to help him aroused his resentment. The narrator was a spoiled brat, egotistic, vain, and overbearing, but he comes to see, although he will not admit the fact to himself, in the other boy all that he ought to be and is not. He had no recourse but to hate him. His fear and hate of his namesake eventually produce the psychosis which enables him to believe that they are not two persons but somehow aspects of the same person. He leaves the academy at the age of fifteen and never really sees the other William Wilson again, yet from time to time when he does something that he knows the other William Wilson would have disapproved, he fancies that he sees and hears him, although no other person is ever aware of him.

In the end, William Wilson is represented as having advanced so far in his insanity that he imagines that he confronts his counterpart in a duel and kills him with a sword. That this is a hallucination is proved by what followed. Thinking he heard someone trying the door, he turned to secure it. When he faced the room again his antagonist was not there; instead, he found himself facing a large mirror and his own image reflected there, with features pale and dabbled with blood. Sanity had returned while his attention had been drawn away to the practical matter of the door, but it lasted only a moment. The hallucination returned, and as he looked at what he supposed to be the other William Wilson he noted that there was "not a thread of all his raiment—not a line in all the marked and singular lineaments of his face" which was not his own. But when the other Wilson spoke he did not whisper, as he had always done before, and the narrator fancied he himself was speaking, as of course he was, saying that in killing the other person he had killed himself. We are to understand, of course, that he had destroyed his own conscience. The story ends thus, but by looking again at the beginning, we see that Wilson afterward recovered his sanity, and possibly also his conscience.

[30] This story first appeared in *Burton's Gentleman's Magazine*, Oct. 1839 (*Works*, III, 299–325).

In the tales I have discussed there is occasional use of what might be called the language of poetry, but the poetic principle inheres chiefly in their symmetry of form and their unity of effect. These, as Poe states in his review of Hawthorne's *Twice-Told Tales*,[31] are characteristics which the short tale has in common with the short poem. The chief difference between the poem and the tale is in their effect. In the poem the effect is beauty, to which rhythm largely contributes; in the tale it may be a number of things—terror, horror, passion, or even truth as in the ratiocinative tale—but it cannot be the purely beautiful, which is best achieved in the metrical poem. There is one attribute which they have in common, namely, imagination, or originality, which displays itself in novelty of tone as well as of matter. These are characteristics which Poe recognizes in Hawthorne's tales, but which are perhaps best exemplified in some of his own, particularly in "Ligeia," "The Fall of the House of Usher," and "William Wilson," all of them written before the Hawthorne review. He also praises in that review what he calls Hawthorne's "essays," such as "Sights from a Steeple" and "A Rill from the Town Pump," and calls them "beautiful." Unlike the tale, they have as their predominant quality repose, not effect, although they may reveal originality of thought. Poe does not mention the term "ideality" in this review, but in an earlier one[32] he identifies it with the sentiment of poetry and defines it as that sense which enables man to appreciate the beauty of nature and which also feeds his desire for knowledge. Moreover, in "The Poetic Principle" he would assert that the poetic sentiment may develop in other arts than poetry, including, as his own work demonstrates, the art of landscape gardening. His statement in the Hawthorne review that beauty can be treated better in the poem than in the prose tale must therefore not be understood as denying altogether to the prose tale the effect of beauty. Certainly Poe's own "Eleonora," to mention only one of many, has a great deal of "ideality," has beauty as one at least of its effects, and in so far as truth is also an effect, subordinates it to the level of an undercurrent. The two early short tales or sketches, "Shadow" and "Silence,"[33] like "Eleonora," make use of the diction and the rhetorical structures commonly associated with

[31] First published in *Graham's Magazine*, May 1842 (*Works*, XI, 104–113).

[32] The review of the poems of Drake and Halleck, published in the *Southern Literary Messenger*, April 1836 (*Works*, VIII, 275–318).

[33] *Works*, II, 147–150; 220–224. "Shadow. A Parable" was first published in the *Southern Literary Messenger* (Sept. 1835). "Silence—A Fable" first appeared in *The Baltimore Book*, 1839, though it was written six or seven years earlier.

poetry. Meanings are conveyed less by logical statement than by moods and language patterns, though the rhythms are irregular and meter does not occur unless by accident.

Other prose tales in which one may discover evidence of the poetic principle in mood, meaning, or form are "MS. Found in a Bottle," "The Assignation," "The Man of the Crowd," "The Oval Portrait," and "The Masque of the Red Death," but these evidences reveal little or nothing that has not already been remarked in other sketches and tales. It is unnecessary, therefore, to extend this essay by a detailed analysis of them. I should point out, however, that in the tales of ratiocination, which are the least poetic because they are the most rational of Poe's prose fiction, the poet, if not the poetic principle, is present. In keeping with the theory, expressed as early as 1836 in the Drake and Halleck review, that the creative poet must be endowed with the faculty of "Causality" (to keep his phrenological term) as well as that of "Ideality,"—the power of analysis as well as the imaginative power—his famous detective, M. Auguste Dupin, is both a poet and a mathematician. The only opponent Dupin finds at all worthy of his respect is the Minister D___, in "The Purloined Letter," who is also a poet and a mathematician. Dupin outwits his less imaginative opponents by his ability to put himself in their places, see things from their point of view, and so anticipate their motives and actions.

Poe himself was scarcely less an analyst than a poet. For his time, and as an amateur, he was very ingenious at solving cryptographic puzzles. Although he had not formally studied mathematics at the University of Virginia, he had done so at West Point, and throughout his life he was intensely interested in the mathematical sciences, especially astronomy. His conception of Dupin very possibly originated in his recognition of his own dual interests. He did not, therefore, betray his poetic genius in turning away, by necessity, from poetry as his primary concern to the writing of tales in which the analytic or constructive talent—the faculty of Causality—was paramount. He was, in his own estimate of himself, and in fact, essentially a poet, and remained so to the end of his life, not only in his poetry, but also in the best of his fiction and his essays on the nature and function of poetry.

Index